Luck: Its Nature and Significance for Human Knowledge and Agency

Palgrave Innovations in Philosophy

Series Editors: **Vincent F. Hendricks,** University of Copenhagen and Columbia University in New York and **Duncan Pritchard,** University of Edinburgh.

Titles include:

Mikkel Gerken
EPISTEMIC REASONING AND THE MENTAL

Kevin Meeker
HUME'S RADICAL SCEPTICISM AND THE FATE OF NATURALIZED EPISTEMOLOGY

Ted Poston
REASON AND EXPLANATION: A Defense of Explanatory Coherentism

Aidan McGlynn
KNOWLEDGE FIRST?

Forthcoming titles:

J. Adam Carter
THE PROSPECTS FOR RELATIVISM IN EPISTEMOLOGY

Annalisa Coliva
THE VARIETIES OF SELF-KNOWLEDGE

Julian Kiverstein
THE SIGNIFICANCE OF PHENOMENOLOGY

Jonathan Matheson
THE EPISTEMIC SIGNIFICANCE OF DISAGREEMENT

David Pedersen
POLITICAL EPISTEMOLOGY: Epistemic Theories and Knowledge Institutions

Christopher Pincock and Sandra Lapointe (*editors*)
INNOVATIONS IN THE HISTORY OF ANALYTICAL PHILOSOPHY

Palgrave Innovations in Philosophy
Series Standing Order ISBN 978–0–230–36085–3 (hardback)
(*outside North America only*)

You can receive future titles in this series as they are published by placing a standing order. Please contact your bookseller or, in case of difficulty, write to us at the address below with your name and address, the title of the series and the ISBN quoted above.

Customer Services Department, Macmillan Distribution Ltd, Houndmills, Basingstoke, Hampshire RG21 6XS, England

Luck: Its Nature and Significance for Human Knowledge and Agency

E.J. Coffman
Associate Professor of Philosophy, University of Tennessee, USA

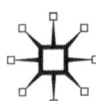

© E.J. Coffman 2015

All rights reserved. No reproduction, copy or transmission of this publication may be made without written permission.

No portion of this publication may be reproduced, copied or transmitted save with written permission or in accordance with the provisions of the Copyright, Designs and Patents Act 1988, or under the terms of any licence permitting limited copying issued by the Copyright Licensing Agency, Saffron House, 6–10 Kirby Street, London EC1N 8TS.

Any person who does any unauthorized act in relation to this publication may be liable to criminal prosecution and civil claims for damages.

The author has asserted his right to be identified as the author of this work in accordance with the Copyright, Designs and Patents Act 1988.

First published 2015 by
PALGRAVE MACMILLAN

Palgrave Macmillan in the UK is an imprint of Macmillan Publishers Limited, registered in England, company number 785998, of Houndmills, Basingstoke, Hampshire, RG21 6XS

Palgrave Macmillan in the US is a division of St Martin's Press LLC, 175 Fifth Avenue, New York, NY 10010.

Palgrave Macmillan is the global academic imprint of the above companies and has companies and representatives throughout the world.

Palgrave® and Macmillan® are registered trademarks in the United States, the United Kingdom, Europe and other countries

ISBN: 978–1–137–32609–6

This book is printed on paper suitable for recycling and made from fully managed and sustained forest sources. Logging, pulping and manufacturing processes are expected to conform to the environmental regulations of the country of origin.

A catalogue record for this book is available from the British Library.

Library of Congress Cataloging-in-Publication Data

E.J. Coffman 1976–
    Luck : its nature and significance for human knowledge and agency /
 E.J. Coffman, Associate Professor of Philosophy, University of Tennessee, USA.
     pages cm. — (Palgrave innovations in philosophy)
   Includes bibliographical references and index.
   ISBN 978–1–137–32609–6
    1. Chance. 2. Fortune. 3. Knowledge, Theory of. 4. Agent (Philosophy)
 5. Act (Philosophy) I. Title.

BD595.C64 2015
123'.3—dc23   2014036783

Transferred to Digital Printing in 2015

Contents

Preface		viii
Acknowledgments		x
1	**Lucky Events: The Current Debate and a New Proposal**	**1**
	1.1 Three leading theories of luck	3
	1.2 Counterexamples to the leading theories of luck	5
	1.3 Lucky events and strokes of luck	13
	1.4 The Strokes Account: further support and defense	19
2	**What Is a Stroke of Luck? Enriching the Strokes Account**	**25**
	2.1 Initial statement of the Analysis and some important implications	25
	2.2 The Analysis: revisions and defense	32
	2.3 Putting it all together: the Enriched Strokes Account of lucky events	37
	2.4 How the Enriched Strokes Account handles the counterexamples to the literature's leading theories of luck	44
3	**Knowledge and Luck I: Gettiered Belief and the Ease of Mistake Approach**	**49**
	3.1 An initial catalog of kinds of epistemic luck	51
	3.2 Pritchard on Evidence Luck and Belief Luck	53
	3.3 The scope of gettiered belief	57
	3.4 The Ease of Mistake Approach to gettiered belief: explanation and support	60
	3.5 Counterexamples to the Ease of Mistake Approach	64
4	**Knowledge and Luck II: Three More Approaches to Gettiered Belief**	**68**
	4.1 From Ease of Mistake to Lack of Credit	68
	4.2 Creditability as explanatory salience	70

	4.3	Creditability as power manifestation	73
	4.4	Two riskier approaches to gettiered belief	77
	4.5	The Risk of Misleading *Dispositions* Approach to gettiered belief	79
	4.6	The Risk of Misleading *Justification* Approach to gettiered belief	81
		4.6.1 Objection 1: Kelp's Demonic Clock	86
		4.6.2 Objection 2: Bogardus's Atomic Clock	90
5	**Freedom, Responsibility, and Luck I: The Possibility of Moral Responsibility and Literal Arguments for the Proximal Determination Requirement**		97
	5.1	Defending the possibility of morally responsible action	101
	5.2	Four different kinds of luck-involving arguments for the Proximal Determination Requirement	115
	5.3	Literal versions of the arguments for the Proximal Determination Requirement	117
		5.3.1 An intriguing attempted counterexample to (IA-2)	118
		5.3.2 Against the 'at least partly a matter of luck' readings of (DA-2) and (IA-2)	120
		5.3.3 Against (DA/IA-1)	124
6	**Freedom, Responsibility, and Luck II: Stipulative Arguments for the Proximal Determination Requirement and Three Arguments against It**		129
	6.1	Stipulative versions of the Direct Argument for the Proximal Determination Requirement	130
	6.2	Stipulative versions of the Indirect Argument for the Proximal Determination Requirement	134
		6.2.1 Five arguments for (MI-2)	136
	6.3	Three arguments against the Proximal Determination Requirement	147
		6.3.1 Objections to the Melean Argument	150
		6.3.2 Objections to Fischer's Argument	153
		6.3.3 Defending the Possibility Argument	158

Coda	164
Notes	167
References	188
Index	195

Preface

This book develops a comprehensive new theory of luck in light of a critical appraisal of the literature's leading accounts (Chapters 1 and 2), then brings this new theory of luck to bear on some central issues in contemporary epistemology (Chapters 3 and 4) and philosophy of action (Chapters 5 and 6). For the benefit of any reader who may want to read only some parts of the book, here is a brief summary of its main results (I provide a more detailed summary in the Coda).

Chapters 1 and 2: Contrary to what recent theorists of luck have assumed, their main target of analysis – the concept of an event's being *lucky for* a subject – is in fact a disjunctive concept that is parasitic on the more fundamental notion of an event's being a *stroke of luck for* a subject. Roughly, a significant event is lucky for you just in case that event is *either* itself a stroke of luck for you *or* due primarily to something that was a stroke of luck for you, where a significant event is a stroke of luck for you just in case the event (a) is modally fragile – in the sense that the event (metaphysically) could well have failed to happen – and (b) is not something that you did intentionally.

Chapters 3 and 4: On the epistemological front, the most charitable reading of the platitude that 'knowledge excludes luck' is both too strong *and* too weak to capture the widespread intuition that knowledge excludes gettiered belief (that is, belief that's relevantly like the ones held by the subjects in those highly influential cases described by Gettier [1963]). The best extant account of gettiered belief – which differs importantly from each of the literature's two leading approaches to gettiered belief – employs only one of the three conditions involved in the best extant analysis of the most basic or fundamental concept of luck.

Chapters 5 and 6: On the action-theoretical front, the relatively weak and plausible thesis that morally responsible action is at least *possible* can help us see not only that all the main luck-involving threats to the scope of free and responsible action among finite, temporal agents such as us ultimately fizzle, but also that luck itself as well as various other luck-related phenomena – including, perhaps most prominently on the contemporary action-theoretical scene, the property of being *proximally undetermined* (that is, not entailed by the immediate past and laws of nature) – are a good deal more congenial to free and responsible action than is typically thought.

As this brief summary indicates, the overall view of luck's significance for human knowledge and agency that emerges over the course of this book is at once both optimistic and pessimistic. The view is optimistic in that it sees knowledge and free, responsible agency as compatible with a surprisingly wide range of luck-related phenomena. The view is pessimistic in that it sees reflection on the concept of luck as unlikely (in and of itself) to shed much light on the nature of knowledge and free, responsible agency or to reveal surprising limits on the scope of these phenomena among people such as us.

Acknowledgments

I'd like to thank Vincent Hendricks and Duncan Pritchard for thinking of me in connection with the *Palgrave Innovations in Philosophy* series. I am confident that I would not have undertaken to write a whole book on the topic of luck without their invitation and encouragement. I am also very grateful to Duncan as well as to Wayne Riggs for early interest in and support of my work on several of the key issues explored in this book.

I am grateful to the following people for various kinds of help on precursors of portions of this book at various times over the last 15 years or so: Richard Aquila, Avery Archer, Amy Atnip, Robert Audi, Andrew Bailey, Jordan Baker, Nathan Ballantyne, Michael Ball-Blakely, Eric Barnes, Nora Berenstain, Justin Biddle, John Bishop, Brian Boeninger, Tomás Bogardus, Rodrigo Borges, Thad Botham, Ayca Boylu, Mary Helen Brickhouse, Devon Bryson, Justin Capes, Al Casullo, Kyle Chapel, Randy Clarke, Nevin Climenhaga, Earl Conee, Adam Cureton, Nena Davis, Claudio de Almeida, Mirja Pérez de Calleja, Mike DePaul, David DiQuattro, Doug Ehring, Richard Feldman, John Martin Fischer, Kamper Floyd, Chris Franklin, Matt Frise, Georgi Gardiner, Jon Garthoff, Sandy Goldberg, Alvin Goldman, Peter J. Graham, John Greco, Chris Green, Jeff Green, Stephen Grimm, Scott Hagaman, Ish Haji, John Hardwig, John Hawthorne, Trevor Hedberg, David Henderson, Chris Hill, Dan Howard-Snyder, Albert Hu, Hud Hudson, Jennifer Jensen, Mark Jensen, Robert Kane, Tomis Kapitan, Matt Kennedy, Brian Kim, Kevin Kimble, Nate King, Peter Klein, Markus Kohl, Peter Kung, Jon Kvanvig, Osup Kwon, Maria Lasonen-Aarnio, Richard Lee, John Lemos, Neil Levy, Clayton Littlejohn, Todd Long, Kirk Ludwig, Yannig Luthra, Jack Lyons, Doug MacLean, Zach Manis, Chad Marxen, James McBain, John McClellan, Aidan McGlynn, Tim McIlrath, Michael McKenna, Al Mele, Caroline Mobley, Andrew Moon, Margaret Moore, Eddy Nahmias, Dana Nelkin, Tim O'Connor, Michael Pace, David Palmer, Matt Pamental, Garrett Pendergraft, Al Plantinga, Duncan Pritchard, Mike Rea, David Reidy, Alex Richardson, Jason Rickman, Wayne Riggs, Naomi Rinehold, Kate Ritchie, Carolina Sartorio, Tom Senor, Seth Shabo, Clerk Shaw, John Shoemaker, J.R. Shrader, Nico Silins, Donald Smith, Ernie Sosa, Dan Speak, Steve Steward, Kevin Timpe, Neal Tognazzini, Dale Tuggy, Roger

Turner, John Turri, Peter van Inwagen, Manuel Vargas, Xinghua Wang, Ted Warfield, Josh Watson, Lee Whittington, Timothy Williamson, Susan Wolf, Lily Ying, Dean Zimmerman, and Michael Zimmerman. Many thanks also to the two anonymous reviewers for Palgrave Macmillan, one of whom provided not only helpful advice on the proposal for this project but also numerous useful suggestions on the penultimate draft of the manuscript.

I presented ancestors of various portions of this book at a number of venues: the University of Arkansas, the University of Notre Dame, the University of Rochester Graduate Conference in Epistemology, Southern Methodist University, the Eastern Division of the Society of Christian Philosophers, the Central States Philosophical Association, the Southwestern Philosophical Society, the Central and Pacific Divisions of the American Philosophical Association, the University of Tennessee (departmental colloquia as well as courses and research seminar meetings), the Inland Northwest Philosophy Conference, and the Midwest Epistemology Workshop. I am grateful to everyone who participated in these meetings and sessions for their stimulating discussion and helpful feedback.

My home institution, the University of Tennessee-Knoxville, has generously supported my work on this project at various stages and in various ways. I am deeply grateful for the following awards that have enabled me to complete this book much more comfortably and quickly than would have been possible otherwise: a Chancellor's Grant for Faculty Research, a College of Arts and Sciences Junior Faculty Fellowship, a College of Arts and Sciences Lindsay Young Professorship, a Humanities Center Faculty Fellowship, and a Faculty Development Leave.

I owe a special debt of gratitude to five of the aforementioned people – Robert Audi, Chris Hill, Al Plantinga, Tom Senor, and Ted Warfield – for much philosophical education and inspiration. Thank you for investing so much in what at times must have seemed a very risky venture.

Last and unquestionably most, thanks to my wife, Sara, and to my children (in chronological order), Evan, Zachary, and Katelyn. It's hard to say exactly where, and how much, luck has been involved in creating and cultivating our vital relationships; but certainly you are, for me, *blessings beyond measure*. Thanks to my mother, Sandra, and to my sister, Louise, for unflagging encouragement and support throughout my whole life and in particular since I set out on the journey to become a professional philosopher. I dedicate this book to them and to the memory of my equally encouraging and supportive father, Eldon.

1
Lucky Events: The Current Debate and a New Proposal

A wide range of important debates across such areas as epistemology, philosophy of action, ethics, political philosophy, and philosophy of law center on luck-involving claims (that is, claims that involve the concept of luck itself, or some other luck-related concept) such as the following:

> If you know that P, then it's not lucky that you believe accurately that P.
>
> If it was lucky that you acted as you did, then you did not freely so act.
>
> If you and I behave in the same way but through sheer bad luck my conduct has worse results than yours, then I am no more blameworthy than you are for so behaving.
>
> We should redistribute resources so as to enhance the prospects of those who, through sheer bad luck, are among our worst off.
>
> We can properly punish successful criminal attempts more severely than ones that fail only by luck.

Reflection on such claims can easily impart a strong sense that '[t]he concept of luck plays a crucial role in many philosophical discussions' (Lackey 2008: 255; cf. Pritchard 2007: 278). Under this impression, several theorists working in one or another of the aforementioned areas have recently begun developing and assessing new, and unusually detailed, accounts of luck.[1] This nascent research program promises dividends, regardless of whether the concept of luck really is as important as it appears to be in light of claims like those above. If the concept actually does play a 'crucial role' in some or other of the indicated debates, then working toward its correct analysis will advance those debates rather directly, by progressively clarifying claims that drive them. But perhaps initial appearances mislead: maybe (at least some of) those discussions don't really revolve around *luck*, but instead revolve around some similar, more or less closely related notion(s). In that case, homing in on the correct analysis of luck should help us recognize that our focus on it has been (at least somewhat) misplaced, and such recognition should in turn lead to beneficial clarification of claims like those listed above.

In this chapter and the next one, I aim to reorient current theorizing about luck as an aid to our discerning the concept's true philosophical importance. Later chapters will bring the analysis of luck developed in the first two chapters to bear on some central debates in epistemology (Chapters 3 and 4) and philosophy of action (Chapters 5 and 6). As will emerge over the course of this book, while I certainly think that luck is a fascinating concept in its own right, I doubt that reflection on it stands much of a chance of illuminating the nature of knowledge and free, morally responsible agency or of revealing surprising limits on the scope of these phenomena among finite, temporal thinkers and agents such as us. Accordingly, this book's overall line of argument will be at least somewhat pessimistic about luck's philosophical importance. This relatively deflationary attitude toward luck runs contrary to certain epistemological and action-theoretical views that many would regard as platitudinous. More on all this in Chapters 3 through 6 below.

Here's an overview of this chapter and the next one.[2] After introducing the literature's leading theories of luck (Section 1.1), I'll present and defend counterexamples to each of them (Section 1.2). Next, I'll argue for the thesis that recent luck theorists' main target of analysis – viz., the concept of an event's being *lucky for* a subject – is actually parasitic on the more fundamental notion of an event's being a *stroke of luck for* a subject. This thesis will serve as at least a partial diagnosis of the leading theories' failure (Sections 1.3 and 1.4). I'll then develop an analysis of *strokes of luck* that utilizes key insights from the recent luck literature (Sections 2.1 and 2.2). Finally, having set out a comprehensive new theory of luck – the **Enriched Strokes Account** of lucky events – I'll return to the initial counterexamples to the literature's leading theories to show that the Enriched Strokes Account can properly handle all of them (Sections 2.3 and 2.4).[3]

Before diving in, let me flag an important assumption and describe how I'll be using some key terms. Following other recent luck theorists, I'll assume that the luck relation(s) can relate (a) individuals for whom things can go better or worse to (b) events proper as well as obtaining states of affairs (or facts). What I call 'events proper' are concrete-object-like entities that have spatiotemporal locations and are denoted by perfect gerundial nominals – for example, 'Ann's catching of the ball', 'the shark's biting of Bob'. By contrast, states of affairs are abstract proposition-like entities that obey Boolean principles (they can be conjoined, disjoined, negated, and so on) and are denoted by imperfect gerundial nominals – for example, 'Ann's catching the ball', 'the shark's biting Bob'.[4] Accordingly – and also in line with other contributors to the recent luck literature – I'll here use 'event' in a relatively broad sense that covers events proper as well as states of affairs. I'll use 'happen' in a correspondingly broad sense to cover both *occurrence* (for events) and *coming to obtain* (for states of affairs). And I'll use 'do' in a broad sense to cover both *performance* (for events) and *actualization* (or *making to obtain* – for states of affairs).

1.1 Three leading theories of luck

Say that possible world W_1 is **close to** possible world W_2 before time t iff W_1 is no more than slightly different from W_2 up to (but not including) t.[5] With this stipulative definition in hand, we can state the literature's three leading accounts of luck as follows:

> **The Modal Account:** Event E is at time t (un)lucky for subject S iff (E happens at t and) (i) E is in some respect good (bad) for S, and (ii) E doesn't happen around t in a wide class of possible worlds that are close to the actual world before t.[6]
>
> **The Control Account:** E is at t (un)lucky for S iff (i) E is in some respect good (bad) for S, (ii) S hasn't successfully exploited E for some purpose, and (iii) E isn't something that S did intentionally.[7]
>
> **The Mixed Account:** E is at t (un)lucky for S iff (i) E is in some respect good (bad) for S, (ii) E doesn't happen around t in a wide class of possible worlds that are close to the actual world before t, and (iii) E isn't something that S did intentionally.[8]

A few remarks about each account's condition (i), and the Modal and Mixed Accounts' condition (ii), are now in order. Condition (i) seems to be the best way to understand the significance or value condition on luck (for the best available discussion of the significance condition, see Ballantyne 2012). Since an event can be good for you in one respect but bad for you in another, accounts of luck that incorporate condition

(i) correctly allow an event to be both lucky *and* unlucky for you (cf. Ballantyne 2012: 331). For example, your lottery win may be good luck in that it enables you to retire early, but bad luck in that it makes you a salient target for extortion.

For expressions of the chanciness condition on luck that resemble the Modal and Mixed Accounts' condition (ii), see Pritchard (2005), Coffman (2007), and Levy (2009, 2011a). It's important to state condition (ii) with *'around* t' instead of *'at* t'. If condition (ii) is stated with 'at', each account's right-to-left conditional will be vulnerable to the following kind of counterexample:

> Under perfectly normal conditions, you (automatically, non-intentionally) inhale wholesome air at t. Inhaling wholesome air is good for you, and it doesn't happen at t in a wide class of worlds that are close to the actual world before t. In most such worlds, you're either exhaling or idle at t.

If condition (ii) is stated with 'at', each account's right-to-left conditional will imply incorrectly that you are at t lucky to be inhaling wholesome air (remember the stipulation that your conditions are perfectly normal). With 'around', each account's right-to-left conditional avoids the implication that you are at t lucky to be inhaling wholesome air (assuming that you inhale wholesome air *around* t in the vast majority of worlds that are close to the actual world before t).[9]

Moreover, since different deterministic worlds may nevertheless be close to each other up to a given time, condition (ii) allows the Modal and Mixed Accounts to countenance lucky events in settings where causal determinism obtains ('causal determinism' here denotes the thesis that 'there is at any instant exactly one physically possible future' [van Inwagen 1983: 3]). Numerous cases illustrate this possibility (cf. Pritchard 2005, Coffman 2007, Levy 2011a). Winning the lottery in a deterministic world is lucky for you, notwithstanding the fact that your lottery win was necessitated by prior events and the laws of nature. For another example, suppose that you live in a deterministic world where your life depends on a certain sphere's remaining perfectly balanced on the tip of a particular cone throughout some temporal interval.[10] We can fill in the details so as to elicit the intuition that you are lucky the sphere remains perfectly balanced on the tip of the cone throughout that interval, notwithstanding the fact that the sphere's remaining so balanced on the cone's tip throughout that interval was necessitated by prior events and the laws of nature.

All three of the literature's leading accounts of luck issue correct verdicts about certain clear cases of luck such as the following:

> ***Good Lottery:*** You habitually play numbers corresponding to your own birthday in the state lottery. On this occasion, however, you seriously contemplate playing numbers corresponding to your mother's birthday. In the end, you stick with standard practice and play your own numbers. Lo and behold, you win!
>
> ***Bad Lottery:*** You live in a corrupt state where citizens are forced to play in a lottery whose winners lose their life savings to the governor. As before, you vacillate between playing your mother's birthday numbers and your own birthday numbers. In the end, you stick with your own numbers. Lo and behold, you win!

In each example, your lottery win isn't something that you did intentionally; you haven't yet exploited your win for some purpose; and, finally, in a wide class of worlds that are close to the actual world before the time at which you win, you don't win around then. To verify that the last condition holds, think about various small changes we could make to the actual world before the time at which you won (I assume here that we share the same birthday, and so that you played '062976'): '6' (rather than '7') is the penultimate number selected; '5' is the penultimate number selected; '4' is the penultimate number selected; and so on. If things had been slightly different in one or another of these ways before the time at which you won, you would not have won around then. Therefore, in a wide class of possible worlds that are close to the actual world before the time at which you won, you don't win around then. So, provided that your win in *Good Lottery* is good for you – and that your win in *Bad Lottery* is bad for you – each of the literature's leading accounts of luck entails that your win is (un)lucky for you.

Alas, as we're about to see, each of the leading accounts is also vulnerable to successful counterexamples.

1.2 Counterexamples to the leading theories of luck

Let's start with the Modal Account. Over the next few paragraphs, I'll defeat Levy's (2011a: 20–2) recent attempted defense of condition (ii)'s necessity for luck from the following counterexample developed by Lackey (2008):

> ***Buried Treasure:*** Sophie buries her treasure at the one spot where rose bushes can grow on the northwest corner of her island. For

personal reasons, Sophie was set on burying her treasure on the island's northwest corner in a spot that supports rose bushes: that's her favorite part of the island, and roses are her favorite flowers. All this is unbeknownst to Vincent, another inhabitant of the island who shows up one month later at the exact same spot where Sophie buried her treasure. Like Sophie, Vincent has personal reasons for digging up that spot – but they're completely different from, and unrelated to, Sophie's: Vincent is set on planting a rose bush in his mother's memory on that part of the island. As Vincent goes about his digging, he's shocked to find buried treasure.

Finding Sophie's treasure when he does clearly seems lucky for Vincent. But given the stipulated details, Vincent finds Sophie's treasure around that time in the vast majority of possible worlds that are close to the actual world before he finds it. *Buried Treasure* thus seems to be a counterexample to condition (ii)'s alleged necessity for luck.

Levy (2011a: 20–2) attempts to defend condition (ii)'s necessity for luck from *Buried Treasure*. We can understand Levy as trying both to undercut and to rebut the judgment that Vincent is lucky to find Sophie's treasure. As for the undercutter, Levy suggests that the critic's judgment that Vincent is lucky to find the treasure stems from the fact that the discovery seems lucky to Vincent. But since E's seeming lucky to S is perfectly compatible with E's not actually being lucky for S, the critic's reason for thinking that the discovery is lucky for Vincent doesn't justify that judgment.

Levy's attempt to rebut the judgment that Vincent is lucky to find Sophie's treasure takes off from the following case (2011a: 21):

Buried Treasure*: Unbeknownst to Vincent, Sophie buried the treasure in the spot at which he found it because Vincent's eccentric great-uncle wanted him to have the riches (perhaps Sophie was unaware of the plan; perhaps Vincent's great-uncle is a neuroscientist with the power to implant in Sophie a love of roses, knowing it will lead her to bury her treasure in the one spot where he knows Vincent will dig). In that case, it will seem to Vincent very lucky that there was treasure in the precise spot at which he dug, but luck has nothing to do with it; his finding the treasure was planned. Indeed, that might be precisely how Vincent's great-uncle thinks of his plan: he has, as he might say, 'left nothing to chance'.

According to Levy, if Vincent knew all the details of *Buried Treasure* and how that case relates to *Buried Treasure** – in which Vincent clearly isn't lucky to find the treasure – Vincent should think he really isn't lucky in *Buried Treasure* after all. And the fact that Vincent should think this in light of such knowledge is a good reason to think he isn't lucky in *Buried Treasure*.

Levy's attempted undercutter can be circumvented by deleting from *Buried Treasure* the unnecessary detail that Vincent is surprised to find Sophie's treasure and stipulating instead that Vincent was extremely confident that he'd make such a discovery despite having no evidence at all for this proposition. The discovery no longer seems lucky *to* Vincent, but it still seems lucky *for* him (cf. Steglich-Petersen 2010: 365ff.). Thus, the basis for our intuition that the discovery is lucky for Vincent can't be just that it seems lucky to him. As for the attempted rebutter, note that we must give its occurrences of 'should' an epistemic reading. (If we don't give Levy's 'should' an epistemic reading, then we should [epistemically] reject his assumption that a subject's being such that s/he should[n't] self-ascribe luck reliably indicates that s/he is[n't] in fact lucky.) But since there's a highly relevant difference between *Buried Treasure* and *Buried Treasure** – viz., the presence of the great-uncle's planning/design – it's not at all clear that Vincent should (epistemically) infer, from the details of *Buried Treasure* and its relation to *Buried Treasure**, that he's not lucky in the former. Indeed, that seems like a pretty weak analogical inference given the highly relevant difference between the two cases in terms of overall planning/design (cf. Lackey 2008: 262–3).

As I see it, then, Levy's attempt to defend condition (ii)'s necessity for luck from Lackey's *Buried Treasure* example fails. Before moving on to the Control Account of lucky events, I want to (a) briefly mention – and then temporarily bracket – one *alleged* consequence of the success of counterexamples, such as *Buried Treasure*, to condition (ii)'s necessity for luck and (b) address at somewhat greater length Riggs' (2007) criticism of a certain kind of counterexample to the Modal Account's right-to-left conditional.

First, some theorists have inferred – from the success of counterexamples such as *Buried Treasure* to condition (ii)'s necessity for luck – that the kind of chance or improbability related to luck is not *metaphysical* but is instead *epistemic*. One prominent recent proponent of this type of view is Steglich-Petersen (2010: 369; cf. Rescher 1995: 28–34), who ultimately endorses the following 'ignorance' requirement on luck:

S is lucky with respect to E at t only if, just before t, S was not in a position to know that E would occur at t.

This ignorance requirement on luck enjoys confirmation from numerous cases, including *Good Lottery* and *Buried Treasure*. In the former, you were lucky to win the lottery, but were not (just before you won) in a position to know you'd soon win. In the latter, Vincent was lucky to find the buried treasure but was not (just before his discovery) in a position to know he'd soon make such a discovery. Should this persuade us that luck-related chance is *epistemic* rather than *metaphysical*? No, because the proposed ignorance requirement on luck is false, given minimally antiskeptical assumptions. I'll be in a better position to press this objection at the beginning of Section 1.4 below, and so I'll set Steglich-Petersen's proposal aside until then.

I turn now to the aforementioned criticism from Riggs (2007) of a certain kind of counterexample to the Modal Account's right-to-left conditional. Contrary to the relevant portion of the Modal Account, a morally significant yet modally fragile choice needn't be a lucky occurrence (cf. Latus 2003, Coffman 2007, Lackey 2008). Suppose that you choose at t to make a substantial donation to Oxfam, where there was right before t a large chance you would not so choose at t (you had fairly strong self-interested reasons to omit such a choice, and so on). The Modal Account entails that your choosing to donate was lucky for you. But suppose your relevant reasons inclined you at least somewhat toward making the donation and that the choice and subsequent donation were made intentionally, freely, and knowingly.[11] Then your choosing to donate wasn't – or at least, it needn't have been – *lucky* for you, notwithstanding the fact that your choice was both modally fragile and good for you.

It looks, then, as though we have here a clear counterexample to the Modal Account's claim of sufficiency for luck. But Riggs suggests the following defense to the Modal Account's proponent (2007: 338, italics added):[12]

> It seems that [the Modal Account's proponent] has only to insist that the circumstances, whatever they were, that led our reluctant philanthropist to *donate the money* are part of the "relevant initial conditions" that must be the same in the nearest possible worlds in which the lucky event must not occur. But if the prompting events are present, then the action will be present. So, the event will not count as lucky on [the Modal Account], thus saving the view from the purported counterexamples.

The suggested defense's key claim is the following counterfactual conditional (which has a true antecedent): *S would have donated to Oxfam had the pertinent prompting events occurred*. Now, what are the donation's prompting events? Presumably, the donation's prompting events are S's having the relevant reasons to donate and choosing to donate for those reasons. More fully, then, the key claim of Riggs' suggested defense of the Modal Account is this: *S would have donated to Oxfam had S chosen, for the relevant reasons, to donate to Oxfam*. But the Modal Account's critic can happily accept the indicated counterfactual. What the critic claims is that S might well have failed to *choose* to donate – and so, might well have failed to donate – had S possessed the relevant reasons for donating. That claim is perfectly consistent with S's being such that she would have donated had she possessed the relevant reasons *and chosen to donate on their basis*. So, the objector's key claim turns out to be perfectly consistent with the case's refuting the Modal Account's right-to-left conditional. Close inspection reveals that Riggs' suggested defense of the Modal Account fails to engage the putative counterexample.

Let's turn now from the Modal Account to the Control Account – specifically, to this nuanced version recently developed by Riggs (2009a: 220):

> E is at t (un)lucky for S iff (i) E is in some respect good (bad) for S, (ii) S hasn't successfully exploited E for some purpose, and (iii) E isn't something that S did intentionally.

Riggs' addition of condition (ii) to earlier, simpler versions of the Control Account immunizes his analysis against cases involving certain significant states of affairs that you didn't actualize intentionally but are nevertheless *not* lucky for you, given their modal stability. Consider: despite the fact that you didn't intentionally bring about the sun's rising this morning or the continued functioning of the electricity in the room you're now in, neither of these states of affairs counts as *lucky* for you. While such examples refute simpler species of the Control Account, they don't refute Riggs' version (assuming you've successfully exploited the indicated states of affairs for some purpose or other, which you presumably have). Moreover, Riggs' inclusion of condition (ii) is quite well motivated because he adds it in light of intuitions about the following fascinating case (2009a: 216):

> ***African Expedition:*** Smith plans an expedition into the wilds of Africa where certain tribes of Africans with exotic customs were known to live. Smith is constrained...to make this trip during a particular month of a particular year. He proposes the trip to his fellow adventurer Jones, including the specific times that he means to travel. Jones agrees to tag along. As it happens, the particular tribe that lives in the area that Smith and Jones visit has a custom of sacrificing people

from outside the tribe on the equinoxes of the year. The autumnal equinox happens to fall during the time that Smith and Jones are in the area, so they are captured and held until that day so that they can be sacrificed... As the tribesmen approach to kill them..., there is a total eclipse of the sun. The members of this tribe always take such exotic natural occurrences to signal the anger of their gods at them for whatever they happen to be doing at the moment. Consequently, they set their captives free.... Smith says to Jones, 'that solar eclipse was an amazing stroke of good luck!' Jones replies, 'Don't be absurd! There was nothing lucky about it. I knew all along that these people would likely try to sacrifice us on the equinox if we were captured, but I also knew that there was a total eclipse of the sun due on that very day and that this tribe would react to that event by letting us go. Did you really think I would be stupid enough to fall into such a situation without having a plan to extricate myself?'

According to Riggs, 'Smith was lucky that the eclipse happened, and Jones was not' (2009a: 217). Obviously, neither adventurer intentionally brought about the eclipse, so we'll need something other than condition (iii) to capture our sense that the eclipse was lucky for Smith but not for Jones. Here, of course, is where condition (ii) comes in. Since only *Jones* successfully exploited the eclipse for some purpose – that is, only Jones 'planned a course of action that assumed that [the eclipse] would occur', which secured his survival (2009a: 218) – (ii) and (iii) together imply that the eclipse was lucky for only *Smith*.

Alas, Riggs' Control Account's right-hand-side doesn't suffice for luck. Suppose that Katelyn lives and works in an underground facility that is, *unbeknownst to her*, solar-powered. This morning's sunrise was good for Katelyn (it kept her facility running), not intentionally brought about by her, and not successfully exploited by her for some purpose: having been underground for so long, Katelyn has become totally oblivious to sunrises, and so she doesn't plan any courses of action assuming that the sun will rise. Riggs' Control Account implies, incorrectly, that Katelyn was lucky the sun rose this morning.

As for the left-to-right conditional of Riggs' Control Account, cases such as the following show that condition (ii) isn't required for luck:

Kidnapping: My son Zachary is kidnapped. The kidnappers communicate to me that I can have Zachary back as soon as I tell them that I can pay a huge ransom. Once I tell them this, I'll have 24 hours to deliver the payment; if I don't get the money to them before the deadline, they'll recapture Zachary and increase the ransom. An informant I know to be extremely reliable tells me that tonight's lottery will be rigged in my favor. According to my informant, the lottery officials have heard about my family's plight and want to help us out. So, I form a justified belief that I'll win tonight's lottery. Now, on this occasion, my reliable informant is mistaken: tonight's lottery *won't* be rigged in my favor. As it happens, though, I'm going to win the lottery fair and square! So, I have a justified and *true* belief that I'm going to win tonight's lottery. I phone the kidnappers to tell them that I can pay the ransom. They release Zachary, reminding me that if they don't have the money in 24 hours, they'll recapture him and increase the ransom. All along, I'm thinking: 'No problem – I'll have my lottery winnings in hand with plenty of time to spare!' I win the large, fair lottery that evening.

My lottery win was clearly a stroke of good luck for me. And it's a fact that I successfully exploited for the purpose of getting Zachary back: I planned a course of action that assumed I would win, and this course of action resulted in Zachary's safe return (compare Jones' parallel relation to the eclipse in Riggs' *African Expedition*). Moral: An event can be lucky for you *even if* you successfully exploit the event for some purpose.

As for condition (iii) of the Control Account, cases such as the following show that it's not a requirement on luck (for two additional structurally similar examples, see Lackey's [2008: 259–260] 'Demolition Worker' and 'Derek' cases):

Distracted Driver: Our department meeting just happens to end early for once. As a result, I'm early to pick up my son Evan from school. Upon arriving, I spot him playing in the street. A car, whose distracted driver is texting on her cell phone, speeds toward Evan. But I'm in a position to push Evan out of the car's path, and I of course do so. Hugging Evan tightly moments later, I say: 'I'm so lucky you are safe!'

If your intuitions follow mine here, the self-ascription of luck regarding Evan's safety will strike you as true *on balance* (more on this qualification momentarily). The seeming truth (on balance) of that self-ascription of luck can be bolstered by (i) the even *stronger* sense that the self-ascription of luck is fully appropriate, combined with (ii) the 'general presumption that, where speakers are not basing their claims on some false beliefs they have about underlying matters of fact, how they naturally and appropriately describe a situation...will be a true description' (DeRose 2009: 51). I conclude, therefore, that I was (at the indicated time) lucky that Evan was safe. Note, finally, that we can understand this case so that Evan's safety is something I brought about intentionally (by pushing him out of the car's path). Moral: An event can be lucky for you *even if* it's something you brought about intentionally.

Now, why the 'on balance' qualification? Because I expect that some theorists will feel some inclination to deny that I am (at the relevant time) *lucky* that Evan is safe (cf. Levy 2011a: 222–3). I can understand such doubt, having harbored it myself in the recent past (cf. Coffman 2009: 503). But I now view such doubt as a mistaken response to a different, though (I hasten to add) closely related, fact – viz., that it's not (at the relevant time) a *stroke of good luck* for me that Evan is safe. To be sure, Evan is safe then *by* a stroke of good luck for me (and for him) – viz., my becoming positioned to save him; but Evan's safety (at the relevant time) isn't *itself* a stroke of good luck for me (or for him). In what remains of this chapter, I'll bolster the error theory I've just sketched by more fully clarifying and defending the distinction between *lucky events* and *strokes of luck* on which the error theory depends.[13] In the next chapter (Section 2.3) I'll return to *Distracted Driver* to show that my overall account of luck yields (what I've here claimed are) the correct verdicts about the case.

We've now seen counterexamples to both directions of both the Modal Account and the Control Account. As for the Mixed Account, *Buried Treasure* and *Distracted Driver* together show that neither (ii) nor (iii) is necessary for an event's being lucky for you. Now, from the success of counterexamples such as *Buried Treasure* and *Distracted Driver* to conditions (ii) and (iii), Lackey has inferred that 'the conditions proposed by [the literature's leading accounts of lucky events]...fail to capture what is distinctive of, and central to, the concept of luck' (2008: 255). Starting in the next section and continuing throughout the next chapter, I'll be presenting and defending a new account of luck on which conditions (ii) and (iii) are requirements on an event's being a *stroke of luck* for a subject, a notion on which the concept *lucky event* is parasitic. If anything like such an analysis of luck is correct, then there's a clear sense in which the Mixed Account's clauses (ii) and (iii) *are* (in Lackey's words) 'distinctive of, and central to, the concept of luck' after all. By the end of the next chapter, then, I believe we'll be in a position to reject Lackey's inference as invalid.

1.3 Lucky events and strokes of luck

Besides their vulnerability to counterexamples, the leading theories of luck have another – and, as will become clearer as we proceed, related – defect in common: their proponents (including yours truly) have assumed, at least implicitly, that the locution 'is (un)lucky for' expresses the most fundamental or basic luck concept. This assumption should strike us as dubious, however, after some reflection on a different locution we frequently use to ascribe luck: 'is a stroke of good (bad) luck for'.

The locutions in question are not equivalent. To see this, extend *Good Lottery* so that the lottery officials are now handing you the lottery's large cash prize. Clearly, you are lucky to be receiving the lottery prize. But while you are receiving the lottery prize *by* a stroke of good luck (viz., your lottery win), your receiving the prize isn't *itself* a stroke of good luck for you: you're the rightful winner, after all. For another illustration of the point that the indicated locutions aren't equivalent, extend *Bad Lottery* so that the governor is now transferring your life savings into his checking account. Clearly, you are unlucky to be losing your life savings to the governor. But while you are losing your life savings to the governor *by* a stroke of bad luck (viz., your lottery win), the governor's taking your life savings isn't *itself* a stroke of bad luck for you: you're the rightful winner, after all. Moral: An event that isn't itself a stroke of good (bad) luck for you may nevertheless be (un)lucky for you.

Keep reflecting on how *is (un)lucky for* might be related to *is a stroke of good (bad) luck for*, and I predict that you'll eventually be tempted to deem the latter more fundamental than the former. While there are no promising accounts of *is a stroke of luck for* in terms of *is lucky for* on the horizon, there's the following promising analysis of the latter in terms of the former: an event that's *(un)lucky* for you is either *itself* a stroke of good (bad) luck for you, or the event is good (bad) for you and due primarily (chiefly, mainly) to some *prior* stroke of good (bad) luck for you. More precisely:

> Event E is at t (un)lucky for subject S iff (i) E is in some respect good (bad) for S and (ii) there's a stroke of good (bad) luck for S, E*, such that *either* (a) E = E* *or* (b) E* is a primary (chief, main) contributor to E.

Call this the **Strokes Account** of lucky events. This proposal differs crucially from the literature's leading accounts of luck in that it sees *is lucky for* as disjunctive – as admitting a direct/indirect distinction – in a way similar to, for example, *is morally responsible for*: subject S is morally responsible for an action, A, iff S is either directly *or* indirectly morally responsible for A, where (i) S is *directly* morally responsible for A iff S is responsible for A but not in virtue of being responsible for some prior act; and (ii) S is *indirectly* morally responsible for A iff S is responsible for A in virtue of being responsible for some prior act (cf. Mele 2006: 86–7).[14] Similarly, the Strokes Account's proponent distinguishes between (i) lucky events that *do* inherit their status as such from some prior lucky events and (ii) lucky events that *don't* inherit their status as such from any prior lucky events – where the latter notion is, the Strokes Account's proponent suggests, commonly expressed in ordinary discourse by 'is a stroke of good (bad) luck for' and cognate locutions.[15]

Something must be said right away about what's here meant by 'is a primary (chief, main) contributor to'. I intend to use that expression and related ones – for example, 'primarily (chiefly, mainly) because' – in their ordinary senses. Such expressions have the same meanings here as they do in familiar bits of ordinary discourse such as the following:[16]

> My having to study *Julius Caesar* in high school is a primary contributor to my present hatred of the work.
>
> The wind's kicking up when it did was a chief contributor to the fire's spreading into the new timber.
>
> The driver's reckless behavior was a main contributor to Sara's becoming a widow.

Call the relation that 'is a primary (chief, main) contributor to' expresses in the above sentences the **primary contribution relation**; the following claims display this relation's converse:

> I now hate *Julius Caesar* primarily because I had to study the work in high school
>
> The fire's spreading to the new timber was due chiefly to the wind's kicking up when it did.
>
> Sara is a widow mainly because of the driver's reckless behavior.

We can tighten our grip on (what I'm calling) the primary contribution relation by noting that it's neither necessary nor sufficient for *causal* contribution. First, causes needn't be primary contributors. The Big Bang, nearly all theorists of causation will agree, is a cause of every subsequent event. So the Big Bang is among the causes of every human birth and death. But no human birth or death has been due primarily (chiefly, mainly) to the Big Bang. (Writes Lewis [1986: 23]: '[The Big Bang], I take it, is a cause of *every* later event without exception. Then it is a cause of every death. But the Big Bang did not kill anyone.')

Second, primary contributors needn't be causes. Suppose that, at noon, I (Sara's husband) am fatally struck by a reckless driver while crossing the street. Sara becomes a widow at noon, and this is due primarily to the reckless driver's behavior. But while the reckless driver's behavior was surely a cause of my death, it wasn't also a cause of Sara's widowing; the latter is instead a non-causal consequence of the driver's actions. (For starters, since my death arguably doesn't cause Sara's widowing – these happen simultaneously, and possibly at great spatial distance – there seems to be no causal chain connecting the driver's behavior to Sara's widowing [cf. Kim 1974].) I hasten to add, however, that primary contribution is *like* causal contribution in that both are objective, mind-independent, out-in-the-world phenomena (cf. Bennett 1988: 32).

Over the next several paragraphs, I'll further clarify the primary contribution relation – and why I've used *it* in the official statement of the Strokes Account rather than any of a number of similar, and perhaps better understood, generative relations – by raising and answering a series of pertinent pointed questions. Here's the first:

'Why "is a primary contributor to" rather than "is a primary cause of"?'

The latter would make the Strokes Account too *strong*. We can imagine that Sara's widowing is unlucky for her, given the way it relates to a certain stroke of bad luck for her – for example, a reckless driver's fatally striking me as I cross the street. But again, the driver's fatally striking me doesn't *cause* Sara's widowing. So, if we replace 'is a primary contributor to' with 'is a primary cause of', the Strokes Account won't issue the correct verdict that Sara is unlucky to be a widow.

'Why "is a *primary* contributor to" rather than merely "contributes to"?' The latter would make the Strokes Account too *weak*.[17] Suppose you narrowly escaped death once as a toddler; your survival at that time was a stroke of good luck for you. If we go with 'contributes to', the Strokes Account's right-to-left conditional will imply that every later significant event to which your survival contributes is lucky for you. Since your survival presumably contributes to *every* later event that involves you, the Strokes Account's right-to-left conditional will imply that *every* later significant you-involving event is *lucky* for you. But such a proliferation of luck would be wholly unacceptable here (cf. Levy 2009: 497; 2011a: 78, footnote 17). Why so? Because the luck analyst's quarry is a phenomenon one paradigm of which is your winning a large fair lottery and whose presence can arguably keep true beliefs from constituting knowledge, rational actions from qualifying as free, and so on. Assuming that lottery win-type events aren't ubiquitous – and that our ability to gain/retain knowledge, and to act freely, isn't under constant threat from luck (see Chapters 3 through 6 for thorough discussion of the main issues here) – the luck analyst's quarry simply can't be as common a phenomenon as the 'contributes to' version of the Strokes Account would have it (cf. Lackey 2008: 258).

Happily, the right-to-left conditional of the official statement of the Strokes Account doesn't yield the same unacceptable proliferation of luck. In the case under consideration, for example, we can safely suppose that your survival as a toddler isn't a *primary* contributor to *every* later event in which you're involved. Now, it is arguable that in the envisaged case, every later event that involves you – or at least, every such event of which you're the sole subject – counterfactually depends on your survival as a toddler: if you hadn't survived, that event wouldn't have happened. Arguably, then, formulating the Strokes Account in terms of counterfactual dependence would make the account too weak. But counterfactual dependence doesn't suffice for primary contribution. Everything downstream from the Big Bang counterfactually depends on it, but it's not the case that everything downstream from the Big Bang – for example, your currently reading this sentence – is due *primarily* to the Big Bang.

It is also arguable that in the imagined case, for every later moment at which you exist, you exist then primarily because you survived as a toddler. But that too is compatible with the claim that your survival as a toddler isn't a *primary* contributor to *every* later event that involves you. Generally speaking, even if X's *existence* at t is due primarily to Y, some X-involving events at t may not be *at all* due to Y. (Writes Sosa [2007: 95]: 'Something may explain the existence of a certain entity...without even partially explaining why it has a given property. That it was made in a Volvo factory may explain the existence of a certain defective car, for example, without even partially explaining why it is now defective. Indeed it may be defective *despite* being a Volvo. Its being defective is hence not at all attributable to its origin in that Volvo factory.') As far as I can currently see, then, the official statement of the Strokes Account – in terms of the primary contribution relation – doesn't suffer from a problematic over-ascription of luck.

'Why "is a primary contributor to" rather than "is counterfactually necessary for"?' As we saw one paragraph back, the latter would arguably make the Strokes Account too *weak*. I believe it would also make the account too *strong*. Suppose that you alone have been left in charge of the mechanism that will generate tonight's winning lottery number. Here's your dastardly plan: let the mechanism generate its number, then quickly modify the result if it doesn't match the number on your ticket (assume that you could make such a change without risk of detection). Lo and behold, the mechanism generates your number on its own; you win the lottery fair and square! Clearly, the mechanism's generating your number was a stroke of good luck for you. Afterward, the lottery officials hand you the lottery's large cash prize. While you are lucky to be receiving the lottery prize, your receipt of the prize isn't *itself* a stroke of good luck for you: you're the rightful winner, after all.

We've now arrived at a counterexample to the left-to-right conditional of a version of the Strokes Account that employs 'is counterfactually necessary for' instead of 'is a primary contributor to'. Since (i) the mechanism's generating your number is the only stroke of good luck for you in the vicinity, and (ii) you would still have received the prize even if the mechanism hadn't generated your number, the left-to-right conditional of the counterfactual dependence version of the Strokes Account implies incorrectly that you weren't lucky to receive the lottery prize. Happily, the official version of the Strokes Account – in terms of the primary contribution relation – issues the right verdict on this case since the mechanism's generating your number was clearly a primary contributor to your receiving the prize.

'Why "is a *primary* contributor to" rather than merely "is a *large* contributor to"?' Note first this question's presupposition that the primary contribution relation is to be understood (at least partly) in terms of what we might call the **large contribution relation**, which is expressed in ordinary discourse by 'is a large contributor to' and whose converse is expressed in such discourse by 'largely because' and cognate locutions (for example, 'is due largely to'). I accept the question's presupposition: plausibly, E* is a *primary* contributor to E only if E* is at least a *large* contributor to E. So again, why formulate the Strokes Account in terms of *primary* contribution rather than merely *large* contribution?

The latter would make the Strokes Account too *weak*. Suppose that, having just been told that you've won the lottery, you celebrate by eating several pieces of raw broccoli. Winning the lottery was a stroke of good luck for you, and you ate the broccoli largely because you won the lottery. So, assuming that eating the broccoli was good for you, the right-to-left conditional of a version of the Strokes Account that employs 'is a large contributor to' instead of 'is a primary contributor to' implies that you were lucky to eat the broccoli. But we can fill in the details so that you weren't lucky to eat the broccoli: we can safely suppose that there were no hidden obstacles to your eating the broccoli; you ate the broccoli intentionally, knowingly, and freely; and so on. This case constitutes a counterexample to the right-to-left conditional of the envisaged large contributor version of the Strokes Account.[18]

Happily, the official version of the Strokes Account issues the right verdict on such a case since (i) your winning the lottery is the only stroke of good luck for you in the vicinity, and (ii) it's not the case that you ate the broccoli *primarily* because you won the lottery; rather, you ate the broccoli primarily because you were in a celebratory mood.[19] Of course, we can understand this case so that you were in an exceptionally celebratory mood primarily because you'd just been told you'd won the lottery, which in turn happened primarily because you had in fact won the lottery. But these facts don't jointly entail that you ate the broccoli primarily because you won the lottery; there are possible cases in which A is due primarily to B, B is due primarily to C, and C is due primarily to D, but A isn't due primarily to D. Consider a familiar example from the recent literature on causation (cf. Sartorio 2012a, who attributes this case to Ned Hall):

> While hiking, you suddenly notice a boulder rolling toward you. You dodge the boulder, thus surviving your hike. You survived the hike primarily because you dodged the boulder; you dodged the bolder primarily because you saw it rolling toward you; and you saw the boulder rolling toward you primarily because it was in fact rolling toward you; but it's false that you survived your hike primarily because the boulder was rolling toward you.

Finally, I submit that if we change the broccoli case so as to make it clearer that you really did eat the broccoli *primarily because* you won the lottery – imagine, for example, that you simply can't bring yourself to eat raw broccoli unless you're in an *exceptionally* celebratory mood, which only something like a lottery win could engender – it will simultaneously become more plausible that you were in fact lucky to get some broccoli in your system, which is just as the Strokes Account would have it. I conclude, then, that the relevant kind of case doesn't seriously threaten the official version of the Strokes Account.

Over the last several paragraphs, I've (i) provided a sampling of highly intelligible claims in which the primary contribution relation, or its converse, figures prominently; (ii) further clarified the primary contribution relation by distinguishing it from *causal* contribution; and (iii) indicated why I've formulated the official version of the Strokes Account in terms of primary contribution rather than one or another of numerous similar, and perhaps better understood, generative relations. I hope that this material helps persuade any initially skeptical readers that the primary contribution relation is sufficiently intelligible for the work I want it to do here – viz., illuminating the relation expressed by 'is (un)lucky for'.[20]

1.4 The Strokes Account: further support and defense

I turn now to providing further argument for, and defense of, the Strokes Account. The extended versions of *Good Lottery* and *Bad Lottery* described above strongly confirm the Strokes Account. Recall our extended version of *Good Lottery*, wherein the lottery officials have just handed you the lottery's large cash prize. Here are two related facts:

You were lucky that your birthday numbers won.

You were lucky to receive the lottery prize.

The Strokes Account smoothly explains both of these facts. It was a stroke of good luck for you that your birthday numbers won, and you received the lottery prize primarily because your numbers won. Combined with these claims, the Strokes Account entails the above facts. That the Strokes Account so smoothly explains those facts counts significantly in its favor.

Now recall our extended version of *Bad Lottery*, wherein the governor has just transferred your life savings into his checking account. Consider two related facts:

You were unlucky that your birthday numbers won.

You were unlucky to lose your life savings to the governor.

Again, the Strokes Account easily explains both facts. It was a stroke of bad luck for you that your birthday numbers won, and the governor took your savings primarily because your numbers won. Combined with these claims, the Strokes Account entails the above facts. That the

Strokes Account so easily explains those facts further confirms it's on the right track.

Let me pause here to provide an argument, promised back in Section 1.2, against the following 'ignorance' requirement on luck that Steglich-Petersen (2010: 369) proposes in light of *Buried Treasure*-type counterexamples to the alleged necessity for luck of condition (ii) of the Modal Account and the Mixed Account:

> S is lucky with respect to E at t only if, just before t, S was not in a position to know that E would occur at t.

Reflection on some previously discussed cases reveals that Steglich-Petersen's requirement has some counterintuitively skeptical consequences. Recall, for example, *Good Lottery* and *Distracted Driver*. In the former, I was lucky that I received the lottery prize, and in the latter I was lucky that Evan survived his encounter with the distracted driver. The ignorance requirement on luck that Steglich-Petersen endorses therefore implies that, just before the lottery officials handed me the prize, I was not in a position to know that I would soon receive the prize. Similarly, Steglich-Petersen's requirement implies that, just before I saved Evan, I was not in a position to know that Evan would soon be safe. On minimally anti-skeptical assumptions, though, we can understand these cases so that I did know (upon learning of my win) that I'd soon receive the lottery prize and that I did know (upon arriving at the scene) that Evan would soon be safe. So, the particular epistemic improbability requirement on luck that Steglich-Petersen proposes – which he arrives at only after considering several other, even less promising, such requirements (2010: 366–8) – is too strong. In light of its failure (and that of several other similar proposals), we can reasonably continue thinking that the core kind of chance or improbability related to luck is metaphysical.

My overall case for the Strokes Account of lucky events will accumulate gradually over the course of this chapter and the next one as we test the account against several additional cases; enrich the account with an analysis of *strokes of luck*; and show how the enriched account can properly handle all the counterexamples to the leading theories of luck set out back in Section 1.2. I'll close this chapter by defending the Strokes Account from a couple additional challenging objections to its left-to-right conditional. Let's start with this neat attempted counterexample:

> **Drawing Marbles:** An opaque jar holds 99 red marbles and 1 green marble. Each trial consists of drawing, and then replacing, a single

marble. You bet that the green marble will be drawn at least once over the course of 450 trials. The odds are squarely in your favor: there's approximately a 99 percent chance that at least one draw will produce the green marble. All 450 trials take place; alas, the green marble is never drawn!

You were unlucky that the green marble was never drawn. But this case doesn't seem to involve any strokes of bad luck for you; for in each trial, there was only a 1 percent chance that the green marble would be drawn. True, in each trial, it would have been a stroke of *good* luck for you had the green marble been drawn. So in each trial, you failed to enjoy a stroke of good luck. But failing to enjoy a stroke of good luck doesn't suffice for suffering a stroke of *bad* luck. Consider: Winning the lottery is a stroke of good luck, but simply failing to win isn't itself a stroke of bad luck (cf. Levy 2011a: 33). *Drawing Marbles* thus impugns the left-to-right conditional of the Strokes Account.[21]

Reply: The objector must be thinking that the complete 450-trial process couldn't *itself* be a stroke of bad luck for you. But why think that? The reasoning would presumably go something like this:

> None of the individual trials was itself a stroke of bad luck for you. And if none of the individual trials was a stroke of bad luck for you, then neither was the whole process made up of all those individual trials.

I accept the first premise, but reject the second. The general thought underlying the second premise would have to be something like this:

> If E is a composite event none of whose individual parts or steps was a stroke of good (bad) luck for S, then E isn't *itself* a stroke of good (bad) luck for S.

There are clear counterexamples to this principle. Suppose I am truly awful at darts. But I learn that I'll receive a big cash prize if I make a bulls-eye on my next throw. So, I try my hardest to make a bulls-eye; lo and behold, I succeed! We can understand this case so that making the bulls-eye was a stroke of good luck for me. Compatibly with such an understanding of the case, we can fill in the details so that each of the individual parts or steps of making the bulls-eye was itself highly likely to happen, given how things stood just before it happened. What emerges is a case wherein making the bulls-eye was a stroke of good luck for me, even though none of the bulls-eye's individual parts or steps was *itself* a stroke of good luck for me.[22]

In the next chapter, I'll develop an analysis of *strokes of luck* on which composite events, such as making a bulls-eye, or a multi-trial marble-drawing process, can count as strokes of good or bad luck for a subject. Once this analysis is on the table, I'll return to *Drawing Marbles* to verify that the analysis implies that the whole 450-trial process is itself a stroke of bad luck for you. That will complete my defense of the Strokes Account from this case.[23]

Here's another, somewhat simpler attempted counterexample to the Strokes Account's left-to-right conditional. At the conclusion of the extended version of *Good Lottery*, you are lucky that you played your birthday numbers. But playing your birthday numbers needn't *itself* have been a stroke of good luck for you: we can safely suppose that there were no hidden obstacles to your selecting those numbers; that you played those numbers intentionally, knowingly, and freely; and so on. Further, we can safely suppose that your playing those numbers was not due primarily to any *prior* stroke of good luck for you. So, the Strokes Account's left-to-right conditional implies incorrectly that you are *not*, at day's end, lucky that you played your birthday numbers.

Reply: I believe that once we get clear on what's true of this case, and how the Strokes Account bears on it, we'll see that the case doesn't seriously threaten the account. To begin, observe that the objector expresses the objection's first premise by way of a *present tense* ascription of luck regarding an *earlier* event: '... you *are* lucky that you *played* your birthday numbers'. Now, like all the going accounts of luck set out above (Section 1.1), the Strokes Account's analysandum is a relation that a subject S bears to an event E at a time t only if E happens (occurs, comes to obtain) *at t*. Initially, then, it's not at all clear that the Strokes Account's analysandum is the relation at play in the objector's first premise.

This lack of clarity raises the difficult question of how exactly we should interpret the objector's first premise. What makes this question difficult is that we can use *present tense* ascriptions of luck regarding *earlier* events to make any of a number of different claims. Notably, if given a strict and literal reading, I think that any such ascription must be false. If an event has *already happened*, then there's a clear sense in which the event's occurrence is now fixed – this is the status labeled 'the necessity of the past' or 'accidental necessity' in the literature on human freedom and divine foreknowledge.[24] But if an event's occurrence is now fixed in the relevant sense – that is, if the event's occurrence is logically necessary relative to (temporally genuine or non-relational) facts about the past *alone* – then the event's occurrence is not *now* lucky for anyone (though, of course, it may be that the event's occurrence *was* lucky for someone *back when it happened*).

A present tense ascription of luck regarding an earlier event might be either of the following (or something else – I needn't, and so won't try to, exhaust the possibilities here):

> A disguised *past tense* ascription of luck to the pertinent earlier event. For example: by uttering 'I am lucky that I won the lottery', I can convey [Winning the lottery was lucky for me].[25]
>
> A disguised *past tense* ascription of ignorance regarding some of the earlier event's later positive consequences (cf. Levy 2011a: 20). For example: by uttering 'I am lucky that I sold my stocks before the market crashed', I can convey [I unwittingly protected myself from the crash by selling my stocks beforehand].

Reflection on these two different uses of the relevant kind of luck ascription yields what strike me as the two most charitable interpretations of the objector's first premise. On the one hand, the objector's claim might be that, *at the time you played your birthday numbers*, you were lucky to be playing those numbers. If so, then the objector's premise is highly dubious: the very reasons that were given for thinking that playing your birthday numbers wasn't (when you played them) a stroke of good luck for you also support the claim that playing those numbers wasn't (when you played them) *lucky* for you. (Suppose that there were no hidden obstacles to your selecting those numbers; that you played them intentionally, knowingly, and freely; and so on.) On the other hand, the objector might be claiming that, when you played your birthday numbers, you were unwittingly selecting what would turn out to be the lottery's winning numbers. If so, then while the objector's premise is of course true, it's irrelevant to the Strokes Account: on this second interpretation, the relation at play in the objector's premise clearly isn't the Strokes Account's analysandum, ignorance of a current action's later positive consequences being far too common a phenomenon to be the luck analyst's quarry. Upshot: Neither of the suggested interpretations of the objector's first premise yields a successful objection to the Strokes Account.

Having introduced and provided some initial support for and defense of the Strokes Account, I turn in the next chapter to developing and defending an analysis of *strokes of luck* that utilizes key insights from the recent luck literature, and – when combined with the Strokes Account – yields a comprehensive new analysis of lucky events that can properly handle all the counterexamples to the literature's leading accounts presented above (Section 1.2).

2
What Is a Stroke of Luck? Enriching the Strokes Account

According to the Strokes Account of lucky events, the notion *lucky event* is not the most fundamental or basic luck concept; it is instead parasitic on the notion *stroke of luck*. But what, exactly, is a stroke of luck? When, precisely, is an event a *stroke of (good or bad) luck* for a subject?

2.1 Initial statement of the Analysis and some important implications

My favored analysis of strokes of luck will bear a significant resemblance to the Mixed Account of lucky events. Temporarily bracketing a few bells and whistles that will emerge in due course (Section 2.2), we can get the core of my preferred analysis of strokes of luck on the table by simply copying and pasting the right-hand-side of the Mixed Account of lucky events:

> **The Analysis:** Event E is at t a stroke of good (bad) luck for subject S iff (E happens at t and) (1) E is in some respect good (bad) for S, (2) E doesn't happen around t in a wide class of possible worlds that are close to the actual world before t, and (3) E isn't something that S did intentionally.

Note that, according to the Analysis, whether E is at t a stroke of luck for S depends on how things stood *just before* – that is, all the way up to, but not including – t. That's intuitively plausible. Suppose that, while there was around the time of the Big Bang only an infinitesimally small chance that E would eventually happen at t, there was just before t only an infinitesimally small chance that E wouldn't happen at t. Suppose E happens at t. Given that there was, just before t, only an infinitesimally small chance that E *wouldn't* happen at t, E shouldn't count as a stroke of luck for anyone. Moral: Whether E is at t a stroke of luck for S depends (not on how likely it was at, say, some point in the remote past that E would happen at t, but) on how likely it was *just before* t that E would happen at t.[1]

Now let's take a closer look at condition (3). Armed with only (3), can the Analysis capture all there is to the platitude that 'strokes of luck are uncontrolled'? Or must we add more conditions to fully capture the 'out of control' requirement on an event's being a stroke of luck for a subject? I'll explore this relatively large question by way of two comparatively smaller ones:

> **The Connections Question:** Can the Analysis (as currently formulated) honor the most obvious connections among the concepts of *directly free action, knowingly performed action,* and *stroke of luck*?
>
> **The Abilities Question:** How do strokes of luck relate to agents' abilities to produce/prevent events?[2]

Take the Connections Question first. An extremely plausible and popular thought is that *directly* free actions – that is, free actions that don't owe their status as such to any *prior* free actions (cf. Mele 2006: 87) – can't be strokes of luck for their agents.[3] Another natural thought is that no act done *knowingly* can be a stroke of luck for its agent. What's the sober truth here, and can condition (3) alone capture it?

Start with acts performed *knowingly*. Arguably, it's possible that you do something knowingly but not intentionally. This is the line that Mele and Moser (1994: 45) take with respect to what they call 'side-effect actions', such as knowingly alerting enemy forces to your presence by firing on one of their soldiers (Harman 1976: 433) or knowingly wearing down the soles of your expensive sneakers by running a marathon in them (Bratman 1984: 399–400). Suppose this is right – that is, certain clearly foreseen side-effects of intentional actions can count as things one does knowingly but not intentionally.[4] Then, as it stands, the Analysis allows for the following possibility: your performing act A ('A-ing', for short) was a stroke of luck for you, notwithstanding the fact that you A-ed *knowingly*. But is this really possible?

One good strategy for trying to construct an illustrative example of this possibility is to amplify one of the aforementioned side-effect action cases. Suppose that, *unbeknownst to you*, your sworn enemy has injected a poisonous substance into the soles of your expensive sneakers. This poison will render you unconscious at t – and shortly thereafter, dead – *unless* you start wearing your soles down by then. On a whim, you decide just before t to start running in your sneakers at t, and you promptly execute this intention. Intuitively, it is at t a stroke of good luck for you that you're then wearing your soles down, notwithstanding the fact that you're knowingly (though not intentionally) wearing them down then. If that's right, then an act done knowingly may nevertheless be a stroke of luck for you – and so, the possibility of acts performed knowingly but not intentionally does not require that we supplement condition (3) with a similar condition for acts done knowingly.

We turn now to directly free acts. Again, an extremely plausible and popular thought is that no directly free act can be a stroke of luck for its agent.[5] Assuming that's correct, can the Analysis honor this truth as is? Yes, given the intuitively plausible assumption that any directly free action is something its agent does intentionally. Suppose that's right: an agent's action is directly free only if the agent does that action intentionally. The left-to-right conditional of the Analysis obviously entails that nothing an agent does intentionally is a stroke of luck for the agent. And so, given one intuitively plausible assumption about the nature of directly free action, the left-to-right conditional of the Analysis entails that nothing an agent does with direct freedom is a stroke of luck for the agent.[6]

Having considered the Connections Question, let's now take up the Abilities Question. Many theorists of luck endorse something along the following lines: E is a stroke of luck for S *only if* S lacks control over E.[7] Unlike 'control *of*', to say that you have 'control *over*' E implies that you are free to produce and/or to prevent E (where S is 'free to' produce/prevent E iff S both has it within her power and knows how to produce/prevent E).[8] Many theorists thus endorse a requirement for E's being a stroke of luck for S on which S isn't *both* free to produce E *and* free to prevent E. Do strokes of luck really relate to agents' abilities as the theorists currently in focus seem to think?

Over the next several paragraphs, I'll argue for two theses:

Thesis 1: Possibly, E is a stroke of good luck for S, yet S is *both* free to produce E *and* free to prevent E.

Thesis 2: Possibly, E is a stroke of bad luck for S, yet S is *both* free to produce E *and* free to prevent E.

If Theses 1 and 2 are true, then E can be a stroke of luck for S despite the fact that S has control over E, in the sense of 'control over' that proponents of the above popular construal of the 'out of control' requirement on strokes of luck seem to have in mind. In light of the two upcoming examples that I'll call *Rigged Lottery* and *Two Buttons*, we should conclude that strokes of luck do *not* relate to agents' abilities as so many theorists of luck seem to think. (Notably, the thesis that you can be free with respect to – that is, free to produce and free to prevent – an event that is a stroke of luck for you is consistent with the claim that no directly free act can be a stroke of luck for you. The former is consistent with the latter because, as the cases with which I'll establish Theses 1 and 2 illustrate, your being free with respect to an event doesn't suffice for that event's being an action of yours, let alone a directly free one.)

First, a case that supports Thesis 1:

> **Rigged Lottery:** Without your having had any say in the matter, you find yourself holding a ticket in a lottery that has been rigged in your favor. There are two ways you can win: press a button that will make you the (illegitimate) winner, or let the lottery proceed fairly in hopes that your number will be the one selected. For you to win either way, *you must keep your ticket*. Although you're free to make yourself the winner, you refrain from intervening. Indeed, given your character, there was almost no chance you'd exploit the set-up to win illegitimately. Lo and behold, you win fair and square!

Your *legitimate* lottery win was a stroke of good luck for you. But now consider the fact that you won the lottery (period). You were free to make yourself the winner, and you were also free to prevent your winning (by destroying your ticket). So, if your winning (period) was a stroke of good luck for you, then Thesis 1 is true. Was it indeed a stroke of good luck for you that you won (period)?

If we try to *argue for* the conclusion that your winning (period) was a stroke of good luck for you, the following reasoning will occur to us fairly early on:

> It was a stroke of good luck for you that you won *legitimately*. That you won legitimately entails that you won (period). The relation *being a stroke of good luck for* is closed under entailment: if it was a stroke of good luck for you that P *and* P entails Q, then it was also a stroke of good luck for you that Q. Therefore, it was a stroke of good luck for you that you won (period).

But this argument fails since *being a stroke of good luck for* clearly isn't closed under entailment (cf. Dretske 1970: 1008–9). Suppose you legitimately win a large, non-rigged lottery. Your legitimate win is a stroke of good luck for you. That you legitimately win entails that *someone* legitimately wins. But (we can safely suppose) no one is lucky that there's a legitimate winner, not even you (that there would be a legitimate winner was *guaranteed*). Thus, it's not a stroke of good luck for you that *someone* legitimately wins the lottery.

Of course, the fact that the above argument fails is no reason to think your win in *Rigged Lottery* wasn't a stroke of good luck for you. Indeed, although I have explicitly claimed (and in the uncomfortably recent past ...[9]) that your winning (period) *wasn't* a stroke of good luck for you, I now feel no inclination to say this, and I instead feel a strong inclination to say that your win (period) was in fact a stroke of good luck for you – as have many people with whom I've discussed such cases.[10] And so I'm now strongly inclined to think that *Rigged Lottery* establishes Thesis 1: it's possible that an event be a stroke of good luck for you even though you were *both* free to produce the event *and* free to prevent it.

Now let's consider Thesis 2. Before presenting a case in support of Thesis 2, I want to discuss an example that might be thought to provide some evidence for the claim that E is a stroke of bad luck for S only if S wasn't free to prevent E:

> **Schrödinger's Cat:** You've trapped a cat in a box that's equipped with a Geiger counter and connected to a tube containing poisonous gas. There's a 50 percent chance that the Geiger counter will detect a particle within the hour and a 50 percent chance it won't. If – but only if – the counter detects a particle within the hour, the poisonous gas will be released from the tube and the cat will die.

Suppose you're blameworthy for trapping that poor cat in the box. There's a 50 percent chance the cat will survive the hour and a 50 percent chance it won't. Suppose the counter detects a particle and the cat is fatally poisoned. Plausibly, it's not *just* a stroke of bad luck for you that the cat died. Why not? Here's a natural answer: the cat's death is something *you were free to prevent*. We can reasonably generalize, from these two claims about this case, that E is a stroke of bad luck for you *only if* you weren't free to prevent E. Notice that this has all the makings of a counterexample to the right-to-left conditional of the Analysis: since (a) it's bad for you that the cat died, (b) there was a sufficiently large objective chance that the cat wouldn't die, and (c) the cat's death isn't something that you did intentionally,[11] the right-hand-side of the Analysis is satisfied; but, again, the cat's death is plausibly *not* a stroke of bad luck for you.

Careful inspection will reveal, I believe, that the above argument fails because it *generalizes hastily*. Recall the argument's **Central Claim**: because you were free to prevent the cat's death, its death isn't *just* a stroke of bad luck for you. From the Central Claim alone, here's all we can safely generalize to:

If E is *just* a stroke of bad luck for you, then you weren't free to prevent E.

But the above argument generalizes to the following, logically *stronger* claim:

If E is a stroke of bad luck for you, then you weren't free to prevent E.

The latter claim is logically stronger because its antecedent is logically weaker than the former's (while sharing the same consequent). Obviously, if E is *just* a stroke of bad luck for you, then E is a stroke of bad luck for you. But the converse is false. Suppose that E is (for you) a stroke of bad luck *for which you're blameworthy*. Think, in this connection, of *un*lucky agents in familiar resultant moral luck cases – for example, the drunk driver who hits a pedestrian or the successful assassin whose bullet penetrates the intended victim.[12] If E is a stroke of bad luck *that you're blameworthy for*, then while E is of course a stroke of bad luck for you, it's not *just* a stroke of bad luck for you – again, it's one *for which you're blameworthy*.

Note well: in such examples of blameworthiness for strokes of bad luck, the blameworthiness is *indirect* or *derivative*. The agent is blameworthy for the stroke of bad luck in virtue of blameworthiness for some prior event – for example, choosing to drive drunk, to shoot at the intended victim, or to trap a cat in a potentially lethal box.[13] My claim here that you can be *indirectly* or *derivatively* blameworthy for a stroke of bad luck is perfectly compatible with my earlier claim that no *directly free* action can be a stroke of luck for its agent; with the related claim that no *directly blameworthy* action (that is, a blameworthy action that doesn't owe its status as such to any other blameworthy actions) can be a stroke of bad luck for its agent; and, finally, with the view that unlucky agents in familiar resultant moral luck cases are no *more* blameworthy in virtue of their relevant choices than are their lucky counterparts. (I regard the following as an important lesson from some of the best recent work on moral luck [for example, Greco 1995, Zimmerman 2002]: an unlucky agent in a familiar resultant moral luck case is *blameworthy for more things* in virtue of his relevant choice than is his lucky counterpart, but the unlucky agent is not *any more blameworthy for* his choice than is his lucky counterpart. For additional discussion of these and related issues, see Section 5.1 below.)

So: E's being a stroke of bad luck for you doesn't suffice for E's being *just* a stroke of bad luck for you. That E is a stroke of bad luck for you is therefore logically weaker than that E is *just* a stroke of bad luck for you. Accordingly, all we can safely generalize to from the Central Claim is the first, logically weaker conditional claim – viz. that if something is *just* a stroke of bad luck for you, then you weren't free to prevent it.[14] The above argument therefore generalizes hastily to the logically stronger claim that *any* stroke of bad luck for you is such that you weren't free to prevent it. The above argument does not establish that stronger claim, and so it does not refute the Analysis.

Having touched on the logical relations between E's being a stroke of bad luck for S and E's being *just* a stroke of bad luck for S, let me pause briefly here to address the question how a couple of similar relations that figure prominently in the recent literature on free will and moral responsibility (see, for example, Mele 2006) relate to the concepts *stroke of luck* and *lucky event*. The relations I have in mind are E's being *partly* a matter of (good or bad) luck for S and E's being *just* a matter of (good or bad) luck for S. Here's a set of proposed equivalences that are intuitively plausible and square with all the views I'll settle on concerning lucky events and strokes of luck (the following definitions will play an important role later in Chapter 5):

E is *just* a matter of good (bad) luck for S iff E is a stroke of good (bad) luck for S that S isn't in any way praiseworthy (blameworthy) for. E is *only partly* a matter of good (bad) luck for S iff E is (un)lucky for S but isn't itself *just* a matter of good (bad) luck for S – that is, iff either (i) E is a stroke of good (bad) luck for S that S is in some way praiseworthy (blameworthy) for, or (ii) E is (un)lucky for S but is not itself a stroke of good (bad) luck for S. Finally, E is *at least partly* a matter of good (bad) luck for S iff either (i) E is *just* a matter of good (bad) luck for S or (ii) E is *only partly* a matter of good (bad) luck for S.

Returning to the main thread, I'll now further defend the Analysis by describing an example that clearly involves a stroke of bad luck for an agent who was free to prevent it and *also* free to produce it:

Two Buttons: I hand you a device that has two buttons, green and red. If you press the *red* button, you'll immediately suffer a painful sensation (100 percent chance). If you press the *green* button, there's a 99 percent chance you'll enjoy a pleasant sensation and only a 1 percent chance you'll suffer a painful sensation. You're free to do any of the following: press the red button; press the green button; omit pressing either button. Hoping – and reasonably expecting – to enjoy the pleasant sensation, you freely press the green button. You suffer a painful sensation.

Your suffering that painful sensation was a stroke of bad luck. Note that the Analysis entails as much: suffering the painful sensation was bad for you; in a wide class of worlds that are close to the actual world before you suffer the painful sensation, you *don't* subsequently suffer such a sensation; and, finally, suffering the painful sensation wasn't something that you did intentionally. Nevertheless, you were free *both* to produce the painful sensation (you were free to press the red button) *and* to prevent it (you were free to omit pressing either button). So *Two Buttons* establishes Thesis 2.

Over the last several paragraphs, we've been considering whether the Analysis can – armed with only (3) – capture all the truth there is in the platitude that 'strokes of luck are uncontrolled'. We've made progress on that question by answering two comparatively smaller questions: the Connections Question and the Abilities Question. I've argued for an affirmative answer to the Connections Question: the Analysis can capture the most obvious connections among the concepts of *directly free action*, *knowingly performed action*, and *stroke of luck*. And reflection on the Abilities Question has revealed that we shouldn't require, in order for an event to be a stroke of luck for you, that you lack *either* the freedom to produce that event *or* the freedom to prevent it. So, reflection on the Abilities Question hasn't uncovered any new reason to think that the Analysis can't capture all the truth there is in the pertinent platitude.[15] On the basis of these answers to the indicated questions, then, I'm cautiously optimistic that condition (3) exhausts the 'out of control' requirement on an event's being a stroke of luck for a subject.[16]

2.2 The Analysis: revisions and defense

Although the Analysis has proven resilient so far, we'll now meet some examples that force revision, starting with this one (cf. Coffman 2007: 396):

Game Show: You are on a game show. You confront two identical doors: Door A and Door B. Unbeknownst to you, the doors conceal two identical iPads: iPad A and iPad B. At time t, you choose Door B and receive iPad B. Suppose that, just before t, there was absolutely no chance that you would at t fail to receive an iPad – that is, just before t, you were guaranteed to pick one of Doors A and B, and so you were guaranteed to walk away with one or the other of the two identical iPads. Suppose also that, just before t, there was only a small chance that you would pick Door B over Door A.

Your receiving iPad B meets conditions (1) – (3) of the Analysis: it's good for you; there was, just beforehand, a sufficiently large objective chance that it wouldn't happen; and it's not something that you did intentionally. The right-to-left conditional of the Analysis therefore implies, counterintuitively to my mind, that it was a stroke of good luck for you that you received iPad B. We can sidestep this problem by reformulating the Analysis as follows:

> E is at t a stroke of good (bad) luck for S iff (1) E is in some respect good (bad) for S; (2*) no event *as significant as E* happens around t in a wide class of possible worlds that are close to the actual world before t; and (3) E isn't something that S did intentionally.

Because your receiving iPad B doesn't satisfy condition (2*), this reformulation of the Analysis improves on the original statement by issuing the intuitively correct verdict on *Game Show*. Recall that, in the vast majority of possible worlds that are close to the actual world before t, you receive iPad A at t – which, by hypothesis, is just as good for you as is receiving iPad B then. So, the reformulated account implies, correctly to my mind, that your receiving iPad B was not a stroke of good luck for you.

Alas, further reflection shows that (2*) makes the Analysis too *strong*. Consider the following case:

> **Two Lotteries:** You hold tickets in two lotteries (call them 'Lottery 1' and 'Lottery 2') for equivalent prizes whose winning numbers will be drawn at noon. Given the number of tickets you hold in each lottery, you have a one percent chance of winning Lottery 1 and a 99 percent chance of winning Lottery 2. As it happens, you win Lottery 1 but not Lottery 2.

Since an event as significant as your winning Lottery 1 (viz. your winning Lottery 2) happens around noon in a wide class of possible worlds that are close to the actual world before noon, the left-to-right conditional of the revised version of the Analysis implies that your winning Lottery 1 was not a stroke of good luck for you. Intuitively, though, your winning Lottery 1 *was* a stroke of good luck for you. We should therefore replace the second statement of the Analysis with this third and final, official statement:

> **The Analysis:** E is at t a stroke of good (bad) luck for S iff (1) E is in some respect good (bad) for S; (2**) in a wide class of possible worlds that are close to the actual world before t, E doesn't happen around t nor does the process that actually generated E yield around t an event as good (bad) for S as E is; and (3) E isn't something that S did intentionally.

This final version of the Analysis yields correct verdicts about both *Game Show* and *Two Lotteries*. With respect to *Game Show*, it correctly implies that your receiving iPad B wasn't a stroke of good luck for you, since (2**) isn't satisfied: in the vast majority of possible worlds that are close to the actual world before t, the process that actually generated your receiving iPad B (viz. your trying to decide which of the available doors to open) yields around t an event that's as good for you as is receiving iPad B (viz. receiving iPad A). With respect to *Two Lotteries*, the final version of the Analysis correctly implies that your winning Lottery 1 was a stroke of good luck for you. This is because (2**) is satisfied: in a wide class of possible worlds that are close to the actual world before noon, you don't win Lottery 1 at noon, and the process that actually generated your win (viz. the drawing of Lottery 1's winning numbers) doesn't yield around noon an event as good for you as is your win.

The (third and final, official version of the) Analysis is, I submit, a very promising account of an event's constituting a stroke of (good or bad) luck for a subject. In order to further bolster the Analysis, I'll now defend it against an objection that stems from the following influential case described by Lackey (2008: 258, italics added):

> **Demolition Worker:** Ramona is...about to press a button that will blow up an old abandoned warehouse...Unbeknownst to her,...a mouse had chewed through the relevant wires in the construction office an hour earlier, severing the connection between the button and the explosives. But *as Ramona is about to press the button*, her coworker hangs his jacket on a nail in the precise location of the severed wires...As it happens, the hanger...is made of metal, and it

enables the electrical current to pass through the damaged wires *just as Ramona presses the button* and demolishes the warehouse.

A critic of the Analysis may claim that the warehouse's explosion is a stroke of good luck for Ramona, despite the fact that the explosion is something that she did intentionally. If so, then condition (3) is unnecessary for an event's being a stroke of luck for a subject, and the Analysis is too strong.[17]

My defense of the Analysis from this attempted counterexample will have two stages. First, I'll highlight an important ambiguity in *Demolition Worker* and identify two possible interpretations of the case. Second, I'll argue that neither of the two interpretations elicits a trustworthy intuition that the warehouse's explosion is *both* a stroke of good luck for Ramona *and* something that she did intentionally.

To begin, compare the italicized bits in *Demolition Worker*. The initial description of the case doesn't make clear exactly when the button-explosives connection was restored. That's problematic because only one of the two ways to clarify the case stands a chance of eliciting the intuition that the explosion is something that Ramona did *intentionally*. Let me explain.

If we lean on the second italicized bit and interpret the case so that the connection was restored *just as* Ramona pressed the button, then – while we might deem the explosion a stroke of good luck for her – we shouldn't think the explosion is something that Ramona did *intentionally*. In general, you perform an act, A, intentionally by performing an act A* *only if* it's not the case that performing A* is (in the circumstances) an extremely unreliable way to perform A (cf. Mele and Moser 1994: 62). On the interpretation of *Demolition Worker* now under consideration – viz. the one on which the depression and reconnection *occur simultaneously* and *are completely unrelated* – pressing the button is an extremely unreliable way to demolish the warehouse. Therefore, on this interpretation of the case, Ramona did not demolish the warehouse *intentionally*. This interpretation of the case poses no threat to the Analysis. (Of course, we can understand the case so that Ramona intentionally *tries* to demolish the warehouse, by pressing the button. But intentionally *trying* to A, and subsequently A-ing, does not suffice for A-ing intentionally. Consider a simple case from Mele [2003b: 448]: 'Even if, wrongly thinking that she has magical powers over dice, Ann *intends* to throw a six now and does so, she does not intentionally throw a six.' We can understand this example so that Ann intentionally *tries* to throw a six, without weakening at all the intuition that Ann doesn't throw a six *intentionally*.)

For *Demolition Worker* to stand a chance of impugning the Analysis, we'll need to lean on the first italicized bit, interpreting the case so that the connection was restored *before* Ramona pressed the button.[18] For present purposes, I'll simply grant something that I think is not at all obviously true: by pressing the button, Ramona intentionally demolished the warehouse. Let me also endorse two claims that follow from, respectively, the Analysis and the Strokes Account:

> It was a stroke of good luck for Ramona that, just before she pressed it, the button was reconnected to the explosives.
>
> The warehouse explosion was lucky for Ramona.

The button-explosives reconnection was good for Ramona; there was just beforehand a sufficiently large chance that no event like it would happen around the time it did; and it's not something that Ramona did intentionally. The Analysis thus entails that the reconnection was a stroke of good luck for Ramona. Moreover, since the reconnection was a primary contributor to the explosion (which was itself good for Ramona), the Strokes Account entails that the explosion was lucky for Ramona (cf. Lackey 2008: 259). Since both claims above are intuitively correct, their entailment by the Analysis and the Strokes Account provides further confirmation for those theories.

The question to ask now is whether – on the second interpretation of *Demolition Worker* – the explosion, in addition to being lucky for Ramona, constitutes a *stroke of good luck* for her. If so, then the Analysis is in trouble since (I'm conceding) the explosion is something that Ramona did (or, brought about) intentionally. What can be said to a critic who claims to have an intuition that the warehouse explosion is *itself* a stroke of good luck for Ramona?

I can offer a two-part error theory for such an intuition. The resources for this error theory are already on the table. First, Ramona's becoming repositioned to demolish the warehouse *was* a stroke of good luck for her. But Ramona's becoming repositioned to demolish the warehouse is a different event from the explosion itself. Anyone who finds it intuitively obvious that the explosion was a stroke of good luck for Ramona may well be (quite understandably) confusing the explosion itself with Ramona's becoming repositioned to cause the explosion. A second factor that may well encourage one to deem the explosion a stroke of good luck for Ramona is that the explosion is lucky for Ramona. Anyone who finds it intuitively obvious that the explosion itself was a stroke of good luck for Ramona may well be (quite understandably) confusing an event's being lucky for Ramona with the event's being a stroke of good luck for her. So, there are at least two independent but complementary error theories for the envisaged critic's sense that the explosion itself is a stroke of good luck for Ramona. Minimally, presenting these theories suffices to raise a legitimate worry that the objector's judgment about Ramona and the explosion is ill founded, thereby undermining that judgment and defending the Analysis from (the second interpretation of) *Demolition Worker*.

As a rejoinder to my reply, a determined critic may try to bolster the claim that the explosion itself was a stroke of good luck for Ramona by invoking this principle:

> If it was a stroke of good luck for S that S was in a position to A *and* (being so positioned) S A-ed, then it was a stroke of good luck for S that S A-ed.

But there are clear counterexamples to this principle.[19] Recall, for example, *Distracted Driver* from above. It was a stroke of good luck for me that I was positioned to save Evan from the distracted driver, and I took advantage of my opportunity to save him. By the above principle, it was a stroke of good luck for me that I saved Evan from the driver. But that's counterintuitive, given the role that my own actions (mental and overt) played in saving Evan from the driver. (It's not as though I was completely unaware of Evan's dire circumstances and inadvertently nudged him out of the car's path as I walked single-mindedly toward the school building to collect him or was ambivalent about whether to save him and insanely let the situation's outcome be determined by coin flip.) So the above principle is false: it may be that S's A-ing was not itself a stroke of good luck for S *even though* it was a stroke of good luck for S that S was positioned to A. The envisaged attempt to reinstate *Demolition Worker* as a counterexample to the Analysis fails. On the basis of the last several paragraphs' discussion, I conclude that neither of the two possible interpretations of *Demolition Worker* casts serious doubt on the Analysis.

2.3 Putting it all together: the Enriched Strokes Account of lucky events

Call the conjunction of the Strokes Account with the Analysis the **Enriched Strokes Account** of lucky events. Now is as good a time as any to note that, since key notions involved in (1) and (2**) of the Analysis admit of degrees, those conditions allow us to capture the fact that luck itself comes in degrees.[20] To illustrate: a proponent of the Enriched Strokes Account can say that some extremely positive and unlikely event was a huge stroke of good luck for you; that any positive event to which that huge stroke of good luck is a primary contributor is extremely lucky for you; that some slightly positive and fairly likely event was only a small stroke of good luck for you; that any positive event to which that small stroke of good luck is a primary contributor is only slightly lucky for you; and so on.

This section's main aims are (a) to verify that the Enriched Strokes Account captures some key claims that I made about strokes of luck in Chapter 1, and then (b) to defend the account from a disturbing charge of incoherence. Recall the following claims I made back in Chapter 1:

> In *Distracted Driver*, Evan's eventual safety was not (right after I brought it about) a stroke of good luck for me (or for him); however, it *was* a stroke of good luck for me (and for him) that I was *in a position* to save him and lucky for me (and for him) that he ended up safe (Section 1.2).
>
> In *Drawing Marbles*, it was a stroke of bad luck for you that the green marble wasn't drawn in any of the 450 trials (Section 1.4).

Let's start with *Distracted Driver*. Just before saving Evan, I became *positioned* to save him. Once I became so positioned, it was (we can safely suppose) *guaranteed* that I would soon save Evan. Evan's eventual safety therefore does not itself meet condition (2**) of the Analysis, and so the Analysis honors the fact that it wasn't a stroke of good luck for me (or for Evan) that he ended up safe. My becoming positioned to save Evan, however, was clearly a primary contributor to his eventual safety. Further, my becoming so positioned was good for me (and for Evan); we can safely suppose that it doesn't happen around the relevant time in a wide class of worlds that are close to the actual world beforehand; and it's not something that I (or Evan) did intentionally. The Enriched Strokes Account thus implies both that my becoming positioned to save Evan was a stroke of good luck for me (and for him) and that it was lucky for me (and for him) that he ended up safe.

Now recall *Drawing Marbles*. The fact that all 450 trials failed to produce a green marble was bad for you, and it was not something that you did intentionally. So, whether the trials' failure to produce a green marble was a stroke of bad luck for you comes down to whether there was – before the stretch of time over which all those individual trials took place (label it 't') – a sufficiently large objective chance that at least one trial would then produce a green marble. More precisely, we need to ask whether the following statement is true: In a wide class of worlds that are close to the actual world before t, at least one trial produces a green marble during t.

We should affirm this statement. Recall that, before the trials took place, there was roughly a 99 percent chance that at least one trial would produce a green marble during t. So, in almost all of the worlds that are close to the actual world before t, at least *one* of the trials produces a green marble during t. So, the trials' failure to produce a green marble was bad for you; it was not something that you did intentionally; and there was, before the stretch of time over which the failure occurred, a sufficiently large chance that it *wouldn't* happen during that period. The Analysis thus honors my earlier claim that the trials' failure to produce a green marble was *itself* a stroke of bad luck for you. More generally, the Analysis clearly and correctly allows for the possibility that some composite event is itself a stroke of (good or bad) luck for you, despite the fact that none of its individual parts or steps is. This completes the defense of the Strokes Account from *Drawing Marbles* that I started developing back in Section 1.4.

I'll devote the rest of this section to defending the Enriched Strokes Account from a tough objection inspired by both Latus (2003: 467ff.) and Levy (2011a: 16–17, 29ff.). Suppose a subject, S, survives a game of Russian roulette in which only one of the revolver's six chambers is loaded. Alternatively, consider a subject S's being born with an exceptionally happy temperament. It seems that if the Analysis is correct, then we can understand S's case so that it doesn't involve *any* strokes of good luck for S. And if we *can* so understand S's case, yet S was nevertheless *lucky* to survive the game of roulette – or to be born with an exceptionally happy temperament – then the Strokes Account is false. But, it's plausible to think, S *was* lucky to survive the game – or to be born with an exceptionally happy temperament. Therefore, it seems that if the Analysis is true, then the Strokes Account is false. Upshot: The Enriched Strokes Account combines two *incompatible* views.

This nasty objection rests upon two basic premises:

> **Premise 1:** If the Analysis is correct, then S's case needn't involve any strokes of good luck for S.
>
> **Premise 2:** S was lucky to survive the roulette game and/or to be born with an exceptionally happy temperament.

In what follows, I'll defend the Enriched Strokes Account from this objection by arguing that neither of the two envisaged cases is such that *both* Premises 1 and 2 are true of it.

Consider, first, S's surviving the roulette game. As it's described, there was roughly a 17 percent objective chance that S would *not* survive the game. That's a sufficiently large chance of death for S's survival to satisfy my intended reading of condition (2**) of the Analysis.[21] So, contrary to the objector's suggestion, since S's survival is *also* in some respect good for S and not something that S did intentionally, the Analysis issues the intuitively correct verdict that S's survival was a stroke of good luck for him.

Now, the objector might try to sidestep this reply by invoking what I'll call the

Inverse Proportionality Thesis: The degree of chanciness required for an event to count as lucky for one is *inversely proportional* to the degree to which the event is good for one.

Latus (2003: 467–8) explicitly endorses the Inverse Proportionality Thesis.[22] If the Inverse Proportionality Thesis is true, then we can simply modify the Russian roulette case so that there was only an *infinitesimally small* objective chance that S would die. So modified, S's survival will be too probable to satisfy condition (2**) of the Analysis, yet (claims the objector) will *still* count as lucky.

Far from revitalizing the above argument, however, such a move would actually render the argument irrelevant to the Strokes Account. To begin to see this, note that luck *runs riot* under the Inverse Proportionality Thesis: any event E that's extremely significant for – but not intentionally done by – S will count as *lucky* for S provided that there was at least an extremely small objective chance that E wouldn't happen. There's an endless supply of examples that illustrate how luck proliferates given the Inverse Proportionality Thesis; let's consider just one, picked more or less at random. I recently survived a routine flight from Chicago to South Bend (IN). My surviving that flight was extremely significant for me, and it didn't count as something that I did intentionally. Finally, we can suppose that there was at least an extremely small objective chance that I wouldn't survive the flight (think: mechanical problems, pilot errors, wayward geese, blood clots, Large Hadron Collider catastrophe, and so on). The Inverse Proportionality Thesis thus implies that I was lucky to survive my flight from Chicago to South Bend. More generally, the Inverse Proportionality Thesis entails that a truly staggering number and variety of significant events are lucky for us.

But this means that, whatever relation is at play in the Inverse Proportionality Thesis – assuming that this principle is indeed true – it's *not* the Strokes Account's analysandum (cf. Lackey 2008: 258). The luck analyst's quarry, remember, is a phenomenon one paradigm of which is your winning a large fair lottery, and whose presence can arguably keep true beliefs from constituting knowledge, rational actions from qualifying as free, and so on. Accordingly, the luck analyst's quarry simply can't be as pervasive as is the relation at play in the Inverse Proportionality Thesis (again, assuming the principle is indeed true). Tying the above argument to the Inverse Proportionality Thesis would therefore render the argument irrelevant to the Enriched Strokes Account. I conclude, then, that however exactly we fill in its details, the Russian roulette case isn't such that both Premises 1 *and* 2 are clearly true of it.

Now for the happy temperament case. From such claims of constitutive luck as that S was lucky to be endowed with an exceptionally happy temperament, Levy (2011a: 32ff.) infers that the following condition suffices for your being lucky relative to some positive character trait:

> Your having the pertinent trait is good for you; you lack control over having the trait; and the trait is sufficiently rare across human experience.

I agree with Levy that you should think that some such condition suffices for luck with respect to some positive trait *if* you deem S lucky to have his exceptionally happy temperament. But we now have all we need, I believe, for a reductio of the claim that S is lucky to have such a temperament (cf. Rescher 1995: 28–9).

Suppose that, on the basis of firmly held intentions formed long ago, S's parents intentionally engineered S so as to *ensure* that S would be hardwired with an exceptionally happy temperament. We can easily fill in the details so that S isn't *lucky* to have his exceptionally happy temperament.[23] But just as clearly, S's having that rare positive trait may be good for, and uncontrolled by, S. So, the above alleged sufficient condition for luck relative to some positive trait turns out on closer inspection to be *in*sufficient. Finally, since we were led to that mistaken condition by the claim that S is – in the original, manipulation-free case – lucky to have an exceptionally happy temperament, we should conclude that S is *not* in fact lucky to have such a temperament in the original case.

In response, Levy might concede that in the manipulation-involving case, S isn't lucky to have the relevant sort of temperament. Levy might then weaken the above alleged sufficient condition by replacing its antecedent with the following, logically stronger proposition:

> Your having the pertinent trait is good for you; *no one* has direct control over your having the trait; and the trait is sufficiently rare across human experience.[24]

So weakened, the new putative sufficient condition is immune to manipulation-involving examples such as the one deployed above. But the envisaged reply has two problems. The smaller problem is that it would commit Levy to thinking that manipulation-involving and manipulation-free cases are different enough so that we can justifiably ascribe luck in the latter but deny luck in the former. As we saw above in Section 1.2, though, Levy's (2011a: 20–2; cf. 2009: 493ff.) own defense of the necessity of the Mixed Account's condition (ii) from Lackey's (2008) *Buried Treasure* case assumes that we're justified in ascribing luck in manipulation-free cases *only if* we're also justified in ascribing luck in manipulation-involving cases. The envisaged response to the manipulation-involving example above would thus conflict with Levy's own defense of the Mixed View, and so the response would render his overall position unstable.

The bigger problem with the envisaged reply is that there's a plausible counterexample even to the weaker putative sufficient condition for luck relative to a positive trait. Suppose it's at least (conceptually) *possible* that there be a divine human being.[25] If there *were* such a being, s/he would *essentially* or *necessarily* exemplify such features as omniscience, omnipotence, and omnibenevolence. Such traits would be good for their possessor and rare across human experience. So, provided no one has control over properties that a thing exemplifies *essentially* or *necessarily*, the weaker putative sufficient condition implies that a divine human being would be *lucky* to be omniscient, omnipotent, and omnibenevolent. But that's a mistake: if there *were* a divine human being, s/he wouldn't be *lucky* to have such traits.[26] Therefore, the weaker alleged sufficient condition for luck relative to positive traits isn't credible enough to ground a successful objection to the Enriched Strokes Account.

The upshot of the last few paragraphs' discussion is that, while Premise 1 may be true of the happy temperament case, Premise 2 isn't. And yet there does seem to be a kernel of truth in at least many such constitutive luck claims. I'll close this section by offering a pair of complementary error theories for such claims.

To begin to see the first kind of error theory, consider the important distinction between *luck* and *fortune*. Whereas an event is *(un)lucky* only if it's properly related to a stroke of luck, you can be *(un)fortunate* relative to an event even if there are no strokes of luck in its vicinity. Rescher (1995: 28–9) helpfully draws the luck/fortune distinction in this passage:

> You are fortunate if something good happens to or for you in the natural course of things. But you are lucky when such a benefit

comes to you despite its being chancy... Fate and fortune relate to the conditions and circumstances of our lives generally, luck to the specifically chancy goods and evils that befall us. Our innate skills and talents are matters of good fortune; the opportunities that chance brings our way to help us develop them are for the most part matters of luck...

The positive and negative things that come one's way in the world's ordinary course – including one's heritage (biological, medical, social, economic), one's abilities and talents, the circumstances of one's place and time (be they peaceful or chaotic, for example) – all these are matters of what might be characterized as fate and fortune. People are not unlucky to be born timid or ill-tempered, just unfortunate. But the positivities and negativities that come one's way by chance and unforeseen happenstance... are matters of luck.

Despite the fact that luck and fortune can be so distinguished on reflection, they are also (and obviously) closely related – for example, like (un)lucky events, (un)fortunate events must be good (bad) for you and also in some sense uncontrolled. Given the close similarity between *luck* and *fortune*, we shouldn't be too surprised to find theorists sometimes running them together, as Levy seems to do in passages such as the following:

[F]ortunate events... are luck-*involving*. Fortune requires luck in the causal history of an event.... (2009: 495)

Fortunate events... are events with luck in their immediate causal ancestry. (2009: 497)

Plausibly, an event that is 'luck-*involving*' in that it was *directly caused* by a stroke of luck is thereby a strong candidate for being a *lucky* event. While the account of *fortunate* events that Levy here sketches isn't a very promising start toward an account of such events, it *is* a promising start toward a theory of (what we might call 'indirectly' or 'derivatively') *lucky* events.[27] I hypothesize that, in so theorizing *fortunate* events, Levy was really focused on the notion of a(n) (indirectly or derivatively) *lucky* event. In any case, with the luck/fortune distinction in hand, we can plausibly conjecture that Levy has confused these notions in claiming that S is *lucky* to have an exceptionally happy temperament. What's true, rather, is that S is merely *fortunate* to have his exceptionally happy temperament (S 'has been blessed with' such a temperament).

A second kind of error theory for Levy's judgment about the temperament case deploys the familiar distinction between (a) an assertive utterance's having true propositional content and (b) the utterance's conveying some or other true proposition(s) similar to its actual content. We can easily imagine circumstances in which an assertive utterance of a sentence of the form 'S is lucky to have his exceptionally happy temperament' conveys one or another of a range of similar (to the utterance's actual propositional content) truths more effectively (or vividly, or forcefully, or colorfully) than would a counterpart utterance that replaces 'lucky' with 'fortunate'. Such conveyed truths might include any of the following:

In anyone's mouth: S hasn't done anything to earn (deserve, merit) his exceptionally happy temperament.

In S's mouth: S is grateful to have such a temperament; S is sensitive to the fact that many people fail to enjoy such a temperament through no fault of their own.

In someone else's mouth: S should be grateful to have such a temperament; S should be sensitive to the fact that many people fail to enjoy such a temperament through no fault of their own.

Since assertive utterances of sentences of the form 'S is lucky to have his exceptionally happy temperament' can very effectively convey any of the above (and, in all likelihood, various other) kinds of truths, it's quite understandable how one could end up thinking that the actual propositional content of such an utterance is true – even if, as I've suggested, the proposition that such an utterance strictly expresses is false. Perhaps Levy's (and others') sense that such an utterance's actual propositional content is true stems from conflating that content with some or other similar truth(s) conveyed or implicated – though not strictly expressed – by the utterance.[28]

This concludes my defense of the Enriched Strokes Account from the objection discussed over the last several paragraphs. The next section will bring this chapter to a close by showing how the Enriched Strokes Account can properly handle all of the key counterexamples to the literature's leading theories of lucky events.

2.4 How the Enriched Strokes Account handles the counterexamples to the literature's leading theories of luck

There are six examples to discuss here; I'll take them in order of appearance (for a refresher, see Section 1.2 above). First, *Buried Treasure*, which shows that condition (ii) of the Modal and Mixed accounts isn't required for an event's being lucky for an agent. The Enriched Strokes Account vindicates the intuitive claim that Vincent's lucky discovery was due primarily to a stroke of good luck for him – viz. his forming an intention whose execution was counterfactually sufficient for discovering the treasure (that is, an intention such that he would discover the treasure were he to execute it). The Analysis implies that Vincent's forming such an intention – again, one whose execution was counterfactually sufficient for discovering the buried treasure – was a stroke of good luck for him: forming such an intention was good for Vincent; it wasn't something that he did intentionally;[29] and – we can safely suppose – no event as significant as Vincent's forming such an intention happens around the relevant time in a wide class of possible worlds that are close to the actual world just beforehand (more on this claim momentarily). Further, since Vincent's forming such an intention is clearly a primary contributor to his subsequent discovery (which, obviously, is in some respect good for him), the Strokes Account implies that his discovery is itself lucky. Upshot: The Enriched Strokes Account can deliver the correct verdict on *Buried Treasure*.

Pointed question: 'What makes it "safe" to suppose that, in a wide class of possible worlds that are close to the actual world before Vincent makes the relevant choice, he *doesn't* so choose around then?' Here, it's essential to keep in mind that Lackey (2008: 261–2) offers *Buried Treasure* as a clear counterexample to the alleged necessity of the Modal (and Mixed) Account's condition (ii) for an event's being lucky, and that I'm accepting the case as such. Obviously, if *Buried Treasure* is to have any chance of achieving Lackey's aim, it must elicit from us a sufficiently strong sense that Vincent's discovery is lucky. Charity thus demands that we interpret *Buried Treasure* so that it elicits such a sense from us (if at all possible). Now, consider a reading of Lackey's example wherein antecedent factors – personal and/or impersonal – align so as to make Vincent's *choice* (as opposed to the later *discovery*) appear around the time he actually makes it in the vast majority of possible worlds that are close to the actual world just beforehand. I submit that, once we're forced to interpret the case in this way, whatever sense we may initially have had that Vincent's treasure find was *lucky* will start to evaporate – the discovery will instead start seeming *fated*. I read the following portion of Lackey's (2008: 263) own commentary on *Buried Treasure* as an attempt to forestall precisely the sort of interpretation now under consideration:

> counterfactual robustness [of Vincent's discovery] is ensured in BURIED TREASURE through absolutely no deliberate intervention

of any sort; instead, circumstances *just happen to fortuitously combine* in such a way so as to make Vincent's discovery appear both in the actual world and in all of the relevant nearby worlds. Indeed, it is precisely because of this fortuitous combination of circumstances that the discovery of the buried treasure is so clearly a lucky event.

Upshot: We should assume that there are no antecedent factors aligning so as to make Vincent's *choice* appear around the time he actually makes it in the vast majority of possible worlds that are close to the actual world just beforehand. And *that* means we can indeed safely suppose that Vincent's choice doesn't happen around the relevant time in at least a wide class of possible worlds that are close to the actual world just beforehand.

Next, the Oxfam donation case, which refutes the Modal Account's proposed sufficient condition for luck. Since choosing to make the donation is something that you did intentionally, the Analysis entails that your choice to donate wasn't itself a stroke of luck for you. Moreover, the case is naturally understood so that your choice wasn't due primarily to any prior stroke of luck for you. Unlike the Modal Account, then, the Enriched Strokes Account delivers the correct verdict that your choosing to donate was not lucky for you.

Now for *African Expedition*, which also shows that condition (ii) of the Modal Account and the Mixed Account isn't required for an event's being lucky for an agent. The Enriched Strokes Account honors Riggs' suggestion (2009a: 217) that visiting the pertinent area during a period when there would be a life-saving eclipse was lucky for *Smith*, but not for *Jones*. Smith visited that area during a period when there would be a life-saving eclipse primarily because he'd earlier become constrained to visit the area during the indicated period. The Analysis implies that Smith's becoming constrained to visit the area during that period was a stroke of good luck for him: his becoming so constrained was clearly good for him; it wasn't something that he did intentionally; and – we can safely suppose – no event as significant as his becoming so constrained happens around the relevant time in a wide class of possible worlds that are close to the actual world just beforehand.[30] Therefore, since Smith's visiting the area during a period when there would be a life-saving eclipse was clearly good for him, the Enriched Strokes Account implies correctly that Smith's visiting the area during a period when there would be a life-saving eclipse was lucky for him. Note, finally, that the Enriched Strokes Account also implies correctly that *Jones* wasn't lucky to visit the area during such a period, since the case harbors no strokes of good luck for *him*.[31]

We finish with three relatively easy examples: the case of Katelyn's solar-powered underground facility, *Kidnapping*, and *Distracted Driver*. The first of these three examples, remember, refutes Riggs' Control Account's proposed sufficient condition for luck. The Enriched Strokes Account, by contrast, implies correctly that the sun's rising on the morning in question wasn't lucky for Katelyn. The Analysis entails that the sunrise wasn't itself a stroke of luck for Katelyn: it was too objectively likely to meet condition (2**). And the case is naturally understood so that the sunrise wasn't due primarily to any prior stroke of luck for Katelyn. Unlike the Control Account, then, the Enriched Strokes Account issues the correct verdict that the sun's rising on the morning in question was not lucky for Katelyn.

Kidnapping, recall, shows that an event can be lucky for you *even if* you successfully exploit the event for some purpose – and so, the case shows that the Control Account's condition (ii) isn't required for an event's being lucky for a subject. The Enriched Strokes Account, by contrast, entails that my lottery win in this case was a stroke of good luck – and so, was lucky – for me, despite the fact that I exploited it for some purpose (viz. to get my kidnapped son back): the win was good for me; it wasn't something that I did intentionally; and nothing as significant as is the win happens around the relevant time in a wide class of worlds that are close to the actual world just beforehand.

Finally, as for *Distracted Driver* – which shows that condition (iii) of the Control Account and the Mixed Account isn't necessary for an event's being lucky for an agent – I've already argued that the Enriched Strokes Account yields the correct verdicts about this case (Section 2.3). Despite being something that I brought about intentionally, Evan's eventual safety was lucky – though was not *itself* a stroke of good luck – for me since his eventual safety was due primarily to my becoming positioned to save him, which *was* a stroke of good luck for me.

This completes my argument that the Enriched Strokes Account of lucky events properly handles all the cases that make trouble for the literature's three leading theories of luck. As was promised earlier, we now have strong reason to think that Lackey's argument (mentioned in Section 1.2's last paragraph) that conditions (ii) and (iii) of the Mixed Account 'fail to capture what is distinctive of, and central to, the concept of luck' (2008: 255) is *invalid*. We should agree with Lackey (and others) that cases such as *Buried Treasure* and *Distracted Driver* show that conditions (ii) and (iii) of the Mixed Account are unnecessary for an event's being lucky for a subject. But I've now set out a strong cumulative case for the Enriched Strokes Account of lucky events, which – while accepting Lackey-type counterexamples to the Mixed Account's conditions (ii) and (iii) – entails that those conditions are nevertheless (in Lackey's words) 'distinctive of, and central to, the concept of luck': according to the Enriched Strokes Account, conditions (ii) and (iii) are requirements on an event's being a *stroke of luck*, a notion on which the concept *lucky event* is parasitic. In the remainder of this book, we'll explore some central epistemological (Chapters 3 and 4) and action-theoretical (Chapters 5 and 6) issues in light of the Enriched Strokes Account of lucky events.

3
Knowledge and Luck I: Gettiered Belief and the Ease of Mistake Approach

Duncan Pritchard (2007: 277) rightly observes that '[i]t is a platitude in epistemology to say that knowledge excludes luck'. On the reading relevant to present purposes, this epistemological anti-luck platitude is a generalization intended to capture widespread intuitive reactions to **Gettier Cases:** cases similar to those Gettier (1963) employed to show that justified true belief doesn't suffice for knowledge.[1] The pertinent reading of the anti-luck platitude is the one that Dancy (1985: 134) expresses in the following passage:

> This was just the point of the Gettier counterexamples; nothing in the tripartite definition [of knowledge as epistemically justified true belief] excluded knowledge by luck.

Here's a pair of familiar Gettier Cases that I'll refer to, throughout this chapter and the next one, as 'the Classics':

> ***Pocket Change:*** Smith knows that Jones has ten coins in his pocket. Smith also has strong evidence that Jones will get the job they've both applied for. Smith infers that the successful candidate has ten coins in his pocket. In fact, it's *Smith* (not Jones) who will get the job. And, having just grabbed a handful of loose change, Smith happens to now have ten coins in his own pocket. (adapted from Gettier 1963)
>
> ***Sheep Rock:*** Using his reliable perceptual faculties, Roddy...forms a true belief that there is a sheep in the field before him.... Unbeknownst to Roddy,...the object he is looking at in the field is not a sheep at all but rather a sheep-shaped [rock] which is obscuring from view the real sheep hidden behind. (Pritchard 2012a: 251; adapted from Chisholm 1977)

Smith doesn't know that the successful candidate has ten coins in his pocket, notwithstanding the fact that the indicated proposition is true and Smith justifiedly believes it. Likewise, Roddy doesn't know that there's a sheep in the field before him, notwithstanding the fact that the indicated proposition is true and Roddy justifiedly believes it. In light of (a) the important distinction between an event's (merely) being *lucky* for you and its being a *stroke of good luck* for you (Section 1.3), along with (b) the recognition that the epistemological anti-luck platitude is a generalization meant to capture widespread intuitive reactions to Gettier Cases, we can charitably sharpen up the expressions of the anti-luck platitude found in the above quotations from Dancy and Pritchard as follows: Even if you're justified in your true belief that P, you don't know that P so long as it's just a stroke of good luck for you that you believe accurately that P.

Let's say that a **gettiered belief** is one that falls short of knowledge in the way illustrated by cases such as the Classics. What, exactly, has happened to a belief that falls short of knowledge in the way such cases illustrate? What, precisely, is gettiered belief? And does this phenomenon have any *essential* connection to luck, as common luck-involving expressions of widespread intuitive reactions to Gettier Cases so strongly suggest? I'll explore these questions throughout this chapter and the next one.[2] After generating an initial catalog of ways that luck can figure in cognition, I'll argue that each of the indicated ways is compatible with knowledge and thus constitutes a distinct kind of benign epistemic luck (Sections 3.1 and 3.2). Then, after introducing two leading substantive answers to the question what is gettiered belief – the **Ease of Mistake Approach** and the **Lack of Credit Approach** – I'll further explain the former approach and then present examples establishing that it's both too weak *and* too strong (Sections 3.3 through 3.5). Next, after showing how the counterexamples to the Ease of Mistake Approach can motivate the Lack of Credit Approach, I'll explain two versions of the latter approach and then present examples establishing that each version is both too weak *and* too strong (Sections 4.1 and 4.2). I'll then introduce and critically assess two additional, less prominent approaches to gettiered belief – one of which, I'll argue at some length, shows real promise not only of properly handling all the cases that bedevil competing accounts but also of yielding a plausible explanation of the superiority of knowledge to gettiered belief (Sections 4.4 through 4.6). And as I've already indicated, throughout this chapter and the next one, we'll be keeping an eye on the question how helpful or illuminating those common luck-involving expressions of the platitude that knowledge excludes gettiered belief really are.

3.1 An initial catalog of kinds of epistemic luck[3]

One good way to start working toward an account of gettiered belief is to generate an initial catalog of basic ways that luck can figure (or basic roles that luck can play) in cognition. One good way to generate such a catalog is to list several different conditions that any typical instance of knowledge will meet which can also be luckily satisfied. By identifying several such conditions, one identifies several different points along the pathway to knowledge at which luck can affect one's trip. By identifying several such points, one identifies several different basic kinds of epistemic (or knowledge-relevant) luck.

Consider, then, the following five conditions that a typical instance of knowledge, B, held by a subject, S, will meet:

Existence Condition: S is an existing thinker.
Belief Condition: S holds B.
Evidence Condition: S has some evidence for B's propositional content.
Basing Condition: B is based on some portion of S's evidence for B's content.
Truth Condition: B's content is true.

Since each of these conditions is such that it can be a stroke of good luck – and thus, by the Strokes Account of lucky events (Section 1.3), lucky – for S that s/he meets it, there's a different kind of epistemic luck associated with each of these conditions. It can be a stroke of good luck for S that s/he is an existing thinker (call this 'Existence Luck'). It can be a stroke of good luck for S that s/he holds her belief, B (call this 'Belief Luck'). It can be a stroke of good luck for S that s/he has some evidence for B's propositional content (call this 'Evidence Luck'). It can be a stroke of good luck for S that B is based on some portion of S's evidence for B's content (call this 'Basing Luck'). And finally, it can be a stroke of good luck for S that B's content is true (call this 'Truth Luck').

We now have an initial catalog of several different kinds of epistemic luck. A bit of reflection reveals that none of the kinds of epistemic luck in our initial catalog is at all plausibly identified with the knowledge-blocking phenomenon illustrated by Gettier Cases: we can easily see that each of the indicated kinds of epistemic luck is compatible with knowledge possession (cf. Pritchard 2005: 133ff.). Start by recalling our final, official statement of the Analysis of strokes of luck (Section 2.2):

> E is at t a stroke of good (bad) luck for S iff (1) E is in some respect good (bad) for S; (2**) in a wide class of possible worlds that are close to the actual world before t, E doesn't happen at t nor does the process that actually generated E yield around t an event as good (bad) for S as E is; and (3) E isn't something that S did intentionally.

Possibly, some subject S knows that s/he is an existing thinker at a time when s/he *also* meets conditions (1)–(3) with respect to S's being an existing thinker. Suppose, for example, that S is reflecting on S's own existence and cognitive abilities while trapped in a potentially lethal indeterministic device like the one described in *Schrödinger's Cat* (see Section 2.1 above). Readers can easily verify that the possibility of such a state of affairs entails that both Existence Luck and Truth Luck are compatible with knowledge. In particular, such a possibility entails that your justified true belief that P might still constitute knowledge *even if* it's a stroke of good luck for you that you believe accurately that P. Note that, in light of the last point, we already have some reason to doubt whether common luck-involving expressions of our focal epistemological platitude will ultimately be of much help or illumination. Against the backdrop of a plausible analysis of *strokes of luck*, such luck-involving expressions are naturally understood as being *much stronger* (logically speaking) than the platitude that they're meant to capture. For example, unlike our focal platitude, such expressions would seem to incorrectly rule out the possibility of knowledge of one's own existence and cognitive abilities in the recently described *Schrödinger's Cat*-type case.

Now, you might naturally think that, once we've established the compatibility of Existence Luck and Truth Luck with knowledge, we can complete the argument to our desired overall conclusion concerning the remaining three kinds of epistemic luck (Belief Luck, Evidence Luck, and Basing Luck) by invoking something along the lines of the following principle:

> If condition C* entails condition C, it's a stroke of good luck for S that s/he meets C, *and* S also meets C*; then it's a stroke of good luck for S that s/he meets C*.

Necessarily, if S holds a belief or has some evidence, then S is an existing thinker. Therefore, when combined with the claim that, in the envisaged case, it's a stroke of good luck for S that s/he's an existing thinker, the above principle entails that, for each of the remaining three conditions, it's a stroke of good luck for S that s/he meets it with respect to the knowledge that s/he's an existing thinker – and so, that each of the remaining three kinds of epistemic luck is compatible with knowledge.

But this attempt to establish our desired overall conclusion fails because the above principle is false. One way to see this is to recall our discussion of *Distracted Driver* (Section 2.3). In that example, it was a stroke of good luck for me that I was in a position to save Evan, my being so positioned was required for my actually saving Evan, and I did actually save Evan; but, contrary to what the above principle implies concerning this case, it *wasn't* a stroke of good luck for me that I in fact saved Evan. True, I saved Evan *by* a stroke of good luck; but as we've seen, this differs importantly from my saving Evan's being *itself* a stroke of good luck for me. The suggested shortcut to our desired overall conclusion turns out to be a dead end.

Obviously enough, though, there's a different way to reach our target conclusion – viz. by directly applying the Analysis to the Belief, Evidence, and Basing Conditions, as we applied it to the Existence and Truth Conditions above. Assuming that we can coherently add to the case suggested above that it's in some respect good for S that s/he holds B (or has some evidence for B, or bases B on some pertinent evidence) – and it seems clear that we *can* so augment the case – it follows that Belief (and Evidence, and Basing) Luck is also compatible with knowledge. The upshot of our discussion so far, then, is that each of the five different kinds of epistemic luck in our initial catalog is compatible with knowledge. Accordingly, none of those kinds of epistemic luck is even a remotely plausible candidate for the knowledge-blocking phenomenon present in Gettier Cases. We must look elsewhere for a satisfactory account of the ignorance-inducing phenomenon that Gettier Cases illustrate.

Before moving on to explain and evaluate several substantive accounts of gettiered belief, I want to pause briefly to consider an interesting thesis – recently defended by Pritchard (2004, 2005) – according to which two of the five kinds of epistemic luck in our initial catalog are much more closely related than I've been letting on.

3.2 Pritchard on Evidence Luck and Belief Luck

According to Pritchard (2004: 202–4; cf. 2005: 138–41), what I've called 'Evidence Luck' and 'Belief Luck' are necessarily coextensive across cases of knowledge: any possible case of knowledge that involves Evidence Luck must also involve Belief Luck, and any possible case of knowledge that involves Belief Luck must also involve Evidence Luck. In this section, I'll argue that both conjuncts of Pritchard's thesis are false. The distinction between Evidence Luck and Belief Luck has more epistemological significance than Pritchard has allowed.

One half of Pritchard's thesis is the claim that any possible case of knowledge that involves Evidence Luck must also involve Belief Luck. Call this 'Pritchard's First Claim'. Pritchard defends this claim by neutralizing an alleged counterexample to it. The example he considers involves a subject who luckily acquires good evidence for a belief, B, where B was previously based entirely on inadequate evidence. Of course, such an example refutes Pritchard's First Claim only if B constitutes knowledge. Pritchard (2004: 203) denies that B amounts to knowledge:

> [I]f a jury member only comes across the evidence which supports her belief in the defendant's guilt through luck, but would have believed in his guilt in most nearby possible worlds where she lacks this evidence regardless, then it seems that her belief in this respect is just too insensitive to the facts to count as knowledge, even if, as in the actual world, her true belief is well supported by evidence.

I'm willing to concede that no such case impugns Pritchard's First Claim (though I'm not sure we *must* grant this). It doesn't follow, of course, from the failure of such an attempted counterexample that Pritchard's First Claim is true. Indeed, I think there are least two kinds of cases that refute Pritchard's First Claim. Consider first a case in which a subject S luckily acquires additional good evidence, E_2, for a belief B which was already based on some *different* good evidence, E_1. After S acquires E_2, B is based on both E_1 *and* E_2. In such a case, B is an instance of knowledge which isn't itself luckily acquired, though it is based on some luckily acquired evidence. Here's an illustrative case, for concreteness:

> Juror Jenny already knows that Defendant Dan is guilty on the basis of good evidence, E_1. Jenny then luckily overhears a conversation between Dan's attorney and the prosecutor in which additional good (but inadmissible) evidence for Dan's guilt, E_2, is revealed. Jenny's belief that Dan is guilty is subsequently based on both E_1 *and* E_2.

I submit that this is a case of knowledge that involves Evidence Luck but *not* Belief Luck.

Second, consider a case in which a belief that was previously based on good evidence comes to be based entirely on some different luckily acquired good evidence. This is another kind of case where an instance of knowledge which isn't itself luckily acquired is nevertheless based on luckily acquired evidence. An illustrative case:

> Ray is struck by a burst of high-energy cosmic radiation. This radiation has two notable effects on Ray's cognitive faculties. First, the radiation alters Ray's doxastic structure such that no belief therein can be evidentially overdetermined (that is, based on multiple pieces of sufficient evidence). Second, Ray's visual system is now such that, at any given time, the probability of Ray's being blind at that time is 0.99. Subsequently, at t_1, Ray knows that there is a cup on the table solely on the basis of *tactile* sensations. Luckily, Ray's sight returns from t_2 to t_3. Throughout this interval, Ray holds the indicated piece of knowledge solely on the basis of an appropriate *visual* experience.

I submit that this is a second kind of case of knowledge that involves Evidence Luck but *not* Belief Luck.

Pritchard's First Claim has thus been refuted, twice over. The other half of the conjunctive thesis that Pritchard defends is the claim that any possible case of knowledge that involves Belief Luck must also involve Evidence Luck. Call this 'Pritchard's Second Claim'. As before, Pritchard defends this claim by defeating an alleged counterexample to it. The example he considers involves a myopic subject who has good evidence for holding a certain belief but attends to that evidence only by way of a stroke of good luck. Of course, such a case refutes Pritchard's Second Claim only if the belief the myopic subject forms in response to the relevant evidence constitutes knowledge. Pritchard (2004: 203–4) denies that it does:

> Suppose...that the agent had the evidence all along (and acquired it in a non-lucky fashion), but failed to form a belief in response to that evidence because she did not properly attend to it (a kind of epistemic *akrasia*), and only eventually formed the relevant belief because she was lucky enough to reflect on her evidence at a rare moment of lucidity. The problem with such an example is that the very story that has to be told to explain why the acquisition of the evidence did not give rise to the belief undermines the plausibility of supposing that the agent has knowledge in the first place. For if we grant such a story then it follows that in most nearby possible worlds in which the agent has the same evidence as she does in the actual world, she fails to form the relevant belief as a result, and this kind

of insensitivity to the evidence normally suffices to indicate that the agent lacks knowledge.

I'm willing to concede that no such case impugns Pritchard's Second Claim (though I don't think we *must* grant this). It doesn't follow, of course, from the failure of such an attempted counterexample that Pritchard's Second Claim is true. Indeed, I think there are other attempted counterexamples to Pritchard's Second Claim that clearly succeed.

Consider, for instance, a case in which good evidence for a proposition P which was not luckily acquired by S actually issues in a justified belief that P, where there was a large chance that S's so believing in response to that evidence would be precluded by external manipulation of S's faculties. In such a case, an instance of knowledge is luckily acquired, although the evidence on which that knowledge is based was not itself luckily acquired. In short, such a case involves both knowledge and Belief Luck but *not* Evidence Luck. An illustrative example:

> Ned, a nefarious neurosurgeon, installs an Acme Belief Prevention Device in Vic's brain. The device degrades Vic's belief-forming faculties such that, at any given time, the probability that Vic can form the belief that he's appeared to greenly in response to a relevant visual experience is only 0.01. While on his daily stroll through the local rainforest, Vic is appeared to greenly and – in response to his visual experience – *improbably* forms the belief that he's being appeared to greenly.

I submit that this is a clear case of knowledge that involves Belief Luck but *not* Evidence Luck.

My argument against Pritchard's thesis that any possible case of knowledge that involves Evidence Luck must also involve Belief Luck – and vice versa – is now complete. So far as I can see, Pritchard's thesis is false: Evidence Luck and Belief Luck are not necessarily coextensive across cases of knowledge. The distinction between Evidence Luck and Belief Luck has more epistemological significance than Pritchard has allowed.

We've encountered five different kinds of epistemic luck so far. Again, since each is clearly compatible with knowledge, none is even a minimally plausible candidate for the ignorance-inducing phenomenon present in Gettier Cases. After highlighting and motivating an important thesis about the *scope* of gettiered belief (Section 3.3) – a thesis that will frame my upcoming discussion and assessment of substantive accounts of gettiered belief – I'll devote the remainder of this chapter, and the entirety of the next one, to considering several initially promising accounts of gettiered belief, some well established in the literature and some novel. We'll focus first on two of the literature's leading substantive accounts of gettiered belief: what I'll call the 'Ease of Mistake Approach' and the 'Lack of Credit Approach'. The former says that a gettiered belief is justified and true but held in such a way that its subject could easily have believed something *false* instead. The latter says that a gettiered belief is justified and true but such that its *accuracy* (or *truth*) isn't sufficiently creditable to the subject's cognitive ability. I'll devote the last two sections of this chapter to further explaining, and then critically assessing, the Ease of Mistake Approach (Sections 3.4 and 3.5). We'll return to the Lack of Credit Approach in the first two sections of the next chapter (Sections 4.1 and 4.2).

3.3 The scope of gettiered belief

At this juncture, I need to highlight and defend an important thesis that will frame my upcoming discussion and assessment of substantive accounts of gettiered belief.[4] Along with the two cases that I earlier dubbed 'the Classics' (*Pocket Change* and *Sheep Rock*), I'll be classifying as Gettier Cases certain 'fake barn' examples[5] (wherein an unsuspecting thinker confronts, in addition to the genuine article, a number of superficially indistinguishable counterfeits) as well as certain 'hidden helper' cases[6] (wherein one agent makes environmental changes to ensure that another believes accurately). Given my definition of 'Gettier Case' (= case similar to the ones Gettier employed to show that justified true belief doesn't suffice for knowledge), so classifying all these examples commits me to a thesis that I will label

> **Omnipresence:** There's a common ignorance-inducing phenomenon present in the Classics as well as in certain fake barn and hidden helper cases.

If Omnipresence turns out to be no more plausible than its denial, then I'll lose one or another of my objections to requirements that the Ease of Mistake Approach and the Lack of Credit Approach impose on gettiered belief. But if I lose one or another of those objections, then the account of gettiered belief that I champion later on in the next chapter (Section 4.6) won't be motivated quite as well as it would be otherwise. And so, it behooves me to ask: What reasons might there be to accept Omnipresence? In what follows, I'll develop two different lines of support for this thesis.

First, prior to any serious theorizing, all the relevant cases might strike you as involving a common ignorance-inducing phenomenon (the following considerations foreshadow some of the objections that I'll press against extant accounts of gettiered belief in this chapter and the next one).[7] Start with a variant of *Sheep Rock* wherein Roddy infers that there's a sheep in the field, from the (false) proposition that the object he sees there is a sheep. As with the original case, in this inferential variant of *Sheep Rock*, Roddy doesn't know that there's a sheep in the field. Why not? Intuitively, this is because Roddy holds his inferential belief in a way that's *liable to mislead* on its particular subject matter (cf. Plantinga 1996: 316) – viz. the location of nearby sheep. This rough, intuitive diagnosis of Roddy's ignorance should be about as uncontroversial as claims come in this neck of the epistemological woods. The diagnosis is consonant with each of the main general recipes for constructing Gettier Cases[8] as well as with each of the leading accounts of gettiered belief introduced above. Indeed, all these views about gettiered belief can plausibly be understood as different attempts to spell out, more fully and precisely, the above intuitive diagnosis of ignorance.

Let's now bring that intuitive diagnosis to bear on the Classics. Given the similarities between *Pocket Change* and the inferential variant of *Sheep Rock* just described, what we said about the latter applies to the former as well: Smith fails to know that the successful candidate has ten coins in his pocket *because* he holds this belief in a way that's liable to mislead on its particular subject matter – which includes, at least, the number of coins in the successful candidate's pocket. Moreover, since the basis for Roddy's perceptual belief in *Sheep Rock* – viz. his *nonveridical* visual experience as of a sheep – seems as liable to mislead (on the pertinent subject matter) as does the basis for his belief in the inferential variant of that case (the same nonveridical visual experience, *plus* the false belief it prompts that what he sees is a sheep), what we said about the inferential variant applies also to the original case: Roddy lacks perceptual knowledge that there's a sheep in the field *because* he holds this belief in a way that's liable to mislead on its particular subject matter – viz. the location of nearby sheep.

We've reached an important lemma: There's a common ignorance-inducing phenomenon present in the Classics – roughly, holding a belief in a way that's liable to mislead on its particular subject matter. To continue arguing toward Omnipresence, compare *Sheep Rock* with a variant of that case in which someone secretly activates a wireless fence system that keeps the sheep from leaving the field. In this hidden helper variant of *Sheep Rock*, the basis for Roddy's perceptual belief that there's a sheep in the field – again, his *nonveridical* visual experience as of a sheep – is liable to mislead on its particular subject matter (again, the location of nearby sheep). Finally, compare *Sheep Rock* with one last variant of the case in which *both* the sheep-shaped rock *and* the sheep are in Roddy's visual field simultaneously, Roddy's gaze just happens to settle on the *sheep*, and he comes thereby to believe that there's a sheep in the field. In this fake barn variant of *Sheep Rock*, the kind of ground on which Roddy bases his belief – viz. visual experience as of a sheep – doesn't reliably indicate the location of sheep in the field. Hence, with respect to both the hidden helper and fake barn variants of *Sheep Rock*, it's plausible to think that the way Roddy holds his sheep belief – viz. directly in response to visual experience as of a sheep – is liable to mislead on its particular subject matter. And since a belief's being so held keeps it from constituting knowledge in the Classics, it's plausible to think that Roddy also fails to know that there's a sheep in the field in both the hidden helper and fake barn variants of *Sheep Rock*. We've now arrived at Omnipresence.

I for one find the argument for Omnipresence developed over the last few paragraphs quite compelling. But there's a second, somewhat simpler argument for Omnipresence worth considering, one you might accept even if you have doubts about one or another of the steps in the first argument for it. Suppose you at least agree that each of the relevant cases – *Pocket Change* along with *Sheep Rock* and its three variants – seems to involve *some or other* odd, ignorance-inducing phenomenon. Such a sense will, I think, be widely shared.[9] Now, obviously, we want to avoid introducing unnecessary complexity into our analyses of knowledge. To avoid introducing such unnecessary complexity, we should avoid needlessly multiplying odd, ignorance-inducing phenomena. To avoid such needless multiplication, we should accept Omnipresence *absent good objections to it*. In this way, considerations of theoretical simplicity can support grouping all the relevant cases (again, *Pocket Change* along with *Sheep Rock* and its three variants) together – at least until we confront good reasons *against* such assimilation. And now we're back at Omnipresence, by a somewhat different and less circuitous route.

Having introduced Omnipresence and presented two arguments for it, I must leave discussion of it here for now. I'll pick up this thread in each of the next two sections, where I'll defend Omnipresence from what strike me as the two strongest reasons to deny it.

3.4 The Ease of Mistake Approach to gettiered belief: explanation and support

We start with a leading approach to gettiered belief initially proposed by Engel (1992) and recently advanced by Pritchard (2004, 2005, 2007, 2012a). Writes Engel (1992: 67):

> There is, I submit, an epistemologically relevant difference between a person who is epistemically lucky in virtue of the fact that, given her evidential situation, it is simply a matter of luck that her belief turns out to be true, and a person who is epistemically lucky in virtue of the fact that she is lucky to be in the evidential situation she is in but that, given her evidential situation, it is *not* a matter of luck that her belief is true. I call the kind of epistemic luck had by the former "veritic luck" because it is just a matter of luck that her belief is *true* and the kind had by the latter "evidential luck" because it is just a matter of luck that she has the *evidence* she does.... [O]f these two kinds of luck, *only* veritic luck is incompatible with knowledge.

Engel (1992: 69–70) goes on to identify what he calls 'veritic luck' with the knowledge-blocking phenomenon present in Gettier Cases.

More recently, Pritchard has advanced views about gettiered belief that are very similar to Engel's. Writes Pritchard (2004: 204–5):

> We must...look more specifically at the sort of luck that affects this epistemic relation between the knowing subject and the fact known. We can express this type of luck in terms of how, even if all the relevant epistemic conditions on knowledge demanded by the epistemological theory in question are met, it is still a matter of luck that the belief is true...We will call this type of luck 'veritic' luck. So construed, veritic luck clearly constitutes one sense in which luck can be epistemologically significant. Indeed, this is the type of luck that is famously at issue in the Gettier counterexamples to the classical tripartite account of knowledge [as epistemically justified true belief].

Elsewhere, Pritchard (2005: 146–8) claims that what he calls 'veritic luck' occurs when an

> agent's belief is true in the actual world, but...in a wide class of near-by possible worlds in which the relevant initial conditions are the same as in the actual world – and this will mean, in the basic case,

that the agent at the very least forms the same belief in the same way as in the actual world ... – the belief is false. ... [I]t is veritic luck that is at issue in the counterexamples to the classical tripartite account of knowledge that were famously advanced by Edmund Gettier.

According to Engel and Pritchard, then, a gettiered belief is (roughly) one that's justified and true but held in such a way that its subject only luckily avoided believing something *false* instead. Hawthorne (2004: 56, footnote 17) makes a suggestion along these same lines:

> Insofar as we withhold knowledge in Gettier cases, it seems likely that 'ease of mistake' reasoning is at work, since there is a very natural sense, in such cases, in which the true believer forms a belief in a way that could very easily have delivered error.

We can state the indicated account of gettiered belief – what I will (following the quotation from Hawthorne) call the 'Ease of Mistake Approach' – a bit more precisely as follows. Say once again that possible world W_1 is **close** to possible world W_2 before time t iff W_1 is no more than slightly different from W_2 up to (but not including) t. And say that **S could easily have had property Q at t** iff, in some possible world that's close to the actual world *before* t, S has Q *at* t. We can now state the **Ease of Mistake Approach** to gettiered belief like this:

> S's belief B that P, held in way W, is gettiered at t iff (B is justified and true but) S could easily have believed a falsehood that is similar to P, in a way like W, at t. (cf. Engel 1992; Hawthorne 2004; Pritchard 2004, 2005, 2007, 2012a)

The Ease of Mistake Approach gets the Classics right since each of the salient beliefs could easily have been false while held in the same way at the relevant time. Starting with *Pocket Change:* Let **t** be a time when Smith holds his successful candidate belief, and let **t*** be the period when Smith grabs (and drops in his pocket) ten coins. Now consider a world, β, that's identical with the actual world, α, before t except for this: during t*, Smith grabs (and drops in his pocket) only *nine* coins. β is only slightly different from α before t. But in β, Smith *falsely* believes at t that the successful candidate has ten coins in his pocket. So, in some world that's close to α *before* t, Smith's belief is false yet held in the same way *at* t. The Ease of Mistake Approach's right-to-left conditional therefore implies that Smith's belief is gettiered.

Turning to *Sheep Rock:* Let **t** be a time when Roddy holds his sheep belief, and let **t*** be the period when Roddy's gaze settles on the sheep-shaped rock. Consider a world, β, that's identical with the actual world, α, before time t except for this: during t*, the real sheep is slipping just beyond the field's boundaries. β is only slightly different from α before t. But in β, Roddy *falsely* believes at t that there's a sheep in the field. So, in some world that's close to α before t, Roddy's belief is false yet held in the same way at t. The Ease of Mistake Approach's right-to-left conditional therefore implies that Roddy's belief is gettiered.

Unfortunately, its smooth treatment of the Classics notwithstanding, the Ease of Mistake Approach is false. Indeed, the Ease of Mistake Approach is both too weak *and* too strong. In the next section, I'll present and defend counterexamples to both its right-to-left conditional and its left-to-right conditional. First, though, I want to defend the former from one kind of alleged counterexample prominent in the recent literature on epistemic luck. Here's an instance of the kind of case I have in mind, adapted from Sosa (2010: 471; cf. Sosa 2011: 84–5):[10]

> **Lucky Subitizer:** Ernie drinks from one cup out of several available on a table. All the other cups contain a drug that degrades subitizing ability (that is, the ability to discern the cardinality of a perceived collection without having to count). So Ernie might easily have lowered his subitizing competence. He might thus easily have believed incorrectly since his competence might easily have been degraded. There were many equally available cups, after all; only by luck did Ernie drink from the one without the drug.

Sosa offers the following commentary on his case: 'Does the fact that [Ernie] *might* have suffered that fate [that is, believing incorrectly as a result of ingesting the drug] deny him subitizing knowledge if *in fact* he does not suffer it? I can only report that to me that seems implausible' (2010: 471).

Do cases such as *Lucky Subitizer* really refute the Ease of Mistake Approach's claim of sufficiency for gettiered belief, as Sosa and several others would have us think?[11] Let's start by granting that, just after drinking from the untainted cup, Ernie can come to know (via subitizing ability) that, say, three objects are present. Here's the claim we should reject: When Ernie comes to know that three objects are present, he could easily have falsely believed then (via subitizing ability) that three objects were present. To begin to see why we should reject that claim, recall the pertinent definition:

S could easily have had property Q at t iff S has Q at t in some possible world that's close to the actual world before t.

Ernie could easily have falsely believed at t (via subitizing ability) that three objects were present *only if* he so believes in some possible world that's no more than slightly different from the actual world up to (but not including) t. Does Ernie so believe in some such world? The argument for answering affirmatively will presumably go like this:

> Let 't' denote the time when Ernie comes to know (via intact subitizing ability) that there are three objects present. And let 't*' denote the time when Ernie chooses to drink from what is in fact the untainted cup. Now consider a world, β, that's identical with the actual world, α, up to t* when Ernie instead chooses to drink from what is in fact one of the many tainted cups, and shortly thereafter he ingests its contents. In β, Ernie falsely believes at t (via degraded subitizing ability) that three objects are present (assume that the collection of objects before Ernie is somehow sensitive to which cup he drinks from: its cardinality would be three if, but only if, he were to drink from the untainted cup). Moreover, β differs only slightly from α up to t. So, in some world that's close to α before t, Ernie's belief is false yet held in the same way (viz. subitizing ability) at t.

Does this argument succeed? No, because it depends on the following dubious hidden inference:

> β differs only slightly from α all the way through t* (the time shortly before t when Ernie chooses to drink from what is in fact the untainted cup). So, β differs only slightly from α up to t.

We can accept that there's only a small difference between *Ernie's choosing to drink from* **this** *cup* and *Ernie's choosing to drink from* **that** *cup*. So we can accept the above inference's premise. But we should deny that the conclusion follows from the premise. The premise implies the conclusion only if the following general principle is true:

> If W_2 differs only slightly from W_1 all the way through t* *and* t* is only shortly before t, then W_2 differs only slightly from W_1 up to t.

This principle is false: a small change to the front edge of some actual process – even a *relatively brief* process – can yield a counterfactual process that's more than just slightly different from the actual process. But then there should be clear counterexamples to the above principle. Indeed, I think *Lucky Subitizer* itself provides a counterexample to that principle. Let me explain.

We can accept that Ernie's actual choice – that is, his active formation of a certain intention to take a drink, whose object turns out to be the untainted cup – differs only slightly from the choice he would have made had he instead been focused on a different cup just beforehand. If Ernie had chosen to drink from a different cup, he would have ingested liquid from a tainted cup shortly thereafter. The counterfactual process *Ernie's ingesting liquid from a tainted cup* is more than just slightly different from the actual process *Ernie's ingesting liquid from the untainted cup*. In the latter, after all, Ernie's subitizing ability remains perfectly intact, whereas in the former Ernie's subitizing ability is greatly diminished. Here, a small change to the front edge of an actual process yields a counterfactual process that's more than just slightly different overall from the actual process. We therefore have a counterexample to the above principle that underlies the *Lucky Subitizer* objection to the right-to-left conditional of the Ease of Mistake Approach. Contrary to what Sosa and others have suggested, then, the Ease of Mistake Approach survives confrontation with cases such as *Lucky Subitizer*.

3.5 Counterexamples to the Ease of Mistake Approach

Alas, despite its smooth treatment of the Classics and resilience to cases such as *Lucky Subitizer*, the Ease of Mistake Approach is false. Indeed, as I said earlier, this approach to gettiered belief is both too weak *and* too strong. To see that the Ease of Mistake Approach is too *weak*, consider the following case:

> *Coffee Cup:* The nondeterministic interpretation of quantum mechanics is correct. Accordingly, there is just before noon a nonzero – albeit *infinitesimally small* – objective probability that the particles composing John's coffee cup will soon behave in such a bizarre way that they no longer compose a coffee cup but instead a mere cup façade. At noon, the coffee cup is still there. Out of deeply ingrained habit, John looks at the cup then and forms a (justified true) belief that there's a cup on the desk. (adapted from Hawthorne 2004: 4–5)

At noon, John could easily have had a false visual belief that there's a cup on the desk. More fully, in some world that differs no more than slightly from the actual world *before* noon, the cup façade scenario obtains *at* noon, and John then has a false visual belief that there's a cup on the desk. So, the Ease of Mistake Approach's right-to-left conditional classifies John's belief as gettiered. But many will find it plausible that John knows there's a cup on the desk, despite the small prior chance of the cup façade scenario.[12] And even the more skeptically inclined should at least find it plausible that John's belief isn't *gettiered*. So, this case refutes the Ease of Mistake Approach's claim of sufficiency for gettiered belief. With *Coffee Cup* in hand, we can conclude that this approach to gettiered belief is too weak.

The Ease of Mistake Approach is also too *strong*, as reflection on the following case reveals:[13]

> ***Religious Sheep Rock:*** God has always firmly intended that Roddy form a justified true sheep belief – while *actually* viewing a sheep-shaped rock – at a specific time, on a specific day. God ensures that Roddy forms such a belief – *and no related false ones!* – at the appointed time by creating, and then guiding Roddy into, a region whose fields are peppered with sheep-shaped rocks. Each of these sheep-shaped rocks obscures its own morbidly shy sheep that infallibly detects approaching human observers and immediately thereafter hides behind its assigned rock. Looking at one of those rocks, Roddy forms a justified true belief that there's a sheep in the field. (adapted from Stone 2013)

Given all the divine intervention here, Roddy couldn't easily have been mistaken about a similar (to the content of his sheep belief) proposition, in a way similar to how he actually holds his belief. More fully: Any possible world in which Roddy holds at the appointed time, t, a similar (in propositional content and method of formation) *false* belief will be more than just slightly different from the actual world before t. So, the Ease of Mistake Approach's left-to-right conditional classifies Roddy's belief as *un*gettiered. But given Omnipresence and the clear similarities between *Religious Sheep Rock* and the hidden helper variant of *Sheep Rock* described earlier (Section 3.3), it's plausible to think that Roddy's belief *is* gettiered. So, *Religious Sheep Rock* impugns the Ease of Mistake Approach's claim of necessity for gettiered belief. This approach to gettiered belief is also too *strong*.

Objection (cf. Pritchard 2012a: 260–1, 273–4): This argument against the Ease of Mistake Approach's left-to-right conditional obviously depends on Omnipresence. The time has come to challenge

Omnipresence – specifically, the thesis that what induces ignorance in the Classics is also present in hidden helper cases. The subject in a hidden helper case is ignorant *only* because his believing accurately isn't *at all* creditable to his own cognitive ability. By contrast, subjects in the Classics hold beliefs whose accuracy or truth is to at least *some* extent creditable to their cognitive abilities. Hence, what induces ignorance in hidden helper cases – again, *zero* creditability for accuracy – is not also present in the Classics, and vice versa. So, Omnipresence is false, and the above argument against the Ease of Mistake Approach fails.

Reply (inspired by Kelp 2013: 6): Assuming that s/he doesn't mean to be going in for a fairly radical skeptical position here, the critic's overall position is untenable. To begin to see this, note that since *Religious Sheep Rock* is clearly a hidden helper-type case, the objector will have to say that Roddy's true belief there isn't *at all* creditable to his own cognitive ability. And given the objector's general diagnosis of ignorance in hidden helper cases, s/he will also have to say that a belief constitutes knowledge only if its truth is to at least *some* extent creditable to the subject's cognitive ability. Call this the **Minimal Creditability Requirement** on knowledge.[14] Now obviously, in *Religious Sheep Rock*, Roddy's cognitive abilities – for example, his powers of vision – play at least *some* role in his believing accurately that there's a sheep in the field. Indeed, Roddy's cognitive abilities seem to play at least as large a role in his holding the relevant true belief as do those of subjects in everyday examples of relatively easily acquired perceptual, introspective, memorial, rational, and testimonial knowledge. Therefore, to avoid a radical skeptical position, the objector must also *deny* the Minimal Creditability Requirement – which, of course, makes for an incoherent overall position. The objector's position thus turns out to be untenable, and the objection to Omnipresence accordingly fails.

I conclude, then, that *Coffee Cup* and *Religious Sheep Rock* jointly cast real doubt on the Ease of Mistake Approach to gettiered belief. We can also note that, in addition to refuting the Ease of Mistake Approach's claim of necessity for gettiered belief, cases such as *Religious Sheep Rock* provide even more reason to doubt whether common luck-involving expressions of our focal epistemological platitude will ultimately be of much help or illumination (such doubt initially arose in Section 3.1 above). Against the backdrop of a plausible analysis of *strokes of luck* (Section 2.2), cases such as *Religious Sheep Rock* reveal that such luck-involving expressions are naturally read as being *weaker* (logically speaking) than the platitude they're meant to capture. For example, unlike our focal platitude, such expressions fail to rule out Roddy's knowing that there are sheep present in a case such as *Religious Sheep Rock*, since – given all the divine intervention there – it wasn't a stroke of good luck for Roddy that his justified belief in the presence of sheep turned out to be true. In the next chapter, we'll see how *Religious Sheep Rock* and *Coffee Cup* can together point the way toward what is arguably the Ease of Mistake Approach's main competitor: the Lack of Credit Approach to gettiered belief.

4
Knowledge and Luck II: Three More Approaches to Gettiered Belief

Reflection on our two counterexamples to the Ease of Mistake Approach (Section 3.5) raises an important question: What distinguishes *Religious Sheep Rock* from *Coffee Cup* so that only the former involves gettiered belief? As we're about to see, an appealing answer to this question points clearly in the direction of what is arguably the Ease of Mistake Approach's main competitor: the Lack of Credit Approach.

4.1 From ease of mistake to lack of credit

Here's an appealing answer – one inspired by much recent work on virtue-theoretic accounts of knowledge[1] – to the question what epistemically relevant differences there are between *Religious Sheep Rock* and *Coffee Cup*:

> In *Religious Sheep Rock*, Roddy's getting it right that there are sheep in the field has a lot more to do with God's purposes and plans than with Roddy's cognitive ability. Likewise in the Classics: for each of the relevant beliefs, while its *existence* may be sufficiently creditable to its agent's cognitive abilities, its *accuracy* or *truth* is not so creditable to those abilities (cf. Riggs 2007, Sosa 2007, Zagzebski 2009, Greco 2010, Turri 2011). By contrast, in *Coffee Cup*, John gets it right as to whether there's a cup on the desk *by* seeing the cup and thus *through* his powers of vision.

Such reflection on these four cases naturally suggests the **Lack of Credit Approach** to gettiered belief:

> S's belief B in P is gettiered iff (B is justified and true but) B's accuracy isn't sufficiently creditable to S's cognitive abilities.

Sosa (2007: 23) provides a very clear statement of this view: 'Beliefs can be true...independently of the believer's competence in so believing, as in Gettier cases.' So does Greco (2010: 74): 'In Gettier cases, S believes the truth, and S believes from an ability, but S does not believe the truth *because* S believes from an ability.' As does Turri (2011: 7): 'Gettier subjects believe the truth, so they succeed in a sense, but this success...does not manifest their competence.'

Two additional points in favor of the Lack of Credit Approach merit mention here. First, this approach yields the following plausible diagnosis of cases such as *Lucky Subitizer* from Section 3.4 above (cf. Sosa 2010: 471; Neta and Rohrbaugh 2004: 404–5):

> The fact that Ernie believes accurately that there are three objects present is sufficiently creditable to his subitizing competence – which, by luck, remained perfectly intact. So, the Lack of Credit Approach correctly implies that Ernie's belief that there are three objects present is *not* gettiered.

Second, the Lack of Credit Approach offers an important axiological bonus: it nicely explains why knowledge is (other things being equal) better than mere gettiered belief (cf. Greco 2010: 99). Given that knowledge requires ungettiered belief, the Lack of Credit Approach implies that knowledge is sufficiently creditable accurate belief, whereas gettiered belief is not. Intuitively, creditable success is better than non-creditable success (other things being equal). It follows that knowing P is better than having a mere gettiered belief that P (other things being equal).[2]

Given its plausible diagnoses of all the examples discussed above along with its explanation of the superiority of knowledge to mere gettiered belief, the Lack of Credit Approach shows real promise. To make good on that promise, though, we must ask: What is it, exactly, for a belief's *accuracy* or *truth* to be 'sufficiently creditable' to a subject's cognitive abilities? As is indicated by the above quotations from prominent proponents of the approach, we can understand its 'sufficient creditability' relation in terms of either *explanatory salience* (for example, Greco 2010) or *power manifestation* (for example, Sosa 2010). In the next two sections (4.2 and 4.3), I'll explain and critically assess both of these main versions of the Lack of Credit Approach. This critical discussion will help set the stage for the introduction, development, and critical appraisal of two less prominent approaches to gettiered belief (Sections 4.4 through 4.6).

4.2 Creditability as explanatory salience

There are two main strains of the explanatory salience version of the Lack of Credit Approach, both of which have been suggested by Greco:

> **Strain 1:** S's belief B in P is gettiered iff (B is justified and true but) S's cognitive ability is not a salient part of the explanation of B's truth. (Greco 2010: 74)
>
> **Strain 2:** S's belief B in P is gettiered iff (B is justified and true but) S's cognitive ability is not among the *most* salient parts of the explanation of B's truth. (Greco 2003: 130)

Obviously, if S's cognitive ability isn't a salient part of the explanation of B's accuracy or truth, then it's not among the *most* salient parts of that explanation. But the converse is false: even if S's cognitive ability isn't among the *most* salient parts of the explanation of B's accuracy, S's cognitive ability might still be a *somewhat* salient part of that explanation. Strain 1's right-hand-side is therefore logically stronger than Strain 2's. So, Strain 1 makes a logically weaker claim of sufficiency for gettiered belief than does Strain 2, which in turn places a weaker requirement on gettiered belief than does Strain 1. Accordingly, we'll look for a counterexample to Strain 1's claim of sufficiency for gettiered belief, and a counterexample to Strain 2's claim of necessity for gettiered belief. Such a pair of cases would together show that the explanatory salience version of the Lack of Credit Approach is both too weak *and* too strong.

As for Strain 1's right-to-left conditional, consider this slight variation of a widely discussed case from Lackey (2007: 352):

> *Field Trip:* Morris is on a field trip to the Sears Tower. The group has just arrived at the train station in Chicago. Morris runs ahead of his class to ask directions from someone other than his teacher. Morris approaches the first adult passerby he sees and asks how to get to the Sears Tower. As it happens, all the adults in Morris's vicinity are honest Chicago residents who know the city extraordinarily well and gain great satisfaction from helping visitors reach their destinations.[3] The knowledgeable, well-intentioned passerby provides Morris with perfect directions to the Tower by telling him that it's located two blocks east of the train station. Morris unhesitatingly forms the corresponding true belief.

Question: How did Morris come to believe *accurately* as to the Tower's whereabouts? Answer: He approached someone who was in fact a knowledgeable and well-intentioned Chicago resident, asked about the Tower's location, and believed the perfect directions that the resident provided. While Morris's testimony-related abilities do show up in this answer, they aren't a *salient* part of the answer. Rather, what the answer makes salient are certain features of the *Chicago resident:* her knowledge of the city, intentions toward Morris, ability to convey directions, and so on. We should therefore say, in line with the virtue-theoretic treatment of the Classics sketched above (Section 4.1), that while Morris's testimony-related abilities may be a salient part of the explanation of why he now *has a belief* about the Tower's location, his testimony-related abilities aren't a salient part of the explanation of why he now believes *accurately* as to the Tower's location (cf. Lackey 2007: 352ff.). So, since Morris's true belief about the Tower's location is epistemically justified, Strain 1's right-to-left conditional classifies Morris's belief as gettiered. But many will find it plausible that Morris now knows where the Tower is. And even the more skeptically inclined among us should at least find it plausible that Morris's belief isn't *gettiered*. So, *Field Trip* impugns Strain 1's claim of sufficiency for gettiered belief. And recall that Strain 2's claim of sufficiency for gettiered belief is even stronger (logically speaking) than Strain 1's. So, Strains 1 and 2 both misclassify Morris's belief as gettiered. The explanatory salience version of the Lack of Credit Approach is too weak.

Riggs (2009b) suggests the following intriguing argument against the claim that the testifee's belief in a case like *Field Trip* is epistemically justified:

> If Morris really is epistemically justified in his belief that the Tower is two blocks east of the station (T), then he should be positioned to make an assertion of T to others that's proper *at least as far as epistemic considerations go*. But Morris isn't positioned to make such an assertion. To see this, imagine that, shortly after his exchange with the Chicago resident, Morris's teacher asks him where the Tower is. If Morris were to reply by flat-out asserting T, he'd be out of line.[4] After all, Morris hasn't yet been to the Tower, and he can't see it from where they're standing. Given his epistemic situation, the most that Morris could properly say is something like 'Someone just told me that the Tower is *that* way.' So, if Morris were to flat-out assert T, his assertion would be improper and on *epistemic* grounds. It follows that Morris's belief isn't epistemically justified after all. (adapted from Riggs 2009b: 210–11)

This defense of Strain 1 from *Field Trip* fails due to a false premise – specifically, the claim that if S has an epistemically justified belief that P, then S is positioned to make an assertion that P to others which is proper *at least as far as* **epistemic** *considerations go*. Recent literature on the epistemology of assertion provides a number of counterexamples to such claims. Consider, for instance, another case from Lackey (2011: 253):

> *Doctor:* Matilda is an oncologist at a teaching hospital who has been diagnosing and treating various kinds of cancers for the past fifteen years. One of her patients, Derek, was recently referred to her office because he has been experiencing intense abdominal pain for a couple of weeks. After requesting an ultrasound and MRI, the results of the tests arrived on Matilda's day off; consequently, all of the relevant data were reviewed by Nancy, a competent medical student in oncology training at her hospital. Being able to confer for only a very brief period of time prior to Derek's appointment today, Nancy communicated to Matilda simply that her diagnosis is pancreatic cancer, without offering any of the details of the test results or the reasons underlying her conclusion. Shortly thereafter, Matilda had her appointment with Derek, where she truly asserts to him purely on the basis of Nancy's reliable testimony, 'I am very sorry to tell you this, but you have pancreatic cancer.'

Surely, we can understand *Doctor* so that Matilda's belief about Derek's condition is epistemically justified. So, by the relevant premise of the above defense of Strain 1 from *Field Trip*, Matilda's justified belief about Derek's condition positions her to make an assertion of the cancer diagnosis to Derek which is proper *at least as far as* **epistemic** *considerations go*. But Matilda is *not* so positioned at the moment: her assertion of the diagnosis to Derek strikes us as improper precisely because she lacks certain kinds of evidence for its content (cf. Lackey 2011: 255). In light of cases such as *Doctor*, then, we can conclude that the above defense of Strain 1 from *Field Trip* fails due to a false premise.[5]

Moving on to the requirement that Strain 2 places on gettiered belief, consider this case from Turri (2011: 5):

> *Hobbled:* A competent, though not masterful, inspection of the crime scene would yield the conclusion that the murderer limps. Holmes saw through it and had already deduced that Dr. Hubble, who doesn't currently limp, poisoned the victim under pretense of treating her. Holmes also recognized that the scene would fool Watson, whose

own inspection was proceeding admirably competently, though not masterfully. Greatly impressed by Watson's competence, Holmes sprang into action. He disguised himself as a porter, strode across the street to where Dr. Hubble was, and kicked him so hard that Hubble was thereafter hobbled with a limp. Holmes returned to find Watson wrapping up his investigation, having just formed a justified true belief that the murderer limps.

Question: How did Watson end up believing *accurately* that the murderer limps? Answer: His competent investigation so impressed Holmes that Holmes did something to ensure that Watson's impending belief about the murderer would be true. Watson's cognitive ability is among the most salient parts of the explanation why he now believes *accurately* that the murderer limps. So, Strain 2 implies that Watson's belief that the murderer limps is *un*gettiered. But given Omnipresence and the clear similarities between *Hobbled* and the hidden helper variant of *Sheep Rock* described in Section 3.3 above, it's plausible to think that Watson's belief *is* gettiered.[6] So, *Hobbled* impugns Strain 2's claim of necessity for gettiered belief. And recall that Strain 1's claim of necessity for gettiered belief is even stronger than Strain 2's. So Strains 1 and 2 both misclassify Watson's belief as ungettiered. In addition to being too weak, the explanatory salience version of the Lack of Credit Approach is also too *strong*.

Field Trip and *Hobbled* together cast significant doubt on the explanatory salience version of the Lack of Credit Approach to gettiered belief. Does the power manifestation version of that approach fare any better?

4.3 Creditability as power manifestation

Following Sosa (2011: 82–4; cf. Turri forthcoming), let's suppose that a success (for example, an accurate believing) can manifest its agent's abilities even if exercising those abilities in the agent's current environment won't *reliably* meet with such success. Suppose, in other words, that there can be **environmentally *un*reliable abilities**. The distinction between environmentally reliable and environmentally *un*reliable abilities (powers, virtues, etc.) yields two strains of the power manifestation version of the Lack of Credit Approach:

> **Strain 1:** S's belief B in P is gettiered iff (B is justified and true but) B's truth doesn't manifest *any* of S's cognitive abilities (not even environmentally unreliable ones). (cf. Sosa 2011, Turri 2011)

Strain 2: S's belief B in P is gettiered iff (B is justified and true but) B's truth doesn't manifest any of S's *environmentally reliable* cognitive abilities. (cf. Carter 2013, Kelp 2013)

Obviously, if B's accuracy doesn't manifest *any* of S's cognitive abilities, then it doesn't manifest any of S's *environmentally reliable* cognitive abilities. But the converse is false: even if B's accuracy doesn't manifest any of S's *environmentally reliable* cognitive abilities, it might still manifest some of S's environmentally *un*reliable cognitive abilities. Strain 1's right-hand-side is therefore logically stronger than Strain 2's. So, Strain 1 makes a weaker claim of sufficiency for gettiered belief than does Strain 2, which in turn places a weaker requirement on gettiered belief than does Strain 1. As before, we'll look for a counterexample to Strain 1's claim of sufficiency for gettiered belief and a counterexample to Strain 2's claim of necessity for gettiered belief. Such a pair of cases would together show that the power manifestation version of the Lack of Credit Approach is both too weak *and* too strong.

Starting with Strain 1, we can concede that *Field Trip* doesn't clearly refute its claim of sufficiency for gettiered belief (cf. Orozco 2010, Kelp 2013). While Morris's belief about the Tower's location isn't gettiered, perhaps its accuracy does manifest Morris's fledgling testimony-related abilities. After all, in acquiring his true belief about the Tower, Morris exercises source selection and content monitoring abilities that have been cultivated to at least *some* small degree. If we allow that the truth of Morris's belief about the Tower's location manifests his testimony-related abilities while also standing by our earlier claim (Section 4.2) that those abilities aren't a salient part of the explanation of why Morris believes accurately, then we'll be committed to the following general thesis: An outcome's manifesting an ability doesn't entail that the ability is a salient part of the explanation of why the outcome occurred. But that general thesis is plausible, as the following kind of case from Pritchard (2012a: 271, footnote 38) illustrates: A wine glass falls on a hard tile floor and shatters. The glass's shattering manifests its fragility. But the glass's fragility isn't a salient part of the explanation of why the glass shattered: the glass shattered because it struck the hard tile floor.

So, it seems plausible enough to say that while *Field Trip* shows that the explanatory salience version of the Lack of Credit Approach is too weak, it doesn't also establish that the power manifestation version is too weak. But there are other cases that arguably do reveal such weakness. Consider, for example, a possible case involving a divine testifier and a human testifee:

Divine Revelation: God directly causes a true belief that God exists to be formed in a thinker, Paul, without using any states internal to Paul as intermediate causes of Paul's newly acquired theistic belief. The input that nondeviantly causes Paul's theistic belief is some state or activity in God, and so it is wholly external to Paul. (adapted from Bergmann 2006: 52, 63)

When our subject, Paul, forms his theistic belief in response to the relevant divine input, he exercises an ability to respond to such input, thereby satisfying the Minimal Creditability Requirement (Section 3.5). But – as proponents of the power manifestation version of the Lack of Credit Approach will surely agree – the mere fact that some ability, A, of S's plays a role in S's acquiring a certain true belief, B, doesn't entail that B's accuracy *manifests* A.[7] That Paul's theistic belief results from an ability to respond to relevant divine input therefore leaves it wide open as to whether the accuracy of Paul's belief is a manifestation of said ability.

Our question, then, is this: Is Paul's believing accurately that God exists a manifestation of some cognitive ability of *Paul's*? Arguably, no. In *Divine Revelation*, Paul doesn't get it right as to whether God exists through some God-detection ability of his own; rather, Paul gets it right as to whether God exists through God's own powers of self-revelation. So, Strain 1 of the power manifestation version of the Lack of Credit Approach will classify Paul's theistic belief as gettiered. But many epistemologists – especially those with broadly externalist sympathies, theists and non-theists alike – will think that knowledge acquisition via divine revelation is at least *possible* (cf. Lackey 2007: 354). And even those who are skeptical about the possibility of such knowledge acquisition should at least find it plausible that Paul's theistic belief isn't *gettiered*. So, *Divine Revelation* impugns Strain 1's claim of sufficiency for gettiered belief. And recall that Strain 2's claim of sufficiency for gettiered belief is even stronger than Strain 1's. So, Strain 1 and Strain 2 both misclassify Paul's belief as gettiered. In light of *Divine Revelation*, then, we can see that the power manifestation version of the Lack of Credit Approach is too *weak*.

To see that the power manifestation version of the Lack of Credit Approach is also too *strong*, consider the following case:

Fake Fruits: The Fruit Lovers Association meets for dinner at Doctor Orange's house. In the middle of Orange's dining room table sits a clear glass bowl. In the middle of the bowl sits one real apple. There have never been, and will never be, any fake apples in the region where Orange lives. Fake apples were globally banned years ago, and they haven't been available anywhere since. But there are no similar bans on other kinds of fake fruit. Now, unbeknownst to his friends, Orange is an inveterate practical jokester. Nestled around the real apple are several counterfeit citruses: two fake oranges, a fake grapefruit, three fake lemons, and two fake limes. A member of the Association, Sara – who knows *nothing* about the global ban on fake apples – casts her eyes upon the bowl and forms the belief that it contains an apple.

(adapted from Gendler and Hawthorne 2005: 344)

We can understand *Fake Fruits* so that the accuracy or truth of Sara's apple belief, B, manifests her ability to visually identify apples. Moreover, Sara's visual apple-identification ability seems to be environmentally reliable: after all, even in her overall relatively misleading current circumstances, Sara would definitely believe accurately as to whether there's an apple present were she to form such a belief through her ability to visually identify apples. So, since B's truth manifests an environmentally reliable cognitive ability, Strain 2 classifies B as *un*gettiered. But given Omnipresence and the clear similarities between *Fake Fruits* and the fake barn variant of *Sheep Rock* sketched in Section 3.3 above, it's plausible to think that Sara's apple belief *is* gettiered. So, *Fake Fruits* impugns the requirement that Strain 2 places on gettiered belief. And recall that Strain 1's requirement on gettiered belief is even stronger than Strain 2's. So, Strains 1 and 2 both misclassify Sara's belief as *un*gettiered. In addition to being too weak, the power manifestation version of the Lack of Credit Approach is also too *strong*.

Objection (cf. Turri 2011: 8–9): The time has come to challenge the part of Omnipresence on which the above argument relies – viz. the claim that subjects in fake barn-type cases lack knowledge. Let's start with an argument that Sara *does* know that there's an apple in the bowl after all. Imagine a variant of *Fake Fruits* wherein, simply to spite Doctor Orange – who recently beat her in the Fruit Lovers Association presidential election – Sara aims her DX4 weapon at the bowl on Orange's table and vaporizes the apple (Sara knows that apples are Orange's favorite food). Here, Sara *knowingly* destroys Orange's apple. And one knowingly does an act of type A *only if* one knows that one is A-ing – call this the **Knowledge Requirement on Acting Knowingly (KRAK)**.[8] So, in this variant of *Fake Fruits*, Sara knows that she's destroying Orange's apple. But if Sara knows in this variant that she's destroying Orange's apple, then she knows in the original case that the bowl contains an apple. So, in *Fake Fruits*, Sara knows that there's an apple in the bowl. And note, finally, that we can run the same kind of argument on any fake barn-style example, thereby defeating whatever ignorance intuition one may initially have had about the case. Hence, Omnipresence is false, and the above argument against the power manifestation version of the Lack of Credit Approach fails.

Reply (cf. Coffman 2013: 215–18): The objector's dependence on KRAK is unfortunate since there are plausible counterexamples to that principle. Suppose that a sharpshooter, Gunnar, knows that exactly 99 of his (rather large) revolver's 100 chambers contain live rounds; the remaining chamber contains a blank. Given the similarities between firing live rounds and blank ones, Gunnar can't know that he's fired a live round *unless* he can see what happens to his intended target. Gunnar is now aiming his revolver into a very small, dark room where his sworn enemy, Ridley, is chained tightly to a wall. Given his skill and circumstances, Gunnar knows that Ridley will die if he simply fires a live round in the direction he's now aiming. So, Gunnar gleefully pulls the trigger. Sure enough, the round is live, and Ridley is fatally wounded. Gunnar just killed Ridley and seems to have done so knowingly. At least, this is what we should say *so long as* we accept the objector's premise that Sara knowingly vaporized Orange's apple since Gunnar's killing Ridley seems *at least* as strong a candidate for an act done knowingly as Sara's vaporizing Orange's apple. Intuitively, though, Gunnar doesn't (yet) know that he killed Ridley. In light of such examples, the objector should give up KRAK and with it the above KRAK-dependent objection.[9]

We've now seen (Sections 3.5 through 4.3) that two of the literature's leading approaches to gettiered belief – the Ease of Mistake Approach and the Lack of Credit Approach – face some serious difficulties. In the remainder of this chapter, I'll develop and critically assess a couple of less prominent – but apparently more promising – approaches to gettiered belief, each of which arises naturally from a little more reflection on the intuitive diagnosis of ignorance in the Classics provided in Section 3.3 above.

4.4 Two riskier approaches to gettiered belief

Recall my earlier intuitive diagnosis of ignorance in the Classics (Section 3.3): in each case, the subject holds his belief in a way that's *liable to mislead* on its particular subject matter (cf. Plantinga 1996: 316). A little more reflection reveals that there are in fact two different senses – one psychological, one normative – in which the subject's belief-forming/-sustaining method is liable to mislead on the relevant subject matter.[10] Let's consider the *psychological* sense first. Roughly, in each of the Classics, the subject's holding his belief as he does actually creates – or at least, could easily have created – a psychological push toward many falsehoods that are similar to his actual belief's propositional content. More precisely, the subject holds his belief in a way that could easily have *disposed him to believe* many falsehoods that are similar to his actual belief's content. (Typically, S's believing that P, in way W, will dispose S to believe many propositions that are similar to P. For example, I now believe, on the basis of a relevant visual experience, that there's a coffee cup on my desk. In virtue of so believing, I'm disposed to believe many propositions that are similar to [There's a coffee cup on the desk] – for example, [There's something holding a beverage nearby]. For groundbreaking discussion of dispositions to believe, and their relation to dispositional and occurrent beliefs, see Audi [1994].)

Starting with *Pocket Change:* Let **P** be [The successful candidate has ten coins in his pocket], and let **W** be deduction from [Jones is the successful candidate] and [Jones has ten coins in his pocket]. Smith could easily have had fewer coins in his pocket at the relevant time. If he'd had fewer coins in his pocket, Smith would have been disposed by W to believe many P-like falsehoods – for example, P itself, [The successful candidate has more than nine coins in his pocket], [The successful candidate has a double-digit, even number of coins in his pocket], and so on. Hence, Smith could easily have been disposed, by W, to believe many P-like falsehoods (that is, many falsehoods that are similar to P).

Now for *Sheep Rock:* Let **P** be [There's a sheep in the field], and let **W** be Roddy's visual experience as of a sheep. Presumably, W *actually* disposes Roddy to believe many P-like falsehoods – for example, [There's a *seen* sheep in the field], [There's a *seen* medium-sized wooly mammal in the field], and so on. Moreover, the sheep could easily have slipped outside the field before Roddy came to believe P. If the sheep *had* slipped outside the field before Roddy came to believe P, Roddy would have been disposed by W to believe many P-like falsehoods – for example, P itself, [There's a medium-sized wooly mammal in the field], and so on. Hence, Roddy could easily have been disposed, by W, to believe many P-like falsehoods.

So, there's a clear *psychological* sense in which the Classics' subjects' doxastic methods are liable to mislead on the relevant subject matter. But there's also a *normative* sense in which those subjects' methods are liable to mislead. Roughly, the subject's holding his belief as he does actually creates – or at least, could easily have created – a normative push toward many falsehoods that are similar to his actual belief's propositional content. More precisely, each subject holds his belief in a way that could easily have *justified him in believing* (or, *given him sufficient reason to believe*) many falsehoods that are similar to his actual belief's content.[11]

Starting with *Pocket Change:* Let **P** be [The successful candidate has ten coins in his pocket], and let **W** be deduction from [Jones is the successful candidate] and [Jones has ten coins in his pocket]. Smith could easily have had fewer coins in his pocket at the relevant time. If he'd had fewer coins in his pocket, Smith would have been justified by W in believing many P-like falsehoods – for example, P itself, [The successful candidate has more than nine coins in his pocket], and so on. Hence, Smith could easily have been justified, by W, in believing many P-like falsehoods.

Now for *Sheep Rock:* Let **P** be [There's a sheep in the field], and let **W** be Roddy's visual experience as of a sheep. Presumably, W *actually* justifies Roddy in believing many P-like falsehoods – for example, [There's a *seen* sheep in the field], [There's a *seen* medium-sized wooly mammal in the field], and so on. Moreover, the sheep could easily have slipped outside the field before Roddy came to believe P. If the sheep *had* slipped outside the field before Roddy came to believe P, Roddy would have been justified by W in believing many P-like falsehoods – for example, P itself, [There's a medium-sized wooly mammal in the field], and so on. Hence, Roddy could easily have been justified, by W, in believing many P-like falsehoods.

In each of the Classics, then, there's both a *psychological* and a *normative* sense in which the subject's doxastic method is liable to mislead on the relevant subject matter. Having recognized this, we can start sketching two corresponding accounts of gettiered belief. What I'll call the **Risk of Misleading *Dispositions* Approach** says, roughly, that your (justified true) belief that Q is gettiered just in case you actually are – or at least, you're at real risk of being – *disposed to draw* a largely inaccurate map of the world's Q-related territory. And what I'll call the **Risk of Misleading *Justification* Approach** says, roughly, that your (justified true) belief that Q is gettiered just in case you actually are – or at least, you're at real risk of being – *justified in drawing* a largely inaccurate map of the world's Q-related territory. In the next two sections (4.5 and 4.6), I'll formulate and critically assess more precise statements of these two approaches.

4.5 The Risk of Misleading *Dispositions* Approach to gettiered belief

In light of some tough cases for the Ease of Mistake Approach along with the point that each subject in the Classics holds his belief in a way that could easily have disposed him to believe many relevant falsehoods, I recently proposed something along the lines of the following strain of the Risk of Misleading Dispositions Approach (cf. Coffman 2010a: 248–9):

> **RMDA:** S's belief B that P held in way W is gettiered at t iff (B is justified and true but) S could easily have been disposed at t, in a way like W, to believe many P-like falsehoods.

Arguably, RMDA can correctly classify Roddy's belief in *Religious Sheep Rock* (Section 3.5) as gettiered, thereby gaining an important advantage over the Ease of Mistake Approach. Recall that, given all the divine intervention, Roddy couldn't easily have *believed* any falsehoods similar to [There's a sheep in the field]. Presumably, though, Roddy's visual experience as of a sheep actually has – and so, could easily have – disposed him to believe many such falsehoods, such as [There's a *seen* sheep in the field] and [There's a *seen* medium-sized wooly mammal in the field]. Unlike the Ease of Mistake Approach, then, RMDA seems able to correctly classify Roddy's belief in *Religious Sheep Rock* as gettiered.

Unfortunately, I missed (at least) two crucial things when I proposed that earlier account of gettiered belief. First, RMDA suffers the same fate as the Ease of Mistake Approach when it comes to cases such as *Coffee Cup* (Section 3.5). In that example, recall, it could easily have happened that there was only a cup façade on John's desk at noon. If there *had* been only a cup façade on John's desk at noon, John would then have been disposed – by his visual experience as of a cup – to believe many falsehoods like [There's a cup on the desk]. So, John could easily have been disposed, by his relevant visual experience, to believe many falsehoods that are similar to [There's a cup on the desk]. Like the Ease of Mistake Approach, RMDA misclassifies John's cup belief as gettiered.

Second, we can easily convert *Religious Sheep Rock* into a counterexample to RMDA's claim of necessity for gettiered belief. We can simply add the following detail to the original case: beyond ensuring that Roddy's visual experience as of a sheep doesn't prompt him to actually form any relevant false beliefs, God *also* ensures that Roddy's visual experience doesn't even *dispose him to believe* any relevant falsehoods. In response to this objection, one might try (as I once did) to defend RMDA by arguing that, contrary to initial appearances, such cases really aren't possible. The envisaged argument would invoke a principle such as this one:

> Necessarily, if S has a visual experience as of an X, then (other things being equal) S is at least *disposed to believe* [There's a *seen* X].

But such a principle is ultimately untenable.[12] For one thing, it's extremely plausible that a thinker who lacks the concept of objectual seeing may nevertheless have visual experiences. Assuming that one is disposed to believe P only if one grasps all P's conceptual components, such a thinker constitutes a counterexample to the above principle: our thinker has visual experiences, all right, but due to conceptual impoverishment, isn't disposed to believe any propositions of the form [There's a *seen* X].

What's more, even if we grant that any host of visual experience can believe propositions of the relevant form, there will still be persuasive counterexamples to the above principle. Imagine, for example, a relatively immature or unsophisticated thinker who lacks facility with the concept of objectual seeing, despite having at least some grasp of it. As a result, this thinker isn't disposed – merely by having visual experiences – to believe any propositions of the form [There's a *seen* X].

So, RMDA turns out to be both too weak *and* too strong. Might some version of the Risk of Misleading *Justification* Approach fare better, at least relative to *Coffee Cup* and *Religious Sheep Rock*?

4.6 The Risk of Misleading *Justification* Approach to gettiered belief

Yes, I think so. To begin working toward a version of the Risk of Misleading Justification Approach that will correctly classify both *Coffee Cup* and *Religious Sheep Rock*, let's invoke a somewhat stronger notion than that of *easy* possibility, one we might label '*decent* possibility'. Say that S **could well** have had property Q at time t iff, in a *wide class* of possible worlds that are close to the actual world *before* t, S has Q *at* t. With this stipulative definition of 'S could well have had Q at t' in hand, we can get our first strain of the Risk of Misleading Justification Approach:

> **RMJA$_1$**: S's belief B that P held in way W is gettiered at t iff (B is justified and true but) S could well have been justified at t, in a way like W, in believing many P-like falsehoods.

RMJA$_1$ issues the right verdict on *Coffee Cup*. John isn't in fact justified – by the relevant visual experience, at noon – in believing many falsehoods that are similar to [There's a cup on the desk]. And while it could *easily* have happened that there was only a cup façade on John's desk at noon, it's false that this could *well* have happened then. That is, it's false that there's just a cup façade on John's desk at noon in a *wide class* of possible worlds that are close to the actual world before noon (remember, the objective chance of the cup façade scenario was infinitesimally small). So, RMJA$_1$ correctly classifies John's belief as *un*gettiered.

Moreover, RMJA$_1$ can also correctly classify Roddy's belief in *Religious Sheep Rock* as gettiered since it's plausible to think that Roddy's visual experience as of a sheep could well have justified him in believing many falsehoods that are similar to [There's a sheep in the field]. That is, in a *wide class* of worlds that differ no more than slightly from the actual world before the time when he forms his belief, Roddy's relevant visual experience justifies him in believing many falsehoods that are similar to [There's a sheep in the field] – for example, [There's a *seen* sheep in the field], [There's a *seen* medium-sized wooly mammal in the field], [There's a sheep in *that* spot] (where '*that* spot' denotes the sheep-shaped rock's location), and so on.

We should pause here to ask whether an analog of the amplified version of *Religious Sheep Rock* that refuted RMDA (Section 4.5) might impugn RMJA$_1$. Can we coherently add to *Religious Sheep Rock* the detail that God ensures that Roddy's visual experience doesn't justify him in believing such propositions as [There's a *seen* sheep in the field]? Arguably, no. To see this, consider the relevant analog of the above principle that I discussed in connection with RMDA:

> Necessarily, if S has a visual experience as of an X, then (other things equal) S is at least *justified in believing* [There's a *seen* X].

This principle has two advantages over its analog, whose consequent concerns being *disposed to believe* a proposition of the form [There's a seen X]. First, this principle isn't impugned by cases that involve hosts of visual experience who lack the concept of objectual seeing: it's plausible to think that one can have justification to believe a proposition which one can't currently believe due to cognitive limitations (cf. Feldman and Conee 1985: 19). Second, the above principle enjoys support from a very plausible general claim about the justificatory power of perceptual experience (cf. Pryor 2004: 357): When one has a perceptual experience as of an X, it feels to one as though one is perceiving an X, and this feeling gives one (prima facie) justification to believe both [There's an X] *and* [There's a perceived X] (even if one currently lacks the concept of objectual perceiving, and so can't now *form a justified belief* that there's a perceived X).

The above putative sufficient condition for being (prima facie) justified in believing propositions of the form [There's a seen X] is therefore quite plausible. But if that principle is true, then we *can't* coherently add to the original version of *Religious Sheep Rock* the further detail that God ensures that Roddy's visual experience as of a sheep doesn't justify him in believing propositions of the relevant form, since the above principle *plus* Roddy's having the relevant visual experience (and the stipulation that ceteris are indeed paribus) *entails* that Roddy has justification to believe such propositions.

Arguably, then, $RMJA_1$ can issue the correct verdicts on both *Coffee Cup* and *Religious Sheep Rock*. Sadly, though, there are cases showing that $RMJA_1$ is too strong. Consider this example from Hawthorne and Lasonen-Aarnio (2009: 104–5; cf. Skyrms 1967):

> **Pyromaniac:** A pyromaniac [Pi] is about to strike a match. At a time t prior to striking the match, she infers, and thereby comes to believe, that it will light when struck from her knowledge that it is a dry match of a brand that has always lit for her when dry and struck. There is a small chance that the particular match she holds will not light by friction when struck. And, in fact, the match does not light by friction. But it lights nevertheless, because of a burst of rare Q-radiation.

At t, Pi's belief that the match will light when struck is gettiered (cf. Hawthorne and Lasonen-Aarnio 2009: 105). But it's false that Pi's inductive reasoning could *well* have justified her in believing many falsehoods that are similar to [The match will light when struck]: in almost all possible worlds that are close to the actual world before t, Pi's match subsequently lights by friction, as usual. And in any such normal world, Pi's inductive reasoning doesn't at t justify her in believing many falsehoods that are similar to [The match will light when struck]. $RMJA_1$ therefore places too strong a requirement on gettiered belief.

The obvious (though, I admit, somewhat inelegant) fix is to go disjunctive as follows:

> **$RMJA_2$:** S's belief B that P held in way W is gettiered at t iff (B is justified and true but) S *either* actually is at t justified, in a way like W, in believing many P-like falsehoods *or* could well have been so justified then.

$RMJA_2$ correctly classifies Pi's belief as gettiered (as it does Roddy's belief in *Religious Sheep Rock*, which we saw a little while ago). After all, Pi is in fact justified at t, by her inductive reasoning, in believing many falsehoods that are similar to [The match will light when struck] – for example, [The match will light *by friction* when struck], [It's false that the match will light when struck due to rare radiation], and so on. RMJA$_2$ also properly handles our four remaining key examples of gettiered belief, which I'll now address in order of appearance:

Pocket Change: P = [The successful candidate has ten coins in his pocket], W = deduction from [Jones is the successful candidate] and [Jones has ten coins in his pocket]. Smith could well have had fewer coins in his pocket at the relevant time. If he'd had fewer coins in his pocket, Smith would have been justified by W in believing many P-like falsehoods – for example, P itself, [The successful candidate has more than nine coins in his pocket], and so on. Hence, Smith could well have been justified, by W, in believing many P-like falsehoods.

Sheep Rock: P = [There's a sheep in the field], W = visual experience as of a sheep. Presumably, W actually justifies Roddy in believing many P-like falsehoods – for example, [There's a seen sheep in the field]. Moreover, the sheep could well have slipped outside the field before Roddy came to believe P. If the sheep had slipped outside the field before Roddy came to believe P, Roddy would have been justified by W in believing many P-like falsehoods – for example, P itself, [There's a medium-sized wooly mammal in the field], and so on. Hence, Roddy could well have been justified, by W, in believing many P-like falsehoods.

Hobbled: P = [The murderer limps], W = abduction from crime scene evidence. Watson's abductive reasoning could well have – and, on a natural interpretation of the case, actually has – justified him in believing many falsehoods that are similar to [The murderer limps], including: [The murderer *had* a limp], [The murderer *was* physically handicapped], and so on.

Fake Fruits: P = [There's an apple in the bowl], W = visual experience as of an apple. Sara could well have believed, on the basis of a visual experience like W (for example, a visual experience as of an orange), that the bowl contained the corresponding kind of fruit (for example, an orange). If Sara had so believed, she would have been justified by a visual experience like W in believing many P-like falsehoods – for example, [There's an orange in the bowl], [There's non-apple fruit in the bowl], [There's citrus fruit in the bowl], and so on. Hence, Sara could well have been justified, in a way like W, in believing many P-like falsehoods.

Upshot: RMJA$_2$'s right-to-left conditional correctly implies that all four salient beliefs are gettiered.

We return now to our four key examples of *un*gettiered belief – viz. *Lucky Subitizer, Coffee Cup, Field Trip,* and *Divine Revelation.* As for each of the latter two cases, there's not even an initially plausible reason to think its subject could *easily* have been justified, in a way similar to how he formed his relevant belief, in believing many falsehoods that are similar to his actual belief's propositional content. *A fortiori,* there's not even an initially plausible reason to think either of those subjects actually is, or could well have been, so justified. As for *Coffee Cup,* we've already noted (in this section's first paragraph) that John's visual experience as of a cup doesn't actually justify him in believing many relevant falsehoods, and there was not a decent chance it would do so. Finally, as for *Lucky Subitizer,* a variant of the argument considered in Section 3.4 above for the conclusion that Ernie could easily have falsely believed that three objects were present *might* provide an initially plausible reason to think that Ernie could well have been justified in believing (via subitizing ability, at the relevant time) many falsehoods like [There are three objects present].[13] But, just like the original argument, the variant will depend on the claim that *Ernie's ingesting liquid from a tainted cup* differs only slightly from *Ernie's ingesting liquid from the untainted cup.* I already explained away, and argued against, this claim in Section 3.4 above. These composite events can seem sufficiently similar because their front edges – *Ernie's choosing to drink from* **this** *cup* vs. *Ernie's choosing to drink from* **that** *cup* – are only slightly different. But a small change at the outset can lead quickly to a rather large difference overall, as is clearly and conveniently illustrated by the two composite events currently in focus (*Ernie's ingesting liquid from the untainted cup* vs. *Ernie's ingesting liquid from a tainted cup*). So, RMJA$_2$'s right-to-left conditional seems not to misclassify any of our four key *un*gettiered beliefs as gettiered.

RMJA$_2$ thus improves significantly on each of the previously discussed accounts of gettiered belief by properly handling *all* the key examples we've considered so far. Further – and perhaps somewhat surprisingly – RMJA$_2$ also yields its own plausible explanation of the (prima facie) superiority of knowledge to mere gettiered belief. To begin to see this, assume RMJA$_2$'s truth for conditional proof. According to RMJA$_2$, if you hold a justified true belief that P in a way that *either* actually has *or* could well have justified you in believing many P-like falsehoods, then your belief that P is gettiered. So, supposing that knowledge is at least ungettiered justified true belief, RMJA$_2$ implies that you know that P only if you hold a justified true belief that P in such a way that you're thereby *neither* actually justified in believing many P-like falsehoods *nor* in real danger of being so justified (say that you're **in real danger** of having property Q at time t iff you could well have had Q at t). Now consider these two states of affairs:

> your holding a justified true belief that P in a way that either actually has, or could well have, justified you in believing many P-like falsehoods
>
> your holding a justified true belief that P in such a way that you're thereby neither actually justified in believing many P-like falsehoods nor in real danger of being so justified

Intuitively, the latter seems better than the former (other things being equal). This comparative value fact is likely underwritten by a deeper axiological fact – viz. that it's always bad to believe falsely (other things being equal).[14] So, given $RMJA_2$, your knowing that P is better than your having a mere gettiered belief that P (other things being equal).

In addition to properly handling all the key cases discussed above, then, $RMJA_2$ also yields its own plausible explanation of the (prima facie) superiority of knowledge to mere gettiered belief. Of course, one can be no more than very cautiously optimistic about the long-term prospects of any particular substantive account of gettiered belief. But $RMJA_2$ is at least shaping up to be a promising new approach to gettiered belief, one that richly deserves further development and exploration. I'll draw this chapter to a close by defending $RMJA_2$'s right-to-left conditional from a pair of challenging attempted counterexamples.

4.6.1 Objection 1: Kelp's Demonic Clock

This imagined objector attacks $RMJA_2$ with an **Epistemic Frankfurt Case** – that is, an example in which (allegedly) a belief constitutes knowledge despite the presence of a counterfactual intervener who makes the belief inevitable for its subject.[15] Here's one widely discussed such case:

> ***Demonic Clock:*** A demon wants Chris to form the belief that the time is 8.22am when he comes down the stairs first thing in the morning (the demon doesn't care whether the belief is true). Since [the demon has] lots of special powers, he is able to ensure that Chris believes this proposition (e.g., by manipulating the clock). Now suppose that Chris happens to come downstairs that morning at exactly 8.22am, and so forms the belief that the time is 8.22am by looking at the accurate clock at the bottom of the stairs. Accordingly, the demon

achieves what he wants without having to do anything. (Pritchard 2012b: 186; adapted from Kelp 2009: 27–8)

RMJA$_2$'s critic can argue as follows for the claim that Chris knows that it's 8:22am: 'The...clock is working reliably as always.... [Chris] has the ability to read the clock, exercises his ability and hits upon the truth through the exercise of this ability' (Kelp 2009: 27). Obviously, if Chris's belief about the time constitutes knowledge, then his belief *isn't* gettiered. But RMJA$_2$'s right-to-left conditional seems to imply that Chris's belief *is* gettiered. While Chris's belief is true and justified, he is – or at least, he could well have been – justified, by reading the clock, in believing many falsehoods like [It's 8:22am], including [It's 8:22am], [The clock wouldn't have read '8:22am' if it had been consulted several minutes ago], [No deceptive demon has any control over the clock's current '8:22am' reading], and so on. Reflection on *Demonic Clock*, the critic concludes, reveals that RMJA$_2$ is too *weak*: the condition that it proposes as sufficient for a belief's being gettiered turns out to be compatible with knowledge, and so, that condition does not suffice for gettiered belief after all.

In defense of RMJA$_2$, I will simply grant that Chris is – or could well have been – justified, by reading the clock, in believing many relevant falsehoods. What I deny is that Chris knows that it's 8:22am (cf. Pritchard 2012b: 187). Note first that the highly positive description of Chris's clock in the above argument for the thesis that Chris knows it's 8:22am actually conflicts with the stipulated details of *Demonic Clock*, making the overall objection incoherent as it currently stands. According to that description, recall, Chris's clock is 'working reliably as always' when Chris reads it. This implies both (i) that Chris can now rely on the clock to provide accurate information about the time ('working reliably') *and* (ii) that the clock hasn't recently suffered any reliability-diminishing changes ('as always'). Since the case's stipulated details clearly imply that both (i) and (ii) are *false*, the case's stipulated details conflict with the claim that Chris's clock is 'working reliably as always'. So, the argument for ascribing knowledge of the time to Chris would seem to reduce to the claim that Chris 'has the ability to read the clock, exercises his ability and hits upon the truth through the exercise of this ability' (Kelp 2009: 27). But, as we've already learned from reflecting on fake barn-type cases such as *Fake Fruits* (Section 4.3), a subject's forming a true belief through the exercise of cognitive ability – even *environmentally reliable* cognitive ability – doesn't suffice for the belief's constituting knowledge.

88 Luck: Its Nature and Significance

The case for attributing knowledge of the time to Chris thus turns out to be considerably weaker than it might initially have appeared. On the other hand, there's this simple but compelling argument *against* ascribing such knowledge to Chris:

> If a clock's reading isn't guided by what time it is, then the clock doesn't enable observers to know what time it is. The reading on Chris's clock is no longer guided by what time it is. Rather, its reading is guided by the truth-indifferent demon. So, Chris's demon-possessed clock doesn't enable him to know what time it is.

I submit that, when combined with the points in the preceding paragraph, this argument serves to render implausible the objector's claim that Chris knows it's 8:22am – and so, the argument serves to defeat the *Demonic Clock*-based objection to RMJA$_2$.

Reply 1: Note that the demon remains *idle* throughout this case – the demon doesn't *do anything* to bring it about that Chris's clock exhibits its actual reading. So, a key premise in the above argument against ascribing knowledge to Chris is false: the demon is *not* guiding the clock's reading.

Rejoinder: The objector's reply assumes that guidance requires *active* causal contribution. But that's a mistake: even if an agent hasn't made an active causal contribution to a state of affairs, that state of affairs may nevertheless be under the agent's guidance. To see this, consider a (less famous) case from Frankfurt (1978: 160):

> A driver whose automobile is coasting downhill in virtue of gravitational forces alone may be entirely satisfied with its speed and direction, and so he may never intervene to adjust its movement in any way. This would not show that the movement of the automobile did not occur under his guidance.

We can understand this example so that the agent was placed in the moving automobile while unconscious. When the agent wakes up and gets his bearings, he *passively* acquires a relevant desire or intention to continue coasting, whose presence then contributes causally to the automobile's subsequent movement (cf. Mele 1997: 9–10). The automobile's movement is now under the agent's guidance, despite the fact that the agent hasn't made an *active* causal contribution to its movement. Given the close similarity between (a) our driver's relation to his car and (b) the demon's relation to Chris's clock, it remains plausible to think that the clock is indeed under the truth-indifferent demon's guidance – and so, it remains plausible to deny that reading the clock enables Chris to know the time.

Reply 2: Let's try this again, a little more subtly. If understood so that its key premises are sufficiently plausible, the above argument for ascribing ignorance of the time to Chris is *invalid*. Here's what we get if we interpret each premise so that it's sufficiently plausible:

(i) If a clock's reading is not *at all* guided by the time, then the clock doesn't enable observers to know the time.
(ii) Chris's clock is not guided *solely* by the time.
(iii) So, Chris's clock doesn't enable observers to know the time.

Claims (i) and (ii) are plausible enough, but they do not jointly entail (iii).

Rejoinder: RMJA$_2$'s proponent has (at least) two possible moves here, one steadfast and one more concessive. The more concessive move is to replace 'at all' and 'solely' with (something like) 'primarily'. This makes for a valid argument with sufficiently plausible premises. The steadfast move asserts that, contrary to the objector's assumption, it's plausible enough to say that Chris's clock isn't *at all* guided by the time. So far as I can see, the only potential reason to think the clock is to *some* extent still guided by the time, post-possession, is this: Because it suits his fancy, the demon is letting the clock continue to accurately depict the time. But, where X and Y are obtaining states of affairs, X may continuously accurately depict Y over a non-trivial stretch of time without being to *any* extent guided by Y at certain times in the relevant period. Here's an illustrative case:

> You unknowingly fall victim to an evil neuroscientist over a certain period of time – say, for one hour on a typical weekday afternoon. The neuroscientist implants a device that gives you randomly selected experience sets (visual, auditory, tactile, and so on) at five second intervals. It just so happens that your actual course of experience over the hour – which is, we may suppose, qualitatively indistinguishable from the course of experience you would have enjoyed had you not been so victimized – continuously accurately depicts your surroundings.

Here, your actual course of experience is guided *entirely* by the neuroscientist's device, not *at all* by your surroundings – notwithstanding the fact that your course of experience continuously accurately depicts your surroundings. Moral: Where X and Y are obtaining states of affairs, X may continuously accurately depict Y over a non-trivial stretch of time without being to *any* extent guided by Y at certain times during the relevant period. So far as I can see, then, the only *potential* reason to think that Chris's demon-possessed clock is to some extent still guided by the time – viz. that it continuously accurately depicts the time since this suits the demon's fancy – is not in the end a *good* reason to think that Chris's clock is still to some extent time-guided.

4.6.2 Objection 2: Bogardus's Atomic Clock

Consider this intriguing example from Bogardus (2014: 300–1):

> *Atomic Clock:* [T]he world's most accurate clock hangs in Smith's office at a cereal factory, and Smith knows this. The clock's accuracy is due to a clever radiation sensor... This radiation sensor is very sensitive, however, and could easily malfunction if a radioactive isotope were to decay in the vicinity (a very unlikely event, given that Smith works in a cereal factory). This morning, against the odds, someone did in fact leave a small amount of a radioactive isotope near the world's most accurate clock in Smith's office. This alien isotope has a relatively short half-life, but – quite improbably – it has not yet decayed at all. It is 8:20am. The alien isotope will decay at any moment, but it is indeterminate when exactly it will decay. Whenever it does, it will disrupt the clock's sensor, and freeze the clock on the reading '8:22'... The clock is in danger of stopping at any moment, even while it currently continues to be the world's most accurate clock. Smith is quite punctual, and virtually always arrives in her office on workdays between 8:20 and 8:25am, though no particular time in that duration is more likely than any other to see her arrive. Upon entering her office, Smith always looks up at her clock and notes the time of her arrival... [T]hat alien isotope has not yet decayed, and so the clock is running normally at 8:22am when Smith enters her office. Smith takes a good hard look at the world's most accurate clock – what she knows is an extremely well-designed clock that has never been tampered with – and forms the true belief that it is 8:22am.

From here, a critic of $RMJA_2$ could argue as follows for the claim that Smith knows that it's 8:22am (Bogardus 2014: 301–2):

> The available evidence supports Smith's belief, and she was within her epistemic rights to form that belief. At many levels of generality,

her belief is formed by a reliable process. Her true belief manifests her intellectual powers, virtues, and abilities... Her belief that P is causally connected in an appropriate way with the fact that P.... [H]er belief results from properly functioning cognitive faculties working in a congenial epistemic environment according to a design plan successfully aimed at truth... Also, it is not an accident that the clock's reading is accurate and that Smith's belief is true... [T]he grounds for her belief do not include any falsehood F such that, if F were removed from her grounds, her belief would no longer be justified. We may also add that there is nothing that Smith believes or that she should believe, given her evidence, which would defeat her justification for her belief that it's 8:22am.

In light of the above considerations, Bogardus (2014: 303–4) concludes that *Atomic Clock* is a counterexample to the 'safety requirement' on knowledge – that is, the thesis that S knows that P only if 'in nearly all... nearby possible worlds in which [S] forms the belief that P in the same way as [S] does in the actual world, that belief is true' (Pritchard 2005: 163). Our imagined critic of RMJA$_2$ can claim, in light of those exact same considerations, that *Atomic Clock* is a counterexample to RMJA$_2$. Obviously, if Smith's belief about the time constitutes knowledge, then her belief isn't gettiered. But RMJA$_2$'s right-to-left conditional seems to imply that Smith's belief *is* gettiered. While Smith's belief is true and justified, she is – or, at least, she could well have been – justified, by reading the clock, in believing many falsehoods like [It's 8:22am], including [It's 8:22am], [The clock wouldn't have read '8:22am' if it had been consulted before 8:22am], and so on. Reflection on *Atomic Clock*, the critic concludes, reveals that RMJA$_2$ is too *weak*: the condition that it proposes as sufficient for a belief's being gettiered turns out to be compatible with knowledge, and so that condition does not suffice for gettiered belief after all.

In defense of RMJA$_2$, I will simply grant that Smith is – or, could well have been – justified, by reading the clock, in believing many relevant falsehoods. What I deny is Bogardus's claim that Smith knows that it's 8:22am. Here, in brief, is my argument against that knowledge attribution. Bogardus's description of *Atomic Clock* is problematic in at least four respects. Accordingly, his description of the example must be revised; and once we've made the required revisions, our epistemic evaluation of Smith's belief must be somewhat more negative than the one that Bogardus offers. So, the case for thinking Smith's belief constitutes knowledge is somewhat weaker than Bogardus's overly positive appraisal suggests. Indeed, on a more accurate assessment, Smith's belief is *at best* epistemically comparable to Sara's apple belief in *Fake Fruits* (Section 4.3). But since the latter falls short of knowledge, the former does as well. I'll devote the rest of this subsection to fleshing out this argument.

To begin, the description of *Atomic Clock* is problematic in at least four respects. First, since the description is supposed to elicit from readers an intuition that Smith knows that it's 8:22am, the stipulation (in the description's first sentence) that Smith knows hers is 'the world's most accurate clock' is improper. (If an example that you're describing is supposed elicit from your audience an intuition that P, you can't properly stipulate that P – or anything that trivially entails P – in setting up the example.) I submit that we should simply ignore this problematic knowledge ascription.

Second, and remaining focused on the claim that Smith's is 'the world's most accurate clock', this claim is liable to mislead in an important way. Often, when we apply the term 'accurate' to a measuring instrument (for example, 'accurate gauge'), we're ascribing to the instrument a (not purely track record) kind of reliability which entails that, if the instrument were to provide a measurement of the relevant quantity, that measurement would probably be true. Now, if we read 'accurate' throughout the example as *reliable* (in the indicated counterfactual or modal sense), then we may well ultimately intuit that Smith knows it's 8:22am. But that obviously can't be Bogardus's intended reading of the term 'accurate', as it appears in 'accurate clock'; otherwise, Smith's belief wouldn't be clearly unsafe, which it must be given Bogardus's aim of constructing a clear counterexample to the safety requirement on knowledge. Rather, we must be very careful to read 'accurate' throughout the description of the case as (something like) *precise* or *exact*.

Third, when we say that something is 'running normally', we often mean that the thing in question isn't currently at serious risk of malfunction. Imagine that you're picking up your previously disabled vehicle from the repair shop. Your mechanic might well say something like 'I've got your van running normally again'. At least part of what she's getting across to you is that your van isn't presently in grave danger of malfunctioning. But that obviously can't be Bogardus's intended reading of 'running normally', since Smith's clock clearly *is* supposed to be at serious risk of malfunction. Rather, we must be very careful to read 'running normally' as (something like) *isn't currently malfunctioning* or *hasn't yet malfunctioned*.[16]

Fourth and finally, recall the stipulation that Smith's clock 'has never been tampered with'. On a natural reading of that expression, putting an instrument under circumstances in which it is at serious risk of malfunction suffices for having tampered with the instrument. Clearly, Bogardus doesn't intend any such reading of the indicated expression. Rather, we must be very careful to read 'has never been tampered with' as (something like) *hasn't yet been made (caused) to malfunction.*

Now suppose that the description of *Atomic Clock* has been revised in the ways I've just argued it must be. Once the description has been duly revised, our epistemic evaluation of Smith's belief about the time must be somewhat more negative than the one that Bogardus offers. At least five of Bogardus's claims about Smith's belief must be clarified, or even simply ignored, in light of the required revisions:

> 'At many levels of generality, [Smith's] belief is formed by a reliable process'. We must keep firmly in mind that Smith's belief is reliably formed *only* in senses compatible with the fact that the instrument on which she's depending for that belief (her testifier) lacks the aforementioned counterfactual or modal kind of reliability.
>
> 'Her true belief manifests her intellectual powers, virtues, and abilities'. Again, we must keep firmly in mind that Smith's belief is formed through intellectual virtues (powers, abilities) *only* in senses compatible with the fact that the instrument on which she's depending for that belief lacks the aforementioned counterfactual or modal kind of reliability.
>
> 'Her belief that P is causally connected in an appropriate way with the fact that P'. It's not at all clear what 'in an appropriate way' is supposed to mean here. Obviously, if it means anything like *knowledge-enabling*, then Bogardus is here improperly stipulating that Smith knows it's 8:22am. I submit that 'in an appropriate way' should simply be deleted from this portion of Bogardus's commentary on Smith's belief.
>
> '[H]er belief results from properly functioning cognitive faculties working in a congenial epistemic environment'. We must proceed cautiously here because there are clear senses in which Smith's belief is *not* held in a 'congenial epistemic environment'.[17] What's true is that Smith holds her belief in what Plantinga (1996: 313) would call an 'appropriate cognitive *maxi*-environment' – that is, a general or global physical environment sufficiently similar to 'the one we enjoy right here on earth, the one for which we were designed by God or

evolution'. But because the instrument on which Smith is depending for her belief lacks counterfactual or modal reliability, Smith does *not* hold her belief in what Plantinga (1996: 327) would call a 'favorable cognitive *mini*-environment' – that is, 'the sort of mini-environment in which [the exercise of cognitive powers by which Smith's belief was produced] can be counted on to produce a true belief'.

'Also, it is not an accident that the clock's reading is accurate and that Smith's belief is true'. It's not at all clear what's being claimed here. If we read 'not an accident that' as *not a stroke of good luck (for Smith) that*, then the claim seems false both intuitively and in light of the Analysis of strokes of luck (Section 2.2). In any event, Bogardus comes very close here to claiming that Smith's belief about the time is non-accidentally true. Given the tight conceptual connection between *non-accidentally true belief* and *knowledge* (cf. Unger 1968), Bogardus thus comes very close here to improperly stipulating that Smith knows it's 8:22am. I submit that we should simply ignore this portion of Bogardus's commentary on Smith's belief.

The upshot of the preceding discussion is that our epistemic assessment of Smith's belief must be somewhat more negative than what Bogardus offers. Accordingly, the case for thinking that Smith's belief constitutes knowledge is somewhat weaker than Bogardus's overly positive epistemic appraisal of the belief suggests. Indeed, I submit that the case for thinking that Smith's belief constitutes knowledge is no stronger than the case for thinking that Sara's apple belief (in *Fake Fruits* [Section 4.3]) constitutes knowledge. As can be easily verified, for each of the epistemic good-making features that Bogardus can properly ascribe to Smith's belief about the time, Sara's apple belief also has that feature:[18]

> The available evidence supports Sara's apple belief, and she was within her epistemic rights to form it. At many levels of generality, Sara's belief is formed by a reliable process. Her belief's accuracy manifests her intellectual powers, virtues, and abilities. Her belief that there's an apple in the bowl is causally connected with the fact that there's an apple in the bowl. Sara's belief results from properly functioning cognitive faculties working in a congenial *maxi*-environment according to a design plan successfully aimed at truth. Sara's grounds for her apple belief do not include any falsehood F such that, if F were removed from those grounds, her belief would no longer be justified. Nothing that Sara in fact believes or that she should believe, given

her evidence, actually does or would defeat her justification for her belief that there's an apple in the bowl.

We can conclude, then, that Smith's belief about the time isn't epistemically superior to Sara's apple belief; *at best*, the former is epistemically comparable to the latter. But since the latter falls short of knowledge (Section 4.3), the former does as well.

I submit that the considerations I've set out in the last several paragraphs serve both to undercut and to rebut any intuitive sense that one may initially have had that Smith knows it's 8:22am in *Atomic Clock*. Those considerations thus jointly constitute a successful defense of RMJA$_2$ from *Atomic Clock*.

* * *

Chapter 3 – the first of two chapters devoted to exploring the relationship between knowledge and luck – began with this quotation from Pritchard (2007: 277; cf. Dancy 1985: 134): 'It is a platitude in epistemology to say that knowledge excludes luck.' We noted that the expression 'knowledge excludes luck' is here meant to capture a widespread intuitive reaction to Gettier Cases, to the effect that gettiered beliefs fall short of knowledge. Assuming that's right, we can learn something important about knowledge through a better understanding of gettiered belief.

We started working our way toward a promising substantive account of gettiered belief by distinguishing among five different basic roles that luck can play in cognition (Sections 3.1 and 3.2), and noting that none of the relevant kinds of epistemic luck is even a minimally plausible candidate for the ignorance-inducing phenomenon present in Gettier Cases, since each is clearly compatible with knowledge. Then, after explaining and critically assessing two of the literature's leading substantive accounts of gettiered belief – the Ease of Mistake Approach and Lack of Credit Approach (Sections 3.3 through 4.3) – I introduced and discussed a couple of less prominent approaches to gettiered belief (Sections 4.4 through 4.6). I argued in some detail that one of these new approaches to gettiered belief – the Risk of Misleading Justification Approach – can properly handle all the cases that bedevil competing accounts while also yielding an explanation of the (prima facie) superiority of knowledge to gettiered belief.[19] Along the way, we saw that even a charitably precisified luck-involving expression of our focal epistemological platitude (*knowledge excludes gettiered belief*) is both too strong (Section 3.2) and too weak (Section 3.5) to fully capture that platitude. Moreover, what ultimately turned out to be our most promising substantive account of gettiered belief, the Risk of Misleading Justification Approach, doesn't utilize the concept of *luck* – though it does employ one of that notion's core conceptual components, what I earlier labeled '*decent* possibility'. I think we can conclude, then, that neither luck-involving expressions of our focal epistemological platitude nor substantive accounts of gettiered belief utilizing the concept of luck are in the end likely to shed much light on the nature of knowledge, in and of themselves (cf. Ballantyne 2011, 2014).

5
Freedom, Responsibility, and Luck I: The Possibility of Moral Responsibility and Literal Arguments for the Proximal Determination Requirement

Luck-involving claims (that is, claims that involve the concept of luck itself or some other luck-related concept) play key roles in contemporary as well as historical debates over the nature and scope of metaphysically free and morally responsible action. On the contemporary scene in philosophy of action, luck-involving claims feature most prominently in arguments for the thesis that no one could be directly morally responsible for an action whose occurrence was not **proximally determined** – that is, logically entailed by the immediate past and laws of nature. We'll call this thesis the **Proximal Determination Requirement** on directly morally responsible action. Again, the Proximal Determination Requirement says that no one could be directly morally responsible for an action whose absence was logically consistent with the immediate past and laws of nature.

Any successful luck-involving argument for the Proximal Determination Requirement will be an elaboration of the following reasoning (cf. Franklin 2011: 201–2):

> If a (morally significant) action A performed by a subject S was not proximally determined, then A's occurrence was a matter of luck for S. But if A's occurrence was a matter of luck for S, then S isn't directly morally responsible for A. Therefore, if S's action A wasn't proximally determined, then S isn't directly morally responsible for A (= the Proximal Determination Requirement).

It's frequently suggested, by theorists of all stripes, that luck-involving arguments for the Proximal Determination Requirement pose an especially serious problem for proponents of what we'll call **standard libertarianism** about moral responsibility and metaphysical freedom, according to which directly morally responsible actions are possible but must be metaphysically free and thus can't be proximally determined.[1] However, as we'll see throughout this chapter and the following one, the widespread 'optimistic' view that luck-involving arguments for the Proximal Determination Requirement threaten only a fairly narrow segment of the whole range of theorists who countenance the possibility of morally responsible action is in fact mistaken (cf. Levy 2011a). Not only do many of these luck-involving arguments contain individual premises that commit those who endorse them to the impossibility of morally responsible action, but the Proximal Determination Requirement itself rules out the possibility of morally responsible action. Therefore, to the extent that one or another luck-involving argument for the Proximal Determination Requirement succeeds, that argument threatens *all* believers in the possibility of morally responsible action, not just proponents of standard libertarianism.

Let me clarify a few key terms before going any further. Say that a (finite, temporal) subject S is **directly morally responsible** for an action A that s/he performed iff S deserves (at least some degree of) moral praise (credit) or blame (criticism) for performing A, where this desert fact doesn't obtain in virtue of S's deserving moral praise or blame for any action(s) other than A.[2] Say that S is **indirectly morally responsible** for A iff S deserves moral praise or blame for performing A, and this desert fact does obtain in virtue of S's deserving moral praise or blame for some action(s) other than A.[3] Alfred Mele (2006: 86, emphasis added) helpfully illustrates these concepts in the following passage (note that Mele says 'inherited' where I say 'indirect'):

> In the typical scenario, the drunk driver is morally responsible for killing the pedestrian because he is morally responsible for driving drunk and because he kills the pedestrian. It is in virtue of the combination of his being morally responsible for driving drunk and of his killing the pedestrian that he does not see while so driving that he is morally responsible for the killing. I mark the existence of an in-virtue-of relation of this sort...by saying that his moral responsibility for Y-ing is *inherited from* his moral responsibility for X-ing. Moral responsibility that is not inherited is *direct*.

Say also that subject S was **free to** perform (omit) an action A iff S both had it within her power and knew how to perform (omit) A.[4] And say, finally, that S was **free with respect to** an action A that s/he performed iff S was, just before s/he performed A, *both* free to perform A *and* free to omit A (that is, to not perform A). While I'm inclined to agree with van Inwagen that the concept here expressed by 'free to' – what I've already been, and will continue, calling **metaphysical freedom** – 'is as clear as any philosophically interesting concept is likely to be' (1983: 8; cf. 2008: 333), it is nevertheless not always trivially easy to fix one's mind on that concept, given the presence of several distinct 'concepts with which the concept of [metaphysical freedom] might be confused, either because they really are similar to the concept of [metaphysical freedom], or because they are sometimes expressed by similar words' (1983: 9; cf. 1998: 366–9). In addition to identifying 'as many as possible of the other simple, ordinary words and phrases that can be used to express the concept of metaphysical freedom' (van Inwagen 1998: 368) – for example, 'can (now)', 'is (now) able to' – one can help interlocutors focus on metaphysical freedom by appealing to the common (in both everyday as well as more formal – for example, decision-theoretical – contexts) notion of a **choice situation**: a situation in which 'an agent...has several options available to her, among which she must decide' (Maier forthcoming: 8). Letting 'A is among S's available options' abbreviate 'S bears to A the species of agentive modality that figures in the framing of a choice situation', one can help interlocutors focus on metaphysical freedom by highlighting its equivalence with the concept expressed by 'A is among S's available options' (cf. Maier forthcoming: 7ff.).

As I said a moment ago, luck-involving arguments for the Proximal Determination Requirement pose a problem for *all* believers in the possibility of morally responsible action, not just standard libertarians: not only do many of these arguments contain individual premises that commit their advocates to the impossibility of morally responsible action, but the Proximal Determination Requirement itself rules out the possibility of morally responsible action. Now, if the relationship between (a) luck-involving arguments for the Proximal Determination Requirement and (b) the thesis that morally responsible action is possible – which I'll often call the **Possibility Thesis** – really is as tense as I'm alleging, then it might (at least in principle) turn out that we can use the Possibility Thesis both to *undermine* and to *rebut* the Proximal Determination Requirement. Indeed, in this chapter and the next one, I will be arguing that the Possibility Thesis can in fact play such defeating roles relative to the Proximal Determination Requirement.

My overall conclusion will be that the Possibility Thesis helps us to see not only that every visible luck-involving argument for the Proximal Determination Requirement ultimately fails,[5] but also that luck itself as well as various other luck-related phenomena are a good deal more congenial to metaphysically free and morally responsible action than is typically thought.

Here's the detailed plan for this chapter and the following one. In Section 5.1, I'll explain and critically evaluate two important arguments against the possibility of morally responsible action, one inspired by Nagel (1979) and the other by Strawson (1994). Discussing these arguments will bring us into contact with important recent work in the moral luck literature. Having defended the possibility of morally responsible action from these two arguments, I'll be in a position to employ the Possibility Thesis in subsequent critical discussion of the main visible luck-involving arguments for the Proximal Determination Requirement. Sections 5.2 through 6.2 will thoroughly explain and critically assess a wide range of such arguments.

In Section 5.2, I will distinguish among four different kinds of luck-involving arguments for the Proximal Determination Requirement. The first of two important distinctions drawn here is that between **indirect** and **direct** luck-involving arguments for the Proximal Determination Requirement. What distinguishes the former from the latter is that the former ('indirect' arguments) employ premises that relate metaphysical freedom to both luck and moral responsibility, whereas the latter ('direct' arguments) do not employ any such freedom-focused premises. The second important distinction drawn here is that between **literal** and **stipulative** luck-involving arguments for the Proximal Determination Requirement. What distinguishes the former from the latter is that proponents of the former ('literal' arguments) would have us interpret and assess their luck-involving claims in light of the best available analyses of luck (for example, Levy 2011a), whereas proponents of the latter ('stipulative' arguments) stipulate readings of their luck-involving claims with little concern for whether such interpretations might constitute tenable analyses of such claims (for example, Mele 2006). Here's another way to put it: literalists intend their luck-involving premises to be read strictly and literally, whereas stipulators intend their luck-involving premises to serve as rather colorful shorthand for claims that may – in light of the correct analysis of luck – turn out to have little to do with luck itself, as opposed to some or other luck-related phenomenon (genuine randomness, say, or having a nonzero objective probability of failing to occur).

In Section 5.3, I will kick off a critical assessment of the main visible luck-involving arguments for the Proximal Determination Requirement; this assessment will continue through the end of Section 6.2 in the next chapter. First, I will explain and evaluate *literal* versions of both indirect and direct luck-involving arguments for the Proximal Determination Requirement. One important finding here will be that a pair, and perhaps even a trio, of initially implausible compatibility claims concerning luck, freedom, and responsibility – compatibility claims that are denied even by some of the staunchest critics of the Proximal Determination Requirement – are in fact true. In Sections 6.1 and 6.2, I will explain and evaluate *stipulative* versions of both indirect and direct luck-involving arguments for the Proximal Determination Requirement. Here, we'll confront the *Mind* Argument (as it's called) and several lines of support for its key premise that no one could be free with respect to an action that, just before it happened, had a nonzero objective probability of failing to happen.

By the end of Section 6.2, I will have defended the possibility of proximally undetermined directly morally responsible action from every visible luck-involving argument against it. The discussion will then turn more 'offensive' in Section 6.3, where I'll explain and assess three different nonpartisan arguments for the possibility of proximally undetermined directly morally responsible action (that is, for the *denial* of the Proximal Determination Requirement):[6] an argument inspired by Mele (2006, 2013), an argument developed by Fischer (2011, 2014), and a novel argument that I'll call the **Possibility Argument** (which, it should be noted, will be neutral on the question whether proximally determined directly morally responsible action is possible). I will argue that whereas the lines of thought suggested by Mele and Fischer fail, the Possibility Argument succeeds. With any luck, the defensive and offensive arguments that I'll develop throughout this chapter and the next one will jointly constitute a significant step in the direction of mitigating worries salient in the contemporary action-theoretical literature regarding the compatibility of metaphysical freedom and moral responsibility, on the one hand, with luck itself and various other luck-related phenomena, on the other.

5.1 Defending the possibility of morally responsible action

In this section, we'll consider two important arguments against the possibility of morally responsible action, one inspired by Nagel (1979) and the other by Strawson (1994).[7] We'll discuss the Nagelian anti-responsibility argument first:[8]

The Nagelian Argument

(NA-1) Necessarily, if subject S is morally responsible for an action A that s/he performed, then S had control over not only A but also over anything on which A's occurrence was contingent.

(NA-2) Necessarily, (finite, temporal) S doesn't have control over everything on which A's occurrence is contingent.

(Impossibility Thesis) So, necessarily, it's false that S is morally responsible for A.

What should we make of this argument? We can start by conceding (NA-2) since it's obviously correct. Obviously, for any action that a (finite, temporal) agent S performs, that action's occurrence will be contingent on a wide variety of things over which S lacks control: S's not being struck by a meteorite or suffering a sudden heart attack or brain aneurysm, S's birth, the Big Bang, and so on. On the other hand, (NA-1) is not at all obviously correct (cf. Zimmerman 1987: 377–8). Again, anything that you do will be contingent on your not then suffering a sudden heart attack or brain aneurysm, on your birth, on the Big Bang, and so on. (NA-1) therefore implies that, to deserve any moral praise or blame for anything you've done, you must have had control over your not then suffering a sudden heart attack or brain aneurysm, your birth, the Big Bang, and so on. Once we've drawn out a few of its most obvious consequences, (NA-1) quickly loses any plausibility it may have enjoyed initially.

Why does Nagel take (NA-1) as seriously as he does? He famously claims that '[p]rior to reflection it is intuitively plausible that people cannot be morally assessed for...what is due to factors beyond their control' (1979: 25). However plausible this 'condition of control' (26) may seem *prior* to reflection, *after* a bit of reflection it's not at all obvious that a person can't be morally assessed for an action whose occurrence was contingent on some things over which s/he lacked control. Given the support that Nagel offers for his 'condition of control', it seems likely that he has conflated this principle with some vaguely similar but logically weaker principle(s) concerning moral responsibility and control.

Consider, for example, this key strand of Nagel's support for his 'condition of control' (1979: 31):

> How is it possible [for a reckless driver, or a professional assassin] to be more or less culpable depending on whether a child gets into the

path of one's car, or a bird into the path of one's bullet? Perhaps it is true that what is done depends on more than the agent's state of mind or intention. The problem then is, why is it not irrational to base moral assessment on what people do, in this broad sense? It amounts to holding them responsible for the contributions of fate as well as for their own – provided they have made some contribution to begin with.

Say that a **resultant moral luck scenario** is a scenario in which (allegedly) some result or outcome, O, of S's behavior, B, *both* depends on some factors beyond S's control *and* makes S more morally responsible (that is, more deserving of moral praise or blame) than S would have been otherwise (that is, had O *not* resulted from B).[9] What reflection on the relevant kind of case pairs – two equally reckless drivers, only one of whom hits a nearby pedestrian; two equally determined assassins, only one of whom succeeds in killing his target – can most directly support is the thesis that *resultant moral luck scenarios are impossible*. More fully, what reflection on such case pairs can most directly support is the thesis that an uncontrolled result of some action of yours can't make you *more* morally responsible (that is, more praiseworthy or blameworthy) than you would have been had your action *not* issued in that uncontrolled result. Since the impossibility of resultant moral luck scenarios would seem to leave open the possibility of a morally responsible action that depends on some uncontrolled factors (for example, the pertinent agent's birth, the Big Bang, and so on), reflection on the kind of case pairs to which Nagel draws our attention fails to adequately support (NA-1). For starters, notice that the claim that there could not be a resultant moral luck scenario concerns moral properties of *outcomes* of agents' actions, whereas the claim that there could be a morally responsible action that depends on some uncontrolled factors concerns moral properties of agents' actions themselves (not their outcomes or results). Moreover, on the plausible assumption that an action which is itself within one's control may nevertheless be contingent on some factors that are themselves beyond one's control (cf. Zimmerman 1987: 377), the impossibility of a morally responsible action that is itself uncontrolled would seem to leave open the possibility of a morally responsible action that depends on some uncontrolled factors.

So much, then, for the Nagelian Argument against the possibility of morally responsible action: it fails due to (NA-1)'s utter lack of plausibility. We turn now to a different – and, I believe, much more interesting and promising – anti-responsibility argument, one inspired by Strawson (1994):[10]

The Strawsonian Argument

(SA-1) Necessarily, if (finite, temporal) subject S is morally responsible for an action A that s/he performed, then S performed a first morally responsible action, A*.

(SA-2) Necessarily, if S was morally responsible for A*, then S was morally responsible for her possession of some reason, R, that influenced A*.

Writes Strawson (1994: 6): '[I]f one is to be truly responsible for how one acts, one must be truly responsible for how one is, mentally speaking – at least in certain respects.'

(SA-3) Necessarily, if S was morally responsible for her possession of some reason R that influenced A*, then S came to have R by way of a prior (to A*) morally responsible action, A**.

Writes Strawson (1994: 6): '[T]o be truly responsible for how one is, mentally speaking, in certain respects, one must have [responsibly] brought it about that one is the way one is, mentally speaking, in certain respects.'

(SA-4) So, necessarily, if S is morally responsible for A, then S performed an action A* that both was *and* wasn't the first morally responsible action that s/he performed. [SA-1, SA-2, SA-3]

(SA-5) Necessarily, it's false that S performed an action that both was *and* wasn't the first morally responsible action that s/he performed.

(**Impossibility Thesis**) So, necessarily, it's false that S is morally responsible for A. [SA-4, SA-5]

The Strawsonian Argument has two basic substantive premises: (SA-2) and (SA-3). Each of these premises is considerably more plausible than is (NA-1) of the Nagelian Argument. The Strawsonian Argument therefore looks to be a much more interesting and promising argument for the impossibility of morally responsible action than is the Nagelian Argument. What should we make of it?

I'll begin my critical assessment of the Strawsonian Argument by explaining and discussing Michael Zimmerman's (2006: 605–6; cf. 2002:

560ff., 1987: 381ff.) argument for the possibility of **responsibility tout court** – that is, moral responsibility in virtue of (certain aspects of) how one is *absent* moral responsibility for anything that one has done. Readers who are already familiar with Zimmerman's fascinating argument may well wonder how it bears on the Strawsonian Argument. Specifically, such readers may wonder whether the possibility of responsibility tout court would impugn (SA-3): if one can be morally responsible *in virtue of* how one is without being morally responsible for anything that one has done, then perhaps one can be morally responsible *for* how one is without coming to be that way via some prior morally responsible action (= ~SA-3). Alternatively, readers who are already familiar with Zimmerman's argument may wonder whether the possibility of responsibility tout court is compatible with the impossibility of morally responsible action – in which case, the Strawsonian Argument, even if successful, would still leave open the possible truth of an important class of responsibility ascriptions. Finally, any readers who are not already familiar with Zimmerman's argument will also benefit from the upcoming discussion: besides being highly interesting in its own right, Zimmerman's argument bears on several issues and topics explored in this chapter and the next one, as well as in Chapters 1 and 2 above.

Along with 'responsibility tout court' and 'resultant moral luck scenario', one more bit of terminology will facilitate statement and discussion of Zimmerman's argument. Say that an **act-focused situational moral luck scenario** is a scenario in which (allegedly) some action A performed by subject S *both* depends on some factors beyond S's control *and* makes S more morally responsible (that is, more deserving of moral praise or blame) than S would have been otherwise (that is, had S *not* performed A). Zimmerman's argument for the possibility of responsibility tout court can now be presented as follows:

Zimmerman's Argument

(ZA-1) Resultant moral luck scenarios are impossible.

(ZA-2) If resultant moral luck scenarios are impossible, then act-focused situational moral luck scenarios are impossible as well.

(ZA-3) So, act-focused situational moral luck scenarios are impossible. [ZA-1, ZA-2]

(ZA-4) If moral responsibility is possible (that is, if it's possible that someone deserves some moral praise or blame) and requires moral responsibility for something that one has done, then act-focused situational moral luck scenarios are possible.

(ZA-5) So, either moral responsibility isn't possible or moral responsibility doesn't require moral responsibility for something that one has done. [ZA-3, ZA-4]

(ZA-6) Moral responsibility is possible (that is, it's possible that someone deserves moral praise or blame).

(ZA-7) So, moral responsibility doesn't require moral responsibility for something that one has done – that is, responsibility tout court is possible: one can deserve moral praise or blame even if one doesn't deserve moral praise or blame for anything that one has done. [ZA-5, ZA-6]

Before critically discussing Zimmerman's Argument and its bearing on the Strawsonian Argument, let's consider what can be said on behalf of (ZA-2) and (ZA-4). Zimmerman's argument for (ZA-2) stems from his argument for (ZA-1). He begins by describing a pair of cases involving two would-be assassins, 'one of whom is successful and the other of whom, due to the fortuitous intervention of a passing bird, is unsuccessful' (2006: 597):

> ***Successful Assassin:*** Successful Assassin decides to shoot at his target. Successful Assassin's decision causes the retraction of his trigger finger, which causes the movement of the trigger, which causes the firing of the gun, which causes the flight of the bullet, which causes the bullet's penetration of the target's body, which causes the target's death.
>
> ***Unsuccessful Assassin:*** This case is just like Successful Assassin, *except* that the bullet is intercepted mid-flight by a passing bird, and thus never penetrates the target.

Here's what Zimmerman says about this pair of cases (2006: 598):

> Let us assume that the successful assassin is culpable for [his decision to shoot at the target, the target's death, and everything in between]. Clearly, the same is not true of the unsuccessful assassin, since [his bullet never even penetrates his target]. Thus it cannot be said that they are culpable for the same things. On the contrary, the successful assassin is *culpable for more things* than the unsuccessful assassin. Nonetheless, if two agents behave in the same way but their behavior, through luck, has different results, then there is nothing to distinguish between *them*, morally speaking. Thus the successful assassin is not *more culpable* than the unsuccessful assassin.

From such claims about such case pairs, Zimmerman generalizes to (ZA-1). I for one find this line of argument compelling. I will simply grant its success in what follows.

Zimmerman then extends his argument for (ZA-1) into an argument for (ZA-2) (2006: 605):

> Return to the case of the Unsuccessful Assassin. I said that the fortuitous intervention of nature in the form of a passing bird, while reducing the scope of the assassin's culpability, would not diminish its degree. But...nature could intervene earlier in the sequence of events from [the assassin's decision to the flight of the bullet]; indeed, it could intervene even *prior* to...the assassin's decision to shoot. For example, it could happen that, just as he is about to make this decision, the assassin is seized by a sudden sneeze that prevents him from making it. If the fortuitous intervention of the bird does not diminish his culpability, I cannot see how the fortuitous intervention of the sneeze could do so.

(ZA-2) is a generalization of the last claim in this passage.[11] I'll return to (ZA-2) in a little while. First, though, I need to finish off this preliminary discussion by setting out the reasoning behind (ZA-4). Suppose that moral responsibility is possible *and* that it requires moral responsibility for something that one has done. In a slogan: Moral responsibility requires morally responsible *action*. Then the following kind of case is possible: A is the first action for which S is morally responsible, and A's occurrence depends on some factors beyond S's control – for example, S's not being seized by a sneeze, interrupted by a colleague, suffering a sudden heart attack, being struck by a wayward meteorite, and so on. Further, if S hadn't performed A when s/he did, S would not then have instead performed some other morally responsible action; rather, S would have continued deliberating about whether to do A, and s/he would not have been morally praiseworthy or blameworthy for so deliberating. Therefore, since A is S's *first* morally responsible action – and since moral responsibility requires morally responsible action – S wouldn't have been morally responsible *at all* if s/he hadn't performed A. S's performing A therefore makes S more morally responsible than s/he would have been otherwise (that is, had s/he *not* performed A). Notice that this case has now grown into an act-focused situational moral luck scenario. We can conclude, then, that act-focused situational moral luck scenarios are possible *provided that* moral responsibility is possible but requires morally responsible action.

Now that we have a reasonably thorough presentation of Zimmerman's Argument before us, we can ask how it bears on the Strawsonian Argument and (in any event) what we should make of it. In what follows, I will argue for three claims concerning Zimmerman's Argument and its relation to the Strawsonian Argument:

Claim 1: Even if Zimmerman's Argument succeeds, it doesn't impugn (SA-3) of the Strawsonian Argument.

Claim 2: The possibility of responsibility tout court entails the possibility of morally responsible action, and so Zimmerman's Argument is not orthogonal to the Strawsonian Argument: Zimmerman's Argument succeeds only if the Strawsonian Argument fails.

Claim 3: Zimmerman's Argument fails because (ZA-2) lacks adequate support.

In sum, while establishing the possibility of responsibility tout court would not defeat the Strawsonian Argument by falsifying (SA-3), establishing this possibility *would* suffice to show that morally responsible action is possible, and so that the Strawsonian Argument has at least one false premise. Unfortunately, as things currently stand, Zimmerman's Argument doesn't establish the possibility of responsibility tout court, and so doesn't presently play its potential defeating role relative to the Strawsonian Argument (alternatively, its potential protective role relative to the Possibility Thesis).

First, an argument for Claim 1. Recall (SA-3) of the Strawsonian Argument:

(SA-3) Necessarily, if S was morally responsible for her possession of some reason R that influenced A*, then S came to have R by way of a prior (to A*) morally responsible act, A**.

One might naturally think that (SA-3) is false *provided that* responsibility tout court is possible. If such a thought were correct, then Zimmerman's Argument would hold the potential to defeat the Strawsonian Argument by rebutting (SA-3). But is the thought in question correct? The argument for it will presumably go like this: Suppose responsibility tout court is possible. Then S could be morally responsible *in virtue of* certain aspects of the way S is – for example, S's possession of certain potentially act-influencing reason states (beliefs, desires, intentions, and so on) – without yet having performed any actions for which s/he is morally responsible. But if S is morally responsible *in virtue of* some aspect of the way s/he is, then S is morally responsible *for* having the pertinent responsibility-grounding feature(s).[12,13] So, S could be morally responsible *for* having the pertinent responsibility-grounding feature(s), without yet having performed any actions for which s/he is morally responsible. And this possibility clearly entails the denial of (SA-3) of the Strawsonian Argument.

Alas, this argument fails, for its second premise (after the initial supposition) is false: being morally responsible *in virtue of* some aspect of the way you are doesn't suffice for your being morally responsible *for* having the relevant responsibility-grounding feature(s) (cf. Zimmerman 2002: 564–5). Consider: It's extremely plausible to think that any morally responsible person is morally responsible at least partly in virtue of having certain responsibility-relevant psychological (intellectual, emotional, and so on) capacities. Supposing that's right, we can clearly imagine a case in which a person is morally responsible at least partly in virtue of having such psychological capacities but isn't at all morally responsible (praiseworthy or blameworthy) for (merely) having such capacities. More generally, one's being morally responsible *in virtue of* (or, *on the basis of*) X doesn't entail that one is morally responsible *for* X. Evidently, then, (SA-3) of the Strawsonian Argument is consistent with the possibility of responsibility tout court, and so the success of Zimmerman's Argument would not threaten that premise in particular.

That's not to say, however, that Zimmerman's Argument is orthogonal to the Strawsonian Argument. On the contrary, the possibility of responsibility tout court entails the possibility of morally responsible action, and thus Zimmerman's Argument succeeds only if the Strawsonian Argument fails. The indicated entailment is fairly easy to see. Suppose, for conditional proof, that responsibility tout court is possible. Necessarily, S is responsible tout court *only if* S is such that she would freely perform some morally significant action, A, were she to be in certain possible circumstances, C (cf. Zimmerman 2002: 564ff.).[14] Now, if S would freely perform some morally significant action A were she to be in certain possible circumstances C, then (obviously) it's possible that S freely performs some morally significant action, A. But, if it's possible that S freely performs some morally significant action A, then surely it's also possible that S freely performs A while meeting whatever epistemic requirements there are on morally responsible action. And, if S freely performs a morally significant action A while *also* meeting whatever epistemic requirements there are on morally responsible action, then S is morally responsible for performing A (cf. Zimmerman 2002: 566).

Thus, if responsibility tout court is possible, then so is morally responsible action. Although your being responsible tout court does not entail that you are *in fact* morally responsible for something you've done, the former does entail that it's at least *possible* that you be morally responsible for something you've done. In a (slightly expanded) slogan: Moral responsibility doesn't require morally responsible action – but it *does* require the *possibility* of morally responsible action. The possibility of responsibility tout court therefore implies, by the reasoning set out in the last paragraph, that the Strawsonian Argument's conclusion is false, and so, that the Strawsonian Argument has at least one false premise. Hence, while a proponent of Zimmerman's Argument cannot sensibly hope to establish the possibility of a kind of moral responsibility that goes unthreatened by the Strawsonian Argument, s/he *can* sensibly hope to defeat the Strawsonian Argument by establishing the possibility of responsibility tout court, since (again) this would entail that at least one of the Strawsonian Argument's premises is false.

And so arises our last question concerning Zimmerman's Argument: to what, if any, extent does this argument succeed? Zimmerman's Argument fails, I'll argue, because (ZA-2) – the claim that if resultant moral luck scenarios are impossible, then act-focused situational moral luck scenarios are also impossible – lacks adequate support. Recall the main reason that Zimmerman offers for (ZA-2): upon considering the *Successful Assassin* and *Unsuccessful Assassin* cases, alongside a third case in which the protagonist's seizure by a sneeze prevents him from ever even *choosing* to kill the target, Zimmerman says that 'if the fortuitous intervention of the bird does not diminish [the assassin's] culpability, I cannot see how the fortuitous intervention of the sneeze could do so' (2006: 605).

I can see at least two reasons to doubt (ZA-2). The first is that the general structure of an act-focused situational moral luck scenario differs significantly from that of a resultant moral luck scenario. In a resultant moral luck scenario, recall, a *non-actional outcome of an agent's prior behavior* – for example, a death that results from a decision to shoot – (allegedly) makes the agent more morally responsible than s/he would have been *had that non-actional outcome not resulted from the agent's behavior*.[15] By contrast, in an act-focused situational moral luck scenario, an *action influenced by some prior non-actional items* – for example, a decision to shoot, based on some of the pertinent agent's prior reason states – (allegedly) makes the agent more morally responsible than s/he would have been *had s/he not performed the action in question*. Given this clear difference in general structure, it's not at all obvious that the impossibility of resultant moral luck scenarios implies that act-focused situational moral luck scenarios are impossible as well.

The preceding paragraph's considerations threaten to undercut (ZA-2). Here's a second reason to doubt (ZA-2), one that threatens to rebut it. Even if we suppose (with the proponent of Zimmerman's Argument) that resultant moral luck scenarios are impossible (= ZA-1) but that moral responsibility is possible (= ZA-6), act-focused situational moral luck scenarios still seem possible (= ~ZA-2). Consider again *Unsuccessful Assassin* (or *Successful Assassin* – the present argument doesn't depend on which of these examples we invoke) along with the modified version described above, in which the protagonist's seizure by a sneeze prevents him from ever even *choosing* to kill the target. Call the main character of the latter example 'Choiceless Assassin' (to mark the fact that he never even *chooses* to kill the target), and call the main character of *Unsuccessful Assassin* 'Choosy Assassin' (to mark the fact that he, like the main character of *Successful Assassin*, actually does choose to kill the target). Choosy Assassin actively forms an intention to kill another person, whereas Choiceless Assassin never makes such a choice.

Now consider the following claim:

> Choosy Assassin's actively forming an intention to kill another person could make him at least a *bit* more deserving of moral criticism than is Choiceless Assassin.

To the extent that you find this claim plausible, you should be inclined to deny (ZA-2) (under the friendly supposition that both ZA-1 and ZA-6 are true). I for one find the claim in question extremely plausible (cf. Davison 1999: 248–9), and so am strongly inclined to deny (ZA-2). But so long as you find that claim at least as plausible as not, you should at best suspend judgment on (ZA-2) and so deem Zimmerman's Argument a failure as it currently stands, due to an inadequately supported key premise.[16]

Before moving on, let's briefly review our main findings in this section so far. Because the Strawsonian Argument features premises that are more plausible than those of the Nagelian Argument, the former is a more interesting and promising argument for the impossibility of morally responsible action than is the latter. Zimmerman's Argument, if successful, would not establish the falsity of any specific premise in the Strawsonian Argument; but it would – via the premise that the possibility of responsibility tout court entails the possibility of morally responsible action – establish the falsity of the Strawsonian Argument's conclusion, thereby showing that at least one of the Strawsonian Argument's premises must be false. Finally, as it currently stands, Zimmerman's Argument fails due to an inadequately supported premise (= ZA-2), and thus does not presently play its potential defeating role relative to the Strawsonian Argument – or, to look at it from another angle, its potential protective role relative to the thesis that morally responsible action is possible (= the Possibility Thesis).

What, then, should we make of the Strawsonian Argument? More specifically, does the Strawsonian Argument cast enough doubt on the Possibility Thesis to keep that thesis from playing the defeating roles, relative to the Proximal Determination Requirement, described in this chapter's introductory section? In what follows, I will argue that it does not: it's more reasonable to accept the Possibility Thesis and reject the Strawsonian Argument than it is to accept the Strawsonian Argument and reject the Possibility Thesis.

To review, the Strawsonian Argument is plainly valid and has four basic premises:

(SA-1) Necessarily, if (finite, temporal) subject S is morally responsible for an action A that s/he performed, then S performed a *first* morally responsible action, A*.

(SA-2) Necessarily, if S was morally responsible for A*, then S was morally responsible for her possession of some reason, R, that influenced A*.

(SA-3) Necessarily, if S was morally responsible for her possession of some reason R that influenced A*, then S came to have R by way of a prior (to A*) morally responsible action, A**.

(SA-5) Necessarily, it's false that S performed an action that both was *and* wasn't the first morally responsible action that s/he performed.

(SA-1) and (SA-5) are trivially true, and (SA-3) is extremely plausible. I will assume that all three of these claims are correct and simplify the Strawsonian Argument as follows:

The Simplified Strawsonian Argument

(SA-2) Necessarily, if S was morally responsible for A* (an arbitrarily selected candidate for S's first morally responsible action), then S was morally responsible for her possession of some reason, R, that influenced A*.

(**Bridge Premise**) Necessarily, if S's being morally responsible for A* strictly implies that S was morally responsible for her possession of some reason that influenced A* (= SA-2), then it's false that S is morally responsible for A (an arbitrarily selected candidate for morally responsible action performed by S).

(**Impossibility Thesis**) So, necessarily, it's false that S is morally responsible for A.

Now consider the following 'reverse' argument that moves from the Possibility Thesis, through the contrapositive of the Bridge Premise, to the *denial* of (SA-2):

The Reverse Argument

(**Possibility Thesis**) Possibly, S is morally responsible for an action A that s/he performed.

(**Bridge Premise Contraposed**) Necessarily, if S is morally responsible for A, then S's being morally responsible for A* does not strictly imply that S was morally responsible for her possession of some reason that influenced A*.

~(**SA-2**) So, possibly, S was morally responsible for A* but not morally responsible for her possession of any reason R that influenced A*.

Which (if either) is the better argument: the Simplified Strawsonian Argument or the Reverse Argument? Obviously, this question quickly boils down to which (if either) of the Possibility Thesis and (SA-2) is more reasonable to accept. Presumably, proponents of the Strawsonian Argument will say that we have better reason to accept (SA-2) than we have to accept the Possibility Thesis. In any event, I take the opposite position: I think that we have better reason to accept the Possibility Thesis than we have to accept (SA-2). Let me explain why I come down as I do here.

Temporarily bracketing the Possibility Thesis, I'm at best inclined to suspend judgment on (SA-2); taken on its own, (SA-2) does not strike me as more plausible than not. Here's a line of reasoning that casts (SA-2) into doubt. Recall Choiceless Assassin from our earlier discussion of Zimmerman's Argument. Imagine now that, by the operations of God or Nature, two new agents who are (to the extent possible) mental duplicates of Choiceless Assassin come to exist at time t1. Call these new agents 'New Assassin 1' and 'New Assassin 2'. Suppose further that, at a slightly later (than t1) time, t2, New Assassin 1 decides (that is, actively forms an intention) to fire at a potential target, whereas New Assassin 2 is at t2 still trying to decide whether to fire at a potential target. Claim: As of t2, New Assassin 1 *could* be at least a *bit* more deserving of moral criticism than is New Assassin 2. That is, there's a coherent way to fill in the details of this case so that New Assassin 1 is, as of t2, at least a *bit* more deserving of moral criticism than is New Assassin 2. But if, as of t2, New Assassin 1 is at least a bit more deserving of moral criticism than is New Assassin 2, then New Assassin 1 must be morally responsible for deciding to fire at a potential target, since this is the only relevant difference between him and New Assassin 2 (the latter, recall, has not yet made any such decision). So, New Assassin 1 must be morally responsible for deciding to fire at a potential target. But, finally, if New Assassin 1 is morally responsible for deciding to fire at a potential target, then (SA-2) must be false, since (by hypothesis) New Assassin 1 is not morally responsible for his possession of any of the reasons that influenced his decision.

I submit that, in light of the above argument, (SA-2) is no more plausible than its denial. By contrast, the Possibility Thesis strikes me as extremely plausible: it clearly seems possible that someone be at least *somewhat* deserving of some moral praise or blame for something that s/he has done (cf. van Inwagen 1983: 208–9). Given its high degree of plausibility, I'm not certain that the Possibility Thesis can be successfully argued for. But suppose we try anyway. Consider, in this connection, the following line of reasoning from van Inwagen (2008: 328):

> It is...evident that moral responsibility does exist: if there were no such thing as moral responsibility nothing would be anyone's fault, and it is evident that there are states of affairs to which one can point and say, correctly, to certain people: 'That is *your* fault.'

I confess that I find this little argument for the existence of morally responsible action quite compelling.[17] In any case, all that's needed to support the Possibility Thesis is the following parallel argument for the *possible* existence of morally responsible action, whose premises are a good deal (logically) weaker – and thus even more plausible – than those in the above argument from van Inwagen:

> If no one even *could* be morally responsible for anything they do, then nothing even *could* be anyone's fault. But surely there at least *could* be a state of affairs to which someone points and says, correctly,

to a certain person: 'That is *your* fault.' So someone at least *could* be morally responsible for something they do (= the Possibility Thesis).

I for one am inclined to judge this argument for the Possibility Thesis successful. However, regardless of whether anyone else shares such an inclination, I think that we should – in light of the above argument against (SA-2) and the high initial plausibility of the Possibility Thesis – accept the Reverse Argument and reject the Simplified Strawsonian Argument. More specifically, we should conclude from the Possibility Thesis that there could be a first morally responsible action influenced by reasons whose possession the relevant agent was not morally responsible for (= ~SA-2). If that's right, then we can reasonably retain the Possibility Thesis and reject the Strawsonian Argument.[18]

Having now defended the Possibility Thesis from both the Nagelian and Strawsonian Arguments, we are in a position to employ the Possibility Thesis in a critical appraisal of the main visible luck-involving arguments for the Proximal Determination Requirement. In the next section, I will distinguish among four different kinds of such arguments: direct, indirect, literal, and stipulative. In Section 5.3, I will kick off my critical evaluation of the main visible luck-involving arguments for the Proximal Determination Requirement. This evaluation will continue through the end of Section 6.2 of the next chapter.

5.2 Four different kinds of luck-involving arguments for the Proximal Determination Requirement

We can draw two important distinctions among the main visible luck-involving arguments for the Proximal Determination Requirement. The first distinction is that between what I will call 'direct' and 'indirect' luck-involving arguments for the Proximal Determination Requirement. On the one hand, some such luck-involving arguments employ premises that posit connections among metaphysical freedom, moral responsibility, and luck (or at least, something luck-related). Call these arguments – ones that involve some freedom-focused premises – **indirect** arguments for the Proximal Determination Requirement. On the other hand, some visible luck-involving arguments for the Proximal Determination Requirement do not employ any such freedom-focused premises. Call an instance of such 'unfree' argumentation a **direct** argument for the Proximal Determination Requirement.[19] Here are two argument templates or schemas, one for each of the two aforementioned kinds of luck-involving arguments for the Proximal Determination Requirement:

The Direct Argument for the Proximal Determination Requirement

(DA-1) Necessarily, if S's (morally significant) action A was not proximally determined, then A was a matter of luck for S.

(DA-2) Necessarily, if A was a matter of luck for S, then S is not directly morally responsible for A.

(**Proximal Determination Requirement**) So, necessarily, if A was not proximally determined, then S is not directly morally responsible for A.

The Indirect Argument for the Proximal Determination Requirement

(IA-1) Necessarily, if S's (morally significant) action A was not proximally determined, then A was a matter of luck for S.

(IA-2) Necessarily, if A was a matter of luck for S, then S was not free with respect to A (that is, S was not, just before s/he performed A, both free to perform A and free to omit A).

(IA-3) Necessarily, if S was not free with respect to A, then S is not directly morally responsible for A.[20]

(**Proximal Determination Requirement**) So, necessarily, if A was not proximally determined, then S is not directly morally responsible for A.[21]

As I noted at the beginning of this section, there's a second important distinction to be drawn among the main visible luck-involving arguments for the Proximal Determination Requirement: there are both literal and stipulative versions of such arguments. What distinguishes the former from the latter is that proponents of the former (**literal** versions) would have us interpret and assess their luck-involving locutions in light of the best available analyses of luck (for example, Levy 2011a); by contrast, proponents of the latter (**stipulative** versions) stipulate readings of their luck-involving locutions with little concern for whether such interpretations might constitute tenable analyses of such expressions (for example, Mele 2006). So, literalists intend their luck-involving locutions to be interpreted strictly and literally, whereas stipulators intend their luck-involving locutions to serve as rather colorful shorthand for claims that may – in light of the correct analysis of luck – ultimately turn out not to be about luck itself, as opposed to some other luck-related phenomenon.

In the next section, I will evaluate literal versions of both the Direct and Indirect Arguments for the Proximal Determination Requirement. In Sections 6.1 and 6.2 of the next chapter, I will critically discuss stipulative versions of those arguments.

5.3 Literal versions of the arguments for the Proximal Determination Requirement

A few preliminary remarks are in order here. First, attentive readers will have noticed that premise (DA-1) of the Direct Argument is identical to premise (IA-1) of the Indirect Argument. Henceforth, I'll refer to this premise as '(DA/IA-1)'. Attentive readers will also have observed that (IA-2) and (IA-3) jointly entail (DA-2), whereas a proponent of (DA-2) needn't accept either (IA-2) or (IA-3). In what follows, I'll focus first on (IA-2) and (DA-2), saving discussion of (DA/IA-1) for later in this section. Finally, when discussing the Indirect Argument, I will make the friendly (to proponents of the Indirect Argument) assumption that (IA-3) is true. I'll discuss and defend (IA-3) in Section 6.3.2 of the next chapter.

Here's an overview of this section's critical appraisal of literal interpretations of (IA-2), (DA-2), and (DA/IA-1). Obviously enough, all these premises involve the expression 'A was a matter of luck for S'. This expression is ambiguous, admitting of these two different readings: *A was **just** a matter of luck for S* and *A was **at least partly** a matter of luck for S*. A bit of further reflection on a case described back in Section 2.1 yields an intriguing attempted counterexample to the 'just a matter of luck' reading of (IA-2). If successful, this attempted counterexample also impugns the 'at least partly a matter of luck' reading of (IA-2), since the 'at least partly a matter of luck' reading entails the 'just a matter of luck' reading. But even if we reject this intriguing attempted counterexample and simply concede the 'just a matter of luck' reading of (IA-2), neither the Indirect Argument nor the Direct Argument succeeds on either the 'at least partly a matter of luck' interpretation or the 'just a matter of luck' interpretation. The 'at least partly a matter of luck' reading of (DA-2) rules out the possibility of morally responsible action, and so can be reasonably rejected on the grounds that such action is possible. The 'at least partly a matter of luck' reading of (IA-2) suffers the same fate (under the friendly assumption that IA-3 is true): it too rules out the possibility of morally responsible action, and so can reasonably be rejected on the grounds that such action is possible. Finally, the 'at least partly a matter of luck' reading of (DA/IA-1) incorrectly implies that proximally undetermined intentional action is impossible. This point impugns the 'just a matter of luck' reading of (DA/IA-1) as well, since the 'just a matter of luck' reading entails the 'at least partly a matter of luck' reading.

5.3.1 An intriguing attempted counterexample to (IA-2)

Again, 'A was a matter of luck for S' admits of two different readings: *A was **just** a matter of luck for S* and *A was **at least partly** a matter of luck for S*. Back in Section 2.1, I proposed the following set of equivalence claims (I now give each claim its own label so that I can easily refer to them individually in what follows):

> **First Proposed Equivalence:** E is *just* a matter of good (bad) luck for S iff E is a stroke of good (bad) luck for S that S is not in any way praiseworthy (blameworthy) for.
>
> **Second Proposed Equivalence:** E is *only partly* a matter of good (bad) luck for S iff E is (un)lucky for S but is not itself *just* a matter of good (bad) luck for S. More fully, E is *only partly* a matter of good (bad) luck for S iff either (i) E is a stroke of good (bad) luck for S that S is in some way praiseworthy (blameworthy) for; or (ii) E is (un)lucky for S but is not itself a stroke of good (bad) luck for S.
>
> **Third Proposed Equivalence:** E is *at least partly* a matter of good (bad) luck for S iff either (i) E is *just* a matter of good (bad) luck for S or (ii) E is *only partly* a matter of good (bad) luck for S.

Call this set of claims the **Proposed Equivalences**. Given the First Proposed Equivalence, the 'just a matter of luck' reading of (IA-2) amounts to the following claim:

> **(IA-2j)** Necessarily, if A was a stroke of good (bad) luck for S that S is not in any way praiseworthy (blameworthy) for, then S was not free with respect to A (that is, S was not, just before s/he performed A, *both* free to perform A *and* free to omit A).

Back in Section 2.1, I described a case that we can now develop into an intriguing attempted counterexample to (IA-2j). Here's the case I have in mind:

> Unbeknownst to you, your sworn enemy has injected a poisonous substance into the soles of your sneakers. This poison will render you unconscious at t – and shortly thereafter, dead – *unless* you start wearing your soles down by then. On a whim, you decide just before

t to start running in your sneakers at t. Accordingly, you start running in your sneakers at t.

At t, you are wearing down the soles of your sneakers. This is what Mele and Moser (1994: 45) call a 'side-effect action', a clearly foreseen side-effect of an intentional action (here, running in your sneakers). Obviously, your wearing the soles down at t is in some respect good for you. Moreover, we can safely assume that you aren't in any way praiseworthy for wearing your soles down then (bear in mind the stipulation that you have no idea your sworn enemy has tampered with your shoes) and also that nothing like this event happens around t in a wide class of possible worlds that are close to (that is, no more than slightly different from) the actual world before t.[22] Finally, although you may well be *knowingly* wearing your soles down at t, it's intuitively plausible that you're not then *intentionally* wearing your soles down (cf. Mele and Moser 1994: 45).[23]

Arguably, then, your wearing the soles down at t is in some respect good for you; nothing like it happens around t in a wide class of possible worlds that are close to the actual world before t; it's not something that you're doing intentionally; and, finally, you're not in any way praiseworthy for it. Now recall the analysis of strokes of luck that I developed and defended in Chapter 2:

> **The Analysis:** E is at t a stroke of good (bad) luck for S iff (1) E is in some respect good (bad) for S; (2**) in a wide class of possible worlds that are close to the actual world before t, E doesn't happen around t nor does the process that actually generated E yield around t an event as good (bad) for S as E is; and (3) E isn't something that S did intentionally.

By the (right-to-left conditional of the) Analysis, your wearing the soles down at t is a stroke of good luck for you. Add the (right-to-left conditional of the) First Proposed Equivalence, and it follows that your wearing the soles down then is *just* a stroke of good luck for you. But, finally, it seems that we can coherently add to this case the detail that you were free with respect to wearing your soles down at t, that just before t you were *both* free to start wearing the soles down *and* free to omit this.

Arguably, then, (IA-2j) is false: it seems, quite surprisingly, that an agent could have been free with respect to an action that was *just* a stroke of good luck for the agent.[24] Moreover, since the 'at least partly a matter of luck' reading of (IA-2) is logically stronger than the 'just a matter of luck' reading, this example impugns *both* readings of (IA-2).

I'm inclined to think that this case falsifies both of the indicated interpretations of (IA-2). But I'm sufficiently uncertain about this that I'm willing to simply set aside the above attempted counterexample and assume that the 'just a matter of luck' readings of both (IA-2) and (DA-2) are true.[25] Given this assumption (and that IA-3 is true), the 'just a matter of luck' versions of the Direct and Indirect Arguments succeed if – but only if – the 'just a matter of luck' reading of (DA/IA-1) is acceptable. I'll return to (DA/IA-1) in Section 5.3.3 after first considering the 'at least partly a matter of luck' readings of (DA-2) and (IA-2).

5.3.2 Against the 'at least partly a matter of luck' readings of (DA-2) and (IA-2)

The 'at least partly a matter of luck' reading of (DA-2) amounts to the following claim:

> **(DA-2p)** Necessarily, if A was at least partly a matter of luck for S, then S isn't directly morally responsible for A.

Even some of the staunchest defenders of the possibility of proximally undetermined directly morally responsible action endorse claims along the lines of (DA-2p). For example, in the course of his recent defense of an action-centered event-causal libertarian account of metaphysically free and morally responsible action from a series of (what I classify as 'stipulative') luck-involving arguments, Christopher Franklin claims that '[i]t is hard to believe that an action that is partly a matter of luck could also be...one for which an agent is morally responsible' (2011: 220–1; cf. Levy 2011a: 42–3, 53–4).[26] In what follows, I'll be arguing that claims along the lines of (DA-2p) actually commit their adherents to the impossibility of morally responsible action. If that's right, then we can reasonably reject (DA-2p) on the grounds that such action is possible.

To begin, recall the analysis of (un)lucky events that I developed and defended above in Chapter 1:

> **The Strokes Account:** Event E is at t (un)lucky for subject S iff (i) E is in some respect good (bad) for S and (ii) there's a stroke of good (bad) luck for S, E*, such that *either* (a) E = E* *or* (b) E* is a primary (chief, main) contributor to E.

By the (right-to-left conditional of the) Strokes Account, A was (un)lucky for S *provided that* A was in some respect good (bad) for S and was due primarily to something that was a stroke of good (bad) luck for S. Further, given the Proposed Equivalences, A was at least partly a matter of luck for S *provided that* A was (un)lucky for S.[27] So, given the Strokes Account and the Proposed Equivalences, (DA-2p) implies the following conditional:

> **(DA-2p*)** Necessarily, if A was due primarily to something that was a stroke of luck for S, then S isn't directly morally responsible for A.

(DA-2p*) implies that S could not be directly morally responsible for her decision to A in a case such as the following:

> *Lucky Reasons:* S is trying to decide whether to perform an action, A, which S recognizes to be morally right (wrong). As S is deliberating, s/he comes to possess at time t a strong reason, R, for performing A. S's acquiring R is in some respect good (bad) for S, not something that S did intentionally, and such that nothing like it happens around t in a wide class of possible worlds that are close to actuality before t. So, it's a stroke of good (bad) luck for S that s/he has reason R to perform action A. S then intentionally chooses to perform A, and S's having R is a primary contributor to this choice.[28]

Arguably, if morally responsible action is possible at all, then S *could* be directly morally responsible for her decision to A in a case such as *Lucky Reasons*. To begin to see this, recall from our earlier discussion of the Simplified Strawsonian Argument (Section 5.1) that the possibility of morally responsible action entails the following claim:

> **~(SA-2)** Possibly, S was morally responsible for A* (an arbitrarily selected candidate for S's first morally responsible action) but *not* morally responsible for her possession of any reason R that influenced A*.

Let me review, briefly: Some (finite, temporal) agent S is morally responsible for some action A that s/he performs only if there was a *first* action, A*, for which S was morally responsible. If A* was the *first* action for which S was morally responsible, then S was not morally responsible for her possession of any of the reasons that influenced her performing A*.[29] Therefore, if it's possible that S is morally responsible for something s/he does, then it's possible that S is morally responsible for an action influenced by reasons the having of which s/he was not morally responsible for (= ~SA-2).

Crucially, though, it seems that if S could be morally responsible for an action influenced by reasons the having of which s/he was not morally responsible for (= ~SA-2), then S could also be directly morally responsible for her decision to A in a case such as *Lucky Reasons*. But, as we've just seen, (DA-2p*) – which, recall, is implied by (DA-2p) – implies that S could *not* be directly morally responsible for her decision to A in a case such as *Lucky Reasons*. Arguably, then, (DA-2p) implies that (SA-2) is true and so that morally responsible action is impossible (= the Impossibility Thesis).

Once it has become plausible that (DA-2p) entails the Impossibility Thesis, the kind of objection pressed against (SA-2) above applies to (DA-2p) as well, *mutatis mutandis*. Again, we confront two competing lines of reasoning:

> (DA-2p) is true. If (DA-2p) is true, then morally responsible action is impossible. So, morally responsible action is impossible.
>
> Morally responsible action is possible. If morally responsible action is possible, then (DA-2p) is false. So, (DA-2p) is false.

Which (if either) of these is the better argument? Obviously, this question quickly boils down to which (if either) of (DA-2p) and the Possibility Thesis is more reasonable to accept. Taken on its own, I'm at best inclined to suspend judgment on (DA-2p). By contrast, the Possibility Thesis strikes me as extremely plausible. I submit, then, that of the two competing arguments set out above, we should accept the second one and reject the first. More specifically, we should conclude from the possibility of morally responsible action that, somewhat surprisingly, there could be a directly morally responsible action whose occurrence was at least partly a matter of luck for its agent (= ~DA-2p). If that's right, then we can reasonably reject (DA-2p) on the grounds that it conflicts with the Possibility Thesis.

Let's turn now to the 'at least partly a matter of luck' reading of (IA-2), which amounts to the following claim (as indicated above, since we're now discussing the Indirect Argument, I'll be operating under the friendly assumption that IA-3 is true):

> **(IA-2p)** Necessarily, if A was at least partly a matter of luck for S, then S wasn't free with respect to A.

Notably, even some of the staunchest defenders of the possibility of proximally undetermined directly morally responsible action endorse claims along the lines of (IA-2p). Again, in the course of his recent defense of action-centered event-causal libertarianism from a series of luck-involving arguments, Christopher Franklin claims that '[i]t is hard to believe that an action that is partly a matter of luck could also be free' (2011: 220–1). However, we're now well positioned to see that claims along the lines of (IA-2p) commit their adherents to the impossibility of morally responsible action – and so, these claims can reasonably be rejected on the grounds that such action is possible.

To begin, recall (from earlier in this section) that the Strokes Account of lucky events and the Proposed Equivalences jointly entail that A was at least partly a matter of luck for S *provided that* A was in some respect good (bad) for S and was due primarily to something that was itself a stroke of good (bad) luck for S. So, given the Strokes Account and the Proposed Equivalences, (IA-2p) implies the following conditional:

Necessarily, if A was due primarily to something that was a stroke of luck for S, then S wasn't free with respect to A.

(IA-2p) therefore implies that S could not have been free with respect to – and so, under the friendly assumption that (IA-3) is true, S could not be directly morally responsible for – her decision to A in a case such as this one, introduced a few paragraphs back:

Lucky Reasons: S is trying to decide whether to perform an action, A, which S recognizes to be morally right (wrong). As S is deliberating, s/he comes to possess at time t a strong reason, R, for performing A. S's acquiring R is in some respect good (bad) for S, not something that S did intentionally, and such that nothing like it happens around t in a wide class of possible worlds that are close to actuality before t. So, it's a stroke of good (bad) luck for S that s/he has reason R to perform action A. S then intentionally chooses to perform A, and S's having R is a primary contributor to this choice.

As we've noted, though, it seems that if S could be morally responsible for an action influenced by reasons the having of which s/he was not morally responsible for (= ~SA-2), then S could be directly morally responsible for her decision to A in a case such as *Lucky Reasons*. But, as we've just seen, (IA-2p) implies that S could *not* be directly morally responsible for her decision to A in a case such as *Lucky Reasons*. Arguably, then, (IA-2p) implies that (SA-2) is true and so that morally responsible action is impossible (given that the Possibility Thesis implies ~SA-2).

Once it has become plausible that (IA-2p) entails the Impossibility Thesis, the kind of objection pressed against (SA-2) and (DA-2p) applies to (IA-2p) as well, *mutatis mutandis*. Once more, we confront two competing lines of reasoning:

> (IA-2p) is true. If (IA-2p) is true, then morally responsible action is impossible. So, morally responsible action is impossible.
>
> Morally responsible action is possible. If morally responsible action is possible, then (IA-2p) is false. So, (IA-2p) is false.

Which (if either) of these is the better argument? Obviously, this question quickly boils down to which (if either) of (IA-2p) and the Possibility Thesis is more reasonable to accept. Taken on its own, I'm at best inclined to suspend judgment on (IA-2p). By contrast, the Possibility Thesis strikes me as extremely plausible. I submit, then, that of the two competing arguments set out above, we should accept the second one and reject the first. More specifically, we should conclude from the possibility of morally responsible action that, somewhat surprisingly, an agent could be free with respect to an action whose occurrence was at least partly a matter of luck for that agent (= ~IA-2p). If that's right, then we can reasonably reject (IA-2p) on the grounds that it conflicts with the Possibility Thesis.

In sum, the Possibility Thesis serves to rebut the 'at least partly a matter of luck' readings of both (DA-2) and (IA-2). Here is one reason, then, why the 'at least partly a matter of luck' interpretations of both the Indirect and Direct Arguments for the Proximal Determination Requirement fail.

5.3.3 Against (DA/IA-1)

We turn now to (DA/IA-1), the 'at least partly a matter of luck' interpretation of which amounts to the following claim:

> **(DA/IA-1p)** Necessarily, if S's (morally significant) action A was not proximally determined, then A was at least partly a matter of luck for S – that is, either (i) E was *just* a matter of good (bad) luck for S, or (ii) E was *only partly* a matter of good (bad) luck for S.

In this subsection, I'll be arguing that we can reasonably reject (DA/IA-1p) on the grounds that it implies, incorrectly, that proximally undetermined intentional action is impossible.

Why should we think that (DA/IA-1p) has this implication or that such an implication would be untoward? I start my argument by introducing a technical term that will prove helpful in what follows. Say that an event, E, is at t **robust** iff E happens around t in *almost* all, if not *all*, of the possible worlds that are close to (that is, no more than slightly different from) the actual world before t. By definition, provided that E is *robust*, E does not meet condition (2**) of the Analysis, and so is not a stroke of (good or bad) luck for anyone. Now assume, for conditional proof, that proximally undetermined intentional action is possible. Given this assumption, the following kind of case would seem to be possible:

> S performs a (morally significant) proximally undetermined intentional action, A, such that all the primary contributors to A were *robust*.

Again, assuming that proximally undetermined intentional action is possible at all, it would seem that there could be a proximally undetermined intentional action all of whose primary contributors were robust. But such a proximally undetermined intentional action would constitute a counterexample to (DA/IA-1p). Let me explain.

Since A was (morally significant but) not proximally determined, A satisfies (DA/IA-1p)'s antecedent. By the (left-to-right conditional of the) Analysis, since S performed A intentionally, A was not itself a stroke of luck for S. Further, since (by hypothesis) all the primary contributors to A were *robust*, none of the contributors to A was a stroke of luck for S either. So, A was not itself a stroke of luck for S (because A was something that S did intentionally), and A was not due primarily to anything that was a stroke of luck for S (because all the primary contributors to A were robust). By the (left-to-right conditional of the) Strokes Account of lucky events, then, A was not (un)lucky for S. And so, by the Proposed Equivalences, A was not even *partly* a matter of luck for S.[30] Thus, A satisfies (DA/IA-1p)'s antecedent but not (DA/IA-1p)'s consequent, and therefore constitutes a counterexample to (DA/IA-1p).

We can conclude, then, that (DA/IA-1p) rules out the possibility of proximally undetermined intentional action. But this implication, that any intentional action must be proximally determined, leads to an extremely dubious under-ascription of intentional action. There are both example-driven and theory-driven ways to bring out the implausibility of this implication.

First, it clearly seems that there could be an action which was done intentionally, whose occurrence was nevertheless not logically entailed by the immediate past and laws of nature (cf. Mele 2003b: 464, Mele and Moser 1994: 61f.). While one's *intentionally* performing an action, A, may well require that one exercise (and thus possess) an environmentally or circumstantially *reliable* ability to perform A, one's performing A intentionally does not seem to require that one exercise (or that one even *possess*) an environmentally or circumstantially *infallible* ability to perform A. Second, on the plausible assumption that 'an agent performs an action that is not intentional only when she does something intentionally' (Clarke 2003: 39, 80), the implication in question entails that there could not be any *actions* (intentional or otherwise) in a world such that every event is proximally undetermined. So, (DA/IA-1p) entails that agency *period* requires the occurrence of some proximally determined events. Besides being implausible on its face, the claim that there could not be any actions whatsoever in (what we might call) a thoroughly indeterministic world will be rejected by proponents of all the leading contemporary theories of action (including advocates of standard noncausalist accounts of action, who simply deny that actions must be caused, as opposed to asserting that actions must be *un*caused [cf. Clarke 2010]).[31]

We can therefore reasonably reject (DA/IA-1p) on the grounds that it conflicts with the extremely plausible thesis that there could be proximally undetermined intentional actions. Of course, this point impugns the 'just a matter of luck' interpretation of (DA/IA-1) as well, since that interpretation entails (DA/IA-1p). It's worth noting, finally, that this kind of criticism applies to a key step of Levy's (2011a: 49–51; cf. 2011b: 179–80) luck objection to action-centered event-causal libertarianism, a view according to which 'free decisions deterministically cause correlative actions, but these decisions are themselves indeterministically caused by mental states of the agent' (2011a: 44).[32] Here is Levy's assertion of the key step in question:

> Because Mike's decision is undetermined, ... Mike lacks direct control over his decision. (2011a: 50; cf. 2011b: 180)

What's meant here by 'direct control'? According to Levy (2011a: 19), 'an agent has direct control over E's occurrence when he can bring about E's occurrence by virtue of performing some basic action which (as he knows) will bring about E's occurrence (the probability of his basic action having the intended effect need not be 100 per cent, but it should be high).'³³ Given his definition of 'direct control', the indicated step in Levy's luck argument commits him to the thesis that no proximally undetermined event could be (near enough) knowingly brought about by way of some basic action.³⁴ Plausibly, though, if proximally undetermined intentional action is possible at all, then there could be a proximally undetermined event (near enough) knowingly brought about by way of some basic action. The indicated step of Levy's luck objection therefore seems to commit him to the impossibility of proximally undetermined intentional action.

It's time to sum up this section's main findings. Each of (IA-2), (DA-2), and (DA/IA-1) involves the expression 'A was a matter of luck for S'. That expression admits of two different readings: *A was **just** a matter of luck for S* and *A was **at least partly** a matter of luck for S*. Further reflection on a case described back in Section 2.1 yields an intriguing attempted counterexample to both readings of (IA-2). But even if we reject this attempted counterexample, neither the Indirect Argument nor the Direct Argument succeeds on either relevant interpretation. The 'at least partly a matter of luck' interpretation of (DA-2) mistakenly rules out the possibility of morally responsible action, and so can be reasonably rejected on the grounds that such action is possible. The 'at least partly a matter of luck' reading of (IA-2) suffers the same fate (under the friendly assumption that IA-3 is true). Finally, on the 'at least partly a matter of luck' reading, (DA/IA-1) mistakenly implies that proximally undetermined intentional action is impossible. This point impugns the 'just a matter of luck' reading of (DA/IA-1) as well, since that reading entails the 'at least partly a matter of luck' reading. All the visible *literal* versions of both the Direct Argument and the Indirect Argument for the Proximal Determination Requirement thus fail due to conflict with the possibility of morally responsible action and/or the possibility of proximally undetermined intentional action.

* * *

Provided that both morally responsible action and proximally undetermined intentional action are at least *possible*, (a) *literal* interpretations of the main visible luck-involving arguments for the Proximal Determination Requirement fail; and (b) an agent could be *both* free with respect to *and* directly morally responsible for an action whose occurrence was at least partly a matter of luck for that agent.³⁵ So, not only do the main visible luck-based threats to the scope of metaphysically free and morally responsible action fail to materialize, but luck turns out to be a good deal more congenial to metaphysically free and morally responsible action than is typically thought (even by some of the staunchest defenders of the possibility of proximally undetermined directly morally responsible action). What remains to be seen is whether some or other *stipulative* luck-involving argument for the Proximal Determination Requirement can successfully justify that requirement, and also what kinds of considerations might support the *denial* of that requirement (that is, the possibility of proximally undetermined directly morally responsible action). These will be our focal questions in the next chapter.

6
Freedom, Responsibility, and Luck II: Stipulative Arguments for the Proximal Determination Requirement and Three Arguments against It

This chapter has two main parts. In the first main part, which comprises Sections 6.1 and 6.2, I will explain and evaluate several prominent recent arguments for the Proximal Determination Requirement, each of which claims that an action's having one or another of the following luck-related properties keeps its agent from being directly morally responsible for it:

being a genuinely random occurrence
lacking any explanation in terms of the process that generated it
lacking a complete explanation in terms of the process that generated it
failing to disclose a moral stand on the part of its agent
having a nonzero objective probability of failing to occur

As noted in the last chapter, I classify these luck-involving arguments for the Proximal Determination Requirement as 'stipulative' since their proponents stipulate readings of their luck-involving claims in terms of one or another of the above properties, with little concern for whether such interpretations might constitute tenable analyses of such claims. Proponents of stipulative versions of the Direct Argument for the Proximal Determination Requirement, which I discuss in Section 6.1, aim to establish that any possible proximally undetermined action will have one or another of the luck-related properties listed above and that an action's having that property is incompatible with its agent's being directly morally responsible for it. Proponents of stipulative versions of the Indirect Argument, which I discuss in Section 6.2, aim to establish that any possible proximally undetermined action will have one or another of the luck-related properties listed above and that an action's having this property is incompatible with its agent's being free with respect to its occurrence – and so, by the additional premise that one is directly morally responsible for an action only if one was free with respect to that action, is incompatible with its agent's being directly morally responsible for it.[1]

Having defended the possibility of proximally undetermined directly morally responsible action from all the main visible luck-involving arguments for the Proximal Determination Requirement, I will get more 'offensive' in the chapter's second main part, Section 6.3. Here, I will explain and assess three different nonpartisan arguments against the Proximal Determination Requirement (that is, for the possibility of proximally undetermined directly morally responsible action):[2] an argument inspired by Mele (2006, 2013); an argument developed by Fischer (2011, 2014); and a novel argument that I will call the 'Possibility Argument' (which, as I mentioned near the beginning of the last chapter, will be neutral on the question of whether proximally determined directly morally responsible action is possible). I will argue that whereas the lines of thought suggested by Mele and Fischer fail, the Possibility Argument succeeds, thus providing good reason to believe in the possibility of proximally undetermined directly morally responsible action.

6.1 Stipulative versions of the Direct Argument for the Proximal Determination Requirement

In this section, I will consider three prominent recent stipulative versions of the Direct Argument for the Proximal Determination Requirement – what I'll call the 'No Explanation Argument', the 'No *Complete* Explanation Argument', and the 'No Moral Stand Argument'. We'll start with the No Explanation Argument, which has been suggested in a number of recent papers by Haji (2006: 186–7, 2012: 195ff.):[3]

The No Explanation Argument

(NE-1) Necessarily, if subject S's action A was not proximally determined, then nothing about the process that generated A explains why A happened.

(NE-2) Necessarily, if nothing about the process that generated A explains why A happened, then S is not directly morally responsible for A.

(**Proximal Determination Requirement**) So, necessarily, if S's action A was not proximally determined, then S is not directly morally responsible for A.

What should we make of this argument? We can start by conceding (NE-2), for it is supported by the following plausible (though by no means completely uncontroversial[4]) line of thought: S is directly morally responsible for A only if S did A for a reason, and S did A for a reason only if something about the process that generated A explains why A happened (cf. Haji 2012: 195–6).

Unfortunately, (NE-1) is not similarly plausible. Clarke (2003: 39) develops and defends the following persuasive line of thought that impugns (NE-1):[5]

> An action that is nondeterministically caused by, among other things, the agent's having certain reasons may be an action performed for those reasons. We can then provide an adequate reason-explanation of it by citing the reasons for which it was performed.

A proponent of (NE-1) must *either* (a) implausibly deny that nondeterministic causation is possible; *or* (b) implausibly deny that a reason-state R's nondeviantly causing an action, A, suffices for A's being done for (or, based on) R; *or* (c) implausibly deny that we can explain why A happened by citing a reason for which A was performed. The No Explanation Argument thus fails due to (NE-1)'s implausibility.

Onward to the No *Complete* Explanation Argument. First, a helpful stipulative definition: say that an event E at t **lacks a complete explanation** iff 'there is no fact or truth to be reported in a correct answer' to the question why E happened at t *rather than* failing to happen then (Mele 2006: 70). The No *Complete* Explanation Argument can now be stated as follows (cf. Waller 1988, Mele 1999, 2006, 2013, Haji 1999, 2001, Cohen 2006, Schlosser 2014):

The No Complete *Explanation Argument*

(CE-1) Necessarily, if S's action A was not proximally determined, then A lacks a complete explanation (that is, 'there is no fact or truth to be reported in a correct answer' to the question why A happened when it did rather than failing to happen then).

(CE-2) Necessarily, if A lacks a complete explanation, then S is not directly morally responsible for A.

(Proximal Determination Requirement) So, necessarily, if S's action A was not proximally determined, then S is not directly morally responsible for A.

What should we make of this argument? I believe that its failure is overdetermined, for both (CE-1) and (CE-2) are highly questionable. As for (CE-1), note that an action A's being proximally undetermined is nevertheless consistent with A's being such that some of its immediate antecedents made A's occurrence at the relevant time more likely than A's *absence* then. In such a case, citing those antecedents – for example, S's firm belief that performing A would be much better than omitting A, coupled with a strong desire to do what's best – may well constitute a correct answer to the question why S performed A rather than omitting A (cf. Clarke 2004: 52–3). To the extent that this reasoning is plausible, (CE-1) is dubious.

As for (CE-2), it is frequently noted that there are two importantly different kinds of requirements on S's performing a directly morally responsible action: what are often called, respectively, epistemic (or, knowledge-relevant) conditions, on the one hand, and control (or, freedom-relevant) conditions, on the other. Presumably, A's lacking a complete explanation need not jeopardize S's meeting whatever *epistemic* requirements there are on her being directly morally responsible for A. The idea behind (CE-2) must instead be that A's lacking a complete explanation would jeopardize S's meeting whatever *control* requirements there are on her being directly morally responsible for A (cf. Mele 2006: 63, 2013: 239–40). So, advocates of (CE-2) must be assuming that there is a tight necessary connection between (a) the obtaining of the relevant control relation(s) between an agent and her action and (b) the availability of a complete explanation for that action.

But, as several contributors to the recent literature on the No *Complete Explanation* Argument have pointed out, the assumption (upon which CE-2 apparently rests) of a tight necessary connection between the pertinent control and explanatory issues is in fact highly questionable. Writes Franklin (2011: 224; cf. Clarke 2003: 81):

> [L]ack of contrastive explanation does not indicate a lack of control. Whether or not an explanation can be given depends on what the explainee knows or is assuming, and precisely because the availability of explanation depends on these epistemic and pragmatic conditions, explanation does not tightly track control: whether I control some outcome does not depend on what some other person knows or

assumes. So, even if nothing accounts for the difference in outcomes between worlds, it does not follow that the agent is subject to ... diminished control ... Since the availability of contrastive explanations depends on pragmatic and epistemic conditions that are irrelevant to control, it is possible for one to control an event even though the event's occurrence does not admit of a certain explanation.

Notably, those who follow theorists such as Franklin (and Clarke) in rejecting (CE-2) on these grounds can offer a plausible error theory for its proponents' mistaken (as they see it) endorsement of it. As I granted above, (NE-2) of the No Explanation Argument is quite plausible. That is, it's quite plausible to think that no one could be directly morally responsible for an action that does not have even a *partial* explanation in terms of the process that generated it. (CE-2) of the No *Complete* Explanation Argument – the claim that no one could be directly morally responsible for an action that does not have a *complete* explanation – is obviously similar to, though considerably logically stronger than, the parallel and quite plausible premise of the No Explanation Argument. Whatever sustained intuitive appeal the second premise of the No *Complete* Explanation Argument has for those who accept it *may* be due to a rather subtle, and thus understandable, confusion between it and the parallel premise of the No Explanation Argument.[6]

We turn now to our third and final stipulative Direct Argument for the Proximal Determination Requirement, which I'll call the No Moral Stand Argument (Haji 2001: 196f.):

The No Moral Stand Argument

(MS-1) Necessarily, if S's action A was not proximally determined, then A does not disclose what S morally stands for.

(MS-2) Necessarily, if A does not disclose what S morally stands for, then S is not directly morally responsible for A.

(**Proximal Determination Requirement**) So, necessarily, if S's action A was not proximally determined, then S is not directly morally responsible for A.

What should we make of this argument? I believe that the No Moral Stand Argument fails at its first step. On what strikes me as the most natural interpretation of 'disclose what S morally stands for', one can simultaneously *take and disclose* a moral stand on some issue or question by making a decision or choice – that is, by actively forming an intention to perform a certain action.[7] So, on the most natural interpretation of 'disclose what S morally stands for', (MS-1) commits its proponent to the thesis that proximally undetermined decisions are impossible. Since it is extremely plausible to think that there *can* be proximally undetermined decisions (see, for example, the above objection to NE-1 of the No Explanation Argument), the No Moral Stand Argument fails at (MS-1) on the most natural interpretation of 'disclose what S morally stands for'.

None of the three prominent stipulative Direct Arguments considered above succeeds. In the next section, we'll consider prominent stipulative *In*direct Arguments for the Proximal Determination Requirement.

6.2 Stipulative versions of the Indirect Argument for the Proximal Determination Requirement

Recall the template for the Indirect Argument that I set out in Section 5.2 above (now slightly expanded with a lemma):

(**IA-1**) Necessarily, if S's action A was not proximally determined, then A was a matter of luck for S.

(**IA-2**) Necessarily, if A was a matter of luck for S, then S was not free with respect to A.

(**Unfreedom Lemma**) Necessarily, if S's action A was not proximally determined, then S was not free with respect to A. [IA-1, IA-2]

(**IA-3**) Necessarily, if S was not free with respect to A, then S is not directly morally responsible for A.

(**Proximal Determination Requirement**) So, necessarily, if S's action A was not proximally determined, then S is not directly morally responsible for A. [Unfreedom Lemma, IA-3]

As in Section 5.3 above, I'll here continue operating under the friendly (to proponents of the Indirect Argument) assumption that one is directly morally responsible for an action only if one was free with respect to that action (= IA-3) – henceforth, the **Freedom Requirement**. As noted earlier, I'll discuss and defend the Freedom Requirement (= IA-3) in Section 6.3.2 below, when I explain and evaluate Fischer's (2011, 2014) recent argument against the Proximal Determination Requirement.[8] In what follows, we'll focus on prominent arguments for the Unfreedom Lemma (= one could not have been free with respect to a proximally undetermined action) that invoke one or another of the luck-related properties listed at the beginning of this chapter. We'll spend the majority of our time exploring several recent attempts to elaborate and defend the following reasoning that van Inwagen (2000: 10; cf. van Inwagen 1983: 16, 2008: 338) has dubbed 'the *Mind* Argument' ('because it has appeared so frequently in the pages of *Mind*'):

> [I]f an agent's acts are undetermined, then *how* the agent acts on a given occasion is a matter of chance. And if how an agent acts on a given occasion is a matter of chance, the agent can hardly be said to have free will.

A bit more formally:

The Mind *Argument*

(MI-1) Necessarily, if S's action A (at t) was not proximally determined, then there was (just before t) a nonzero objective probability that S would not perform A (at t).

(MI-2) Necessarily, if there was (just before t) a nonzero objective probability that S would not perform A (at t), then S was not free with respect to A.

(Unfreedom Lemma) Necessarily, if S's action A was not proximally determined, then S was not free with respect to A.

In what follows, I will grant (MI-1) and consider five prominent recent arguments for (MI-2) – what I'll call, respectively, the 'Device Argument' (van Inwagen 1983, Graham 2010), the 'Promising Argument' (van Inwagen 2000, 2011), the 'Assimilation Argument' (Shabo 2013), the 'Nomological Grounding Argument' (Finch 2013), and the 'Selection Argument' (Haji 2001, Schlosser 2014). Before getting to these five prominent recent arguments for (MI-2), though, I want to briefly discuss two other lines of reasoning for the Unfreedom Lemma that, while historically salient, are much less interesting and promising than the five arguments that we'll focus on.[9]

First, one might infer the Unfreedom Lemma from (i) the premise that any proximally undetermined event must be a genuinely random occurrence, together with (ii) the premise that no one could be free with respect to a genuinely random occurrence.[10] Second, one might argue that since no proximally undetermined event could be an action – or at least not a rational action, an action done for reasons – no proximally undetermined event could be an action with respect to which one was free (= the Unfreedom Lemma).[11] What should we make of these arguments?

Not much, in my estimation. As we saw in Section 6.1 when discussing the No Explanation Argument, the possibility of proximally undetermined rational action (that is, action done for reasons) follows from two extremely plausible and, accordingly, widely accepted theses: (I) nondeterministic causation is possible; (II) a reason-state R's nondeviantly causing an action A performed by a subject S suffices for A's being done by S for R. The conjunction of (I) and (II) directly rebuts the second line of reasoning sketched above, since that reasoning depends on the claim that no proximally undetermined event could be an action done for reasons. Further, given the extremely plausible assumption that S's performing A for a reason suffices for S's exercising a kind of control over A that rules out A's being a genuinely random occurrence (cf. Mele 1992, Clarke 2003),[12] the conjunction of (I) and (II) also rebuts the first argument's premise that any proximally undetermined event must be a genuinely random occurrence.

6.2.1 Five arguments for (MI-2)

We'll start with the Device Argument, which takes off from the following example:[13]

> *Device Scenario:* Let us imagine a mechanism the salient features of which are a red light, a green light, and a button. If one presses the button, we'll suppose, then exactly one of the two lights must flash, but it is causally undetermined *which*.... Now suppose that you must press the button on this mechanism. Have you any choice about which of the lights will flash? It seems obvious that you have no choice about this. (van Inwagen 1983: 142)

From here, the Device Argument runs as follows (cf. Graham 2010: 286–9):

The Device Argument

(DE-1) If a subject S could have been free with respect to an action A such that there was (just before S performed A) a nonzero objective probability that S would not perform A, then the agent in the Device Scenario could have been free with respect to the flashing of whichever light subsequently flashed.

(DE-2) Necessarily, it's false that the agent in the Device Scenario was free with respect to the flashing of whichever light subsequently flashed.

(DE-3) So, S could not have been free with respect to an action A such that there was (just before S performed A) a nonzero objective probability that S would not perform A (which generalizes to MI-2).

What should we make of the Device Argument? To begin, (DE-2) is extremely plausible. By hypothesis, whichever light subsequently flashes, its flashing is a *non-active result of a prior unfree action*. Necessarily, an agent was free with respect to a non-active result of a prior action of hers only if the agent was free with respect to the relevant prior action (cf. Graham 2010: 290). So, necessarily, the agent in the *Device Scenario* was free with respect to the flashing of whichever light subsequently flashes only if she was free with respect to the prior action from which the flash resulted – viz. her pressing the button on the device. But, in the *Device Scenario*, it's stipulated that the agent was *not* free with respect to pressing the button on the device ('...you must press the button on this mechanism...'). Thus, the stipulated details of the *Device Scenario*, together with the above requirement on an agent's being free with respect to a non-active result of some prior action of hers, entail that the agent in the *Device Scenario* was not free with respect to the flashing of whichever light subsequently flashes.

This doesn't mean that the Device Argument succeeds, though, for (DE-1) rests on an assumption that is at best extremely dubious. Again, whichever light subsequently flashes, its flashing is a non-active result of a prior unfree action. On the other hand, we can safely assume (since this is consistent with DE-1's antecedent) that S's action A was a basic action nondeterministically caused by some of S's prior reason states.[14] (DE-1) therefore rests on something like the following assumption:

> A proximally undetermined basic action of S's that was caused by some of S's prior reason states could not be a better candidate for thing with respect to which S was free than is a proximally undetermined non-active result of some prior unfree action of S's.

This assumption is at best extremely dubious (Graham 2010: 292–3; cf. Clarke 2003: 79, Franklin 2011: 213–15). As noted above, an agent's being free with respect to a *non-active result of some prior action of hers* strictly implies that the agent was free with respect to the relevant prior action. But, unless your being free with respect to any given action of yours requires that you perform an infinite regress of free actions – an extremely dubious claim (cf. Graham 2010: 292–3) – your being free with respect to any given action of yours does *not* require your being free with respect to some *prior* action of yours. So, while any non-active result of a prior *unfree* action is obviously disqualified from being something with respect to which its agent was free, the same does *not* hold for every possible action of S's that was nondeterministically caused by some of her prior reasons. Thus, the above assumption upon which (DE-1) rests is extremely dubious: a proximally undetermined basic action of S's that was caused by – and thus, we can safely suppose, based on – some of S's prior reason states *may very well* be a better candidate for thing with respect to which S was free than is a proximally undetermined nonactive result of some prior unfree action of S's. The Device Argument thus fails to adequately support premise (MI-2) of the *Mind* Argument for the Unfreedom Lemma.

Onward, then, to the Promising Argument (van Inwagen 2000: 17–18; 2011), which takes off from the following kind of example:

> **Discreditable Fact:** Ann is a candidate for public office. Bob knows a discreditable fact about Ann's past that, if made public, would – and should – cost Ann the election. Ann and Bob both know that a local reporter will soon ask Bob about the pertinent portion of Ann's past. Ann begs Bob to deny the discreditable fact, to lie to the reporter about her past. Bob is pulled two ways, one way by the claims of citizenship and the other by the claims of friendship. Bob knows that there exist exactly two possible continuations of the present in one of which he tells the reporter the truth about Ann's past and in the other of which he lies to the reporter about Ann's past; and Bob knows that the objective, 'ground-floor' probability of his telling the truth is 0.43 and that the objective, 'ground-floor' probability of his lying is 0.57. (adapted from van Inwagen 2000: 17)

From here, the Promising Argument runs as follows:

The Promising Argument

(PA-1) If a subject S could have been free with respect to an action A such that there was (just before S performed A) a nonzero objective probability that S would not perform A, then in *Discreditable Fact* Bob could (when begged by Ann to lie to the reporter) have been free with respect to whether he later lies to the reporter.

(PA-2) If in *Discreditable Fact* Bob could have been free with respect to whether he later lies to the reporter, then in *Discreditable Fact* Bob could (when begged by Ann to lie to the reporter) have been well positioned to sincerely promise Ann that he will lie to the reporter.

(PA-3) In *Discreditable Fact*, Bob could not (when begged by Ann to lie) have been well positioned to sincerely promise Ann that he will lie to the reporter.

(PA-4) So, S could not have been free with respect to an action A such that there was (just before S performed A) a nonzero objective probability that S would not perform A (which generalizes to MI-2).

What should we make of the Promising Argument? Unfortunately, *Discreditable Fact* leaves a crucial question without a clear answer; and once the indicated question receives a clear answer, either (PA-1) or (PA-3) will be too dubious for the Promising Argument to succeed (cf. Franklin 2011, van Inwagen 2011). Here's the crucial question:

Would Bob's *now* promising to lie to the reporter (in response to Ann's urgent request) substantially increase the likelihood of his *later* lying?

If the answer is yes, then (PA-3) becomes dubious. If it's the case that Bob would (in all probability) later lie were he to now promise Ann that he will lie, then Bob in fact seems to be well positioned to sincerely promise Ann that he will lie (= ~PA-3).

So, suppose we instead answer the crucial question in the negative: Bob's now promising to lie would *not* substantially change the likelihood of his later lying. If that's how we answer the crucial question, then (PA-1) becomes dubious. As before, we can safely assume (since this is consistent with PA-1's antecedent) that S's action A was a basic action nondeterministically caused by some of S's prior reason states. On the other hand, whether Bob lies or tells the truth to the reporter at the appointed time, his behavior then will be a proximally undetermined actional outcome of some prior action of his (as opposed to being a *basic* action). (PA-1) therefore rests on something like the following assumption:

A proximally undetermined basic action of S's that was caused by some of S's prior reason states could not be a better candidate for thing with respect to which S was free than is a proximally undetermined actional outcome of some prior action of S's.

This assumption, like the similar one discussed above in connection with (DE-1) of the Device Argument, is at best extremely dubious (cf.

Graham 2010: 290–1). An agent's being free with respect to an *actional outcome of some prior action of hers* strictly implies that the agent was free with respect to the relevant prior action. But, again, unless your being free with respect to any given action of yours requires that you perform an infinite regress of free actions – which remains an extremely dubious claim – your being free with respect to any given action of yours does *not* require your being free with respect to some *prior* action of yours. So, while your being free with respect to an actional outcome of some prior action of yours strictly implies that you were also free with respect to the pertinent prior action, the same does *not* hold for every possible action of S's that was nondeterministically caused by some of her prior reasons. Hence, the above assumption upon which (PA-1) rests (on the second interpretation of *Discreditable Fact*) is extremely dubious: a proximally undetermined basic action of S's that was caused by – and thus, we can safely suppose, based on – some of S's prior reason states *may very well* be a better candidate for thing with respect to which S was free than is some proximally undetermined actional outcome of some prior action of S's. In sum, however we answer the crucial question, one of the Promising Argument's basic premises will become too dubious for that argument to succeed. The Promising Argument thus fails to adequately support premise (MI-2) of the *Mind* Argument for the Unfreedom Lemma.

Next, the Assimilation Argument, which employs the following series of examples (Shabo 2013: 301ff.):[15]

> *Case 3:* Scientists have placed an interesting device in Alice's brain. This device consists of a particle and a detector that monitors said particle's behavior. The particle will swerve in one direction or another, with each outcome having an equal, objective probability. If the particle swerves one way, this will register with the detector, and the detector will then causally determine Alice's brain to go into a state that is intrinsically indistinguishable from an ordinary, executive intention to tell the truth in response to the question she has been asked. If the particle swerves the other way, this will register with the detector, and the detector will then causally determine Alice's brain to go into a state intrinsically indistinguishable from an ordinary, executive intention to lie in response to the question she has been asked. In the event, the particle swerves in the first direction, with the result that Alice exhibits truth-telling behavior, behavior that is caused in a normal way by the relevant neural state.
>
> *Case 4:* The scientists introduce an upgraded device. The upgraded device harnesses indeterminacy in Alice's own neural pathways.... The

upgraded device can target pathways that are causally inert, pathways that are involved in reflex-type behavior, or pathways that are involved in the formation of intentions. When the pathways in the last of these regions are targeted, the upgraded device charges a particle (or group of particles) in that pathway, causing that particle(s) to behave like the particle in Case 3. That is, the particle(s) will swerve one way or another, with each outcome having an equal, objective probability. In this case, however, the outcome is an intention to lie or an intention to tell the truth – or at least a neural state that is intrinsically indistinguishable from one of these intentions or the other.

Case 5: There is no input from any external device. Due to its ordinary, endogenous workings, Alice's brain state as she mulls her options is such that lying and telling the truth are equally probable outcomes. She intends to make up her mind, and this intention causally contributes to her deciding to tell the truth, a decision that is based on her reasons for doing so.

From here, the Assimilation Argument runs as follows:[16]

The Assimilation Argument

(AS-1) In *Case 3*, Alice could not have been free with respect to her being in the truth-telling-conducive neural state.

(AS-2) If in *Case 3* Alice could not have been free with respect to her being in the truth-telling-conducive neural state, then in *Case 4* Alice could not have been free with respect to her being in the truth-telling-conducive neural state.

(AS-3) If in *Case 4* Alice could not have been free with respect to her being in the truth-telling-conducive neural state, then in *Case 5* Alice could not have been free with respect to her (proximally undetermined) decision to tell the truth.

(AS-4) If in *Case 5* Alice could not have been free with respect to her (proximally undetermined) decision to tell the truth, then no subject S could have been free with respect to an action A such that there was (just beforehand) a nonzero objective probability that S would not perform A.

(AS-5) So, no subject S could have been free with respect to an action A such that there was (just beforehand) a nonzero objective probability that S would not perform A (= MI-2).

What should we make of the Assimilation Argument? Unfortunately, *Case 4* leaves a crucial question without a clear answer; and once the indicated question receives a clear answer, either (AS-2) or (AS-3) will be too dubious for the Assimilation Argument to succeed (cf. Franklin 2012: 400–6). Here's the crucial question:

> Does the charging of the pertinent particle – which, recall, occurs in one of the 'pathways [in Alice's brain] that are involved in the formation of intentions' – constitute a mental event or state of a kind that could issue in a genuine decision?

If the answer is yes, then (AS-2) becomes dubious. On this interpretation of *Case 4*, (AS-2) rests on something like the following assumption:

> A proximally undetermined intrinsically choice-like event caused by a mental event or state of a kind that could issue in a genuine decision could not be a better candidate for thing with respect to which an agent was free than is a proximally determined intrinsically choice-like non-actional event caused by a machine of the kind described in *Case 3*.

Since this assumption – which, again, underlies (AS-2) on the current interpretation of *Case 4* – is extremely dubious, (AS-2) itself lacks adequate support on the indicated interpretation of *Case 4*.

So, suppose we instead answer the crucial question in the negative: the pertinent particle-charging event does *not* constitute a mental event or state of a kind that could issue in a genuine decision. If that's how we answer the crucial question, then (AS-3) becomes dubious. In that case, (AS-3) rests on something like the following assumption:

> A proximally undetermined decision to tell the truth, one that was caused by and thereby based on some of its agent's prior reason states that support telling the truth, could not be a better candidate for thing with respect to which an agent was free than is a proximally undetermined intrinsically choice-like non-actional event that was not caused by a mental event or state of a kind that could issue in a genuine decision.

Since this assumption – which, again, underlies (AS-3) on the current interpretation of *Case 4* – is extremely dubious, (AS-3) itself lacks adequate support on the indicated interpretation of *Case 4*. In sum, however we answer the crucial question, one of the Assimilation Argument's basic premises will become too dubious for that argument to succeed. The Assimilation Argument thus fails to adequately support premise (MI-2) of the *Mind* Argument for the Unfreedom Lemma.

Next, the argument that I earlier dubbed the 'Nomological Grounding Argument' (Finch 2013: 484–6):[17]

The Nomological Grounding Argument[18]

(NG-1) Necessarily, if S was at t1 free with respect to her action A at t2 which had at t1 a nonzero objective probability of not happening at t2, then it was at t1 physically possible that S performs A non-freely at t2.

(NG-2) Necessarily, if S performs A non-freely at t2, then S was not at t1 free with respect to whether s/he performs A at t2.[19]

(NG-3) So, necessarily, if S was at t1 free with respect to her action A at t2 which had at t1 a nonzero objective probability of not happening at t2, then it was at t1 physically possible that S was not then free with respect to whether s/he performs A at t2. [NG-1, NG-2]

(NG-4) Necessarily, if it was at t1 physically possible that S was not then free with respect to whether s/he performs A at t2, then there is a physically possible world that is exactly like the actual world before t2 *except* that S is not at t1 free with respect to whether s/he performs A at t2.

(NG-5) So, necessarily, if S was at t1 free with respect to her action A at t2 which had at t1 a nonzero objective probability of not happening at t2, then there is a physically possible world that is exactly like the actual world before t2 *except* that S is not at t1 free with respect to whether s/he performs A at t2. [NG-3, NG-4]

(NG-6) Necessarily, if S was at t1 free with respect to her action A at t2 which had at t1 a nonzero objective probability of not happening at t2, then any physically possible world that is exactly like the actual world before t2 is such that S is at t1 free with respect to whether s/he performs A at t2.

Letting 'free will' denote the ability or power to act freely (cf. Clarke 2004: 61, footnote 1), we can abbreviate (NG-6) in this (relatively long) slogan: No difference in one's free will (at t) without a difference in either (a) one's properties (at t) or (b) the laws of nature. Or, in a shorter slogan (cf. Finch 2013: 486): Free will is *synchronically nomologically grounded*.

(NG-7) So, necessarily, if S was at t1 free with respect to her action A at t2 which had at t1 a nonzero objective probability of not happening at t2, then there both is *and* is not a physically possible world that is exactly like the actual world before t2 except that S is not at t1 free with respect to whether s/he performs A at t2. [NG-5, NG-6]

(NG-8) Necessarily, it's false that there both is *and* is not a physically possible world exactly like the actual world before t2 except that S is not at t1 free with respect to whether s/he performs A at t2.

(NG-9) So, necessarily, it's false that S was at t1 free with respect to her action A at t2 which had at t1 a nonzero objective probability of not happening at t2 (which generalizes to MI-2). [NG-7, NG-8]

What should we make of the Nomological Grounding Argument? Fascinating as this argument is, I believe that it fails right out of the gate. Recall (NG-1):

(NG-1) Necessarily, if S was at t1 free with respect to her action A at t2 which had at t1 a nonzero objective probability of not happening at t2, then it was at t1 physically possible that S performs A non-freely at t2.

Defenders of the denial of the Proximal Determination Requirement can reasonably maintain that there are metaphysically possible scenarios in which, while S was at t1 free with respect to her action A at t2 which had at t1 a nonzero objective probability of not happening at t2, nevertheless it was at t1 physically necessary that *if* S performs A at t2, then S performs A *freely* at t2 (that is, it was at t1 physically impossible that S performs A non-freely at t2).[20] In the envisaged scenario, then, at t1 the only relevant physical possibilities for t2 are these: *S freely performs A* and *S freely omits A*. Such a scenario would, of course, be a counterexample to (NG-1).

If (NG-1) really is subject to the kind of counterexample just sketched – as I believe it is – the question arises why anyone would be taken in by (NG-1). Fortunately, there's a plausible error theory available here. To begin to see it, consider the following proposition:

(NG-1*) Necessarily, if S was at t1 free with respect to her action A at t2 which had at t1 a nonzero objective probability of not happening at t2, then it was at t1 physically possible that S does not perform A freely at t2.

(NG-1*) is obviously true. Now, if a theorist sensed (NG-1*)'s obvious truth but then went on to conflate *S's **not** performing A freely at t2* with *S's performing A **non-freely** at t2*, then that theorist would end up mistakenly endorsing premise (NG-1). But a theorist who sensed (NG-1*)'s obvious truth might well go on to conflate *S's **not** performing A freely at t2* with *S's performing A **non-freely** at t2*: such conflation would amount to a subtle and understandable kind of scope confusion. I think that something like this has probably happened to any theorist who endorses a claim along the lines of (NG-1).

We turn, finally, to the argument that I earlier dubbed the 'Selection Argument' (Haji 2001: 190ff.; cf. Schlosser 2014: 378–9, Shabo 2013: 297–300):

> *The Selection Argument*[21]
>
> **(SE-1)** Necessarily, if subject S performed an action A at t2 and there was still at t1 a nonzero objective probability that S would not perform A at t2, then S did not ensure A's occurrence by way of performing some prior action, A*.
>
> **(SE-2)** Necessarily, if S did not ensure A's occurrence by way of performing some prior action A*, then A is not a manifestation of S's power to select one course of action rather than another.
>
> **(SE-3)** Necessarily, if A is not a manifestation of S's power to select one course of action rather than another, then S was not free with respect to A.
>
> **(SE-4)** So, necessarily, if subject S performed an action A at t2 and there was still at t1 a nonzero objective probability that S would not perform A at t2, then S was not at t1 free with respect to A (which generalizes to MI-2).

What should we make of the Selection Argument? I believe that anyone who endorses (SE-2) faces a fatal dilemma (cf. Franklin 2011: 211–13). The problem may be a bit easier to see if we start by noting (SE-2)'s contrapositive:

> **(SE-2c)** Necessarily, if A is a manifestation of S's power to select one course of action rather than another, then S ensured A's occurrence by way of performing some prior action, A*.

Either the mandated prior ensuring action, A*, must – in order for A to be a manifestation of S's power to select one course of action rather than another – be free, or A* needn't be free for this. If A* must be free, then (SE-2) and (SE-3) jointly entail that any possible free action is preceded by yet another earlier free action, and so that there can't be a *first* free action, and so that free action is impossible (for finite, temporal agents). Among other problems, this would (given the friendly – to proponents of the Indirect Argument – assumption that the Freedom Requirement is true) commit the Selection Argument's proponent to the impossibility of morally responsible action, and so we could reasonably infer the denial of (the relevant reading of) (SE-2) from the possibility of morally responsible action (since SE-3 is unobjectionable).

On the other hand, if the mandated prior ensuring action A* *needn't* be free, then (SE-2) rests on something like the following assumption:

> A proximally undetermined basic action of S's such that S was (just beforehand) free to omit it could not be a better candidate for being a manifestation of S's power to select which course of action to pursue than is an action of S's whose occurrence was ensured by a prior *unfree* action of S's.

Since this assumption – which, again, underlies the reading of (SE-2) on which the mandated prior ensuring action *needn't* be free – is extremely dubious (cf. Franklin 2011: 212), the second interpretation of (SE-2) is itself extremely dubious. In sum, on the first interpretation, (SE-2) commits the Selection Argument's proponent to the impossibility of morally responsible action (assuming that the Freedom Requirement holds), while on the second interpretation (SE-2) remains too dubious for the Selection Argument to succeed. However we interpret (SE-2), then, the Selection Argument does not adequately support premise (MI-2) of the *Mind* Argument for the Unfreedom Lemma.

Let's pause briefly to take stock. We have now completed a critical discussion, which began back in Section 5.2, of the main visible luck-involving arguments for the Proximal Determination Requirement. We have found, I submit, that none of these arguments constitutes a good reason to believe the Proximal Determination Requirement. The largely critical line of argument developed throughout this and the last chapter amounts, I believe, to a reasonably thorough *defense* of the possibility of proximally undetermined directly morally responsible action. Such a defense, however, provides little positive reason to believe that proximally undetermined directly morally responsible action really is possible. Providing good reason to believe in the possibility of such action (that is, that the Proximal Determination Requirement is *false*) is the aim of the next section. I'll start by setting out three different nonpartisan arguments against the Proximal Determination Requirement:[22] an argument inspired by Mele (2006, 2013), an argument developed by Fischer (2011, 2014), and a novel argument that I'll call the 'Possibility Argument'. I will argue that whereas the lines of thought suggested by Mele and Fischer fail, the Possibility Argument succeeds, thus providing good reason to believe in the possibility of proximally undetermined directly morally responsible action.

6.3 Three arguments against the Proximal Determination Requirement

Here is the argument for the possibility of proximally undetermined directly morally responsible action that I will defend later in this section:

The Possibility Argument

(PO-1) Possibly, some (finite, temporal) agent is directly morally responsible for some action that s/he performed.

(PO-2) If it's possible that some agent is directly morally responsible for some action that s/he performed, then it's possible that some agent is directly morally responsible for a *proximally undetermined* action that s/he performed.

(~Proximal Determination Requirement) So, it's possible that some agent is directly morally responsible for a proximally undetermined action that s/he performed.

The Possibility Argument is clearly valid. On the extremely plausible assumption that some (finite, temporal) agent is morally responsible for some action A only if s/he is *directly* morally responsible for some action A* (where A* may be identical with A), (PO-1) is logically equivalent to the highly intuitively plausible Possibility Thesis (= morally responsible action is possible), which I've already defended from the most likely arguments against it (see Section 5.1 above). Later in this section, I will provide support for and defense of (PO-2) – which, as I've already mentioned a couple times, will be neutral on the question whether proximally determined directly morally responsible action is possible. First, though, it will be instructive to contrast the Possibility Argument with two other recent arguments against the Proximal Determination

Requirement, those suggested by Fischer (2011: 94ff., 2014; cf. Vargas 2012: 424ff.) and Mele (2013: 249ff.; cf. 2006: 129ff.).

We'll start with Fischer's argument against the Proximal Determination Requirement, which he nicely summarizes in the following passage:

> Let's suppose...that we have some sufficiently determinate intuitive notion of 'the way a causal sequence goes,' where this notion abstracts away from whether causal determinism obtains or not. We now suppose that in [possible world] W1 the actual causal sequence goes in the 'normal' way typically thought to ground attributions of moral responsibility, apart from considerations pertinent to causal determination. Now add to W1 that causal determinism does in fact obtain. It should be widely accepted that, whatever the requisite glue (the responsibility-grounding relationship) is, it obtains in W1. Given that the responsibility-grounding relationship is present in W1 and intuitively cannot be expunged simply because of the existence of [a causally indeterministic relationship between the relevant agent's prior mental states and subsequent choice] in W2, it also is present in W2. (Fischer 2011: 97)

We can state Fischer's argument against the Proximal Determination Requirement as follows:

Fischer's Argument

(FA-1) For some possible deterministic causal sequence CS-1 that involves a directly morally responsible action A done by subject S for reasons R, there's a possible causal sequence CS-2 exactly like CS-1 in which A is proximally *un*determined, being *nondeterministically* caused by R.

(FA-2) If S is directly morally responsible for A in CS-1 *and* CS-2 is exactly like CS-1, then (provided that S's epistemic circumstances in CS-2 are identical to those in CS-1) S is directly morally responsible for A in CS-2 as well.[23]

(~Proximal Determination Requirement) So, possibly, S is directly morally responsible for a proximally undetermined action.

Mele (2013: 249ff.; cf. 2006: 129ff.) suggests an interestingly different argument against the Proximal Determination Requirement, one that appeals not to the alleged supervenience of (the control-related element of) moral responsibility on facts about causal sequences, but instead to the alleged proportionality between (a) the degree to which an agent can be morally responsible for an action s/he performed and (b) the degree to which an agent's responsibility-relevant psychological capacities (intellectual, emotional, and so on) are developed. Here's my reconstruction of the argument that Mele suggests:[24]

The Melean Argument

(MA-1) The degree to which an agent can be morally responsible for an action that s/he performed is limited by the degree to which the agent's responsibility-relevant psychological capacities are developed (cf. Mele 2013: 253).

(MA-2) If the degree to which an agent can be morally responsible for an action that s/he performed is limited by the degree to which the agent's responsibility-relevant psychological capacities are developed, then the 'standards for moral responsibility in young children are plausibly regarded as very modest by comparison with standards for normal adults' (Mele 2013: 250).

(MA-3) If the 'standards for moral responsibility in young children are plausibly regarded as very modest by comparison with standards for normal adults', then '[i]t is conceptually possible that some ordinary young children have a small degree of basic moral responsibility for some of what they do (where a necessary condition of an agent's being *basically* morally responsible for A-ing is that the proximal causes of the action do not deterministically cause it)' (Mele 2013: 253, emphasis in original).

(~Proximal Determination Requirement) So, possibly, S is directly morally responsible for a proximally undetermined action.

I believe that the Possibility Argument stands a better chance of rebutting the Proximal Determination Requirement than do the arguments that Fischer and Mele suggest. To begin to see this, focus on premise (FA-1) of Fischer's Argument and on premise (MA-1) of the Melean Argument:

(FA-1) For some possible deterministic causal sequence CS-1 that involves a directly morally responsible action A done by subject S for reasons R, there's a possible causal sequence CS-2 exactly like CS-1 in which A is proximally *un*determined, being *nondeterministically* caused by R.

(MA-1) The degree to which an agent can be morally responsible for an action that s/he performed is limited by the degree to which the agent's responsibility-relevant psychological capacities are developed.

Each of (FA-1) and (MA-1) is logically stronger than (PO-1) of the Possibility Argument: each of (FA-1) and (MA-1) entails (PO-1), but a proponent of (PO-1) needn't endorse either (FA-1) or (MA-1). So, provided that there's strong reason to accept (PO-2) – as indeed there is, which we'll see in Section 6.3.3 below – the Possibility Argument stands a better chance of rebutting the Proximal Determination Requirement than do the arguments suggested by Fischer and Mele. In fact, I believe that the Possibility Argument is *considerably* stronger than either of these other arguments against the Proximal Determination Requirement, since each of those arguments involves at least one highly questionable premise, as I'll argue in the next two subsections.

6.3.1 Objections to the Melean Argument

Consider again premise (MA-1) of the Melean Argument. (MA-1) seems plausible initially, and it enjoys widespread acceptance across a broad range of theorists working throughout different areas of value theory. However, as Ryberg (2014) brings out in a fascinating recent paper, (MA-1) is by no means obviously true – even on the assumption, which I do regard as obviously correct, that 'there are certain mental capacities that are necessary for the possession of moral...responsibility' (Ryberg 2014: 394). In this subsection, I will present considerations that jointly serve to at least partially undermine, as well as rebut, (MA-1). I believe that these considerations cast enough doubt on (MA-1) to keep the Melean Argument from succeeding to any significant extent (at least in its current state).

To begin, why might (MA-1) initially strike us as plausible? I follow Ryberg (2014: 395) in thinking that the reasoning behind (MA-1) must be something like this:

(I) If S1 and S2 perform morally responsible actions of the same type in a common choice situation *but* S1's responsibility-relevant capacities are less developed than are S2's, then S1 wasn't equipped as well as S2 was to face their common choice situation.[25] (II) If S1 wasn't equipped as well as S2 was to face their common choice situation, then S1 is less morally responsible for the action he performed in that situation than S2 is for the action she performed in that situation. (III) So, if S1 and S2 perform morally responsible actions of the same type in a common choice situation *but* S1's responsibility-relevant capacities are less developed than are S2's, then S1 is less morally responsible for the action he performed in that situation than S2 is for the action she performed in that situation (which is near enough to MA-1).

I have at least two worries about this reasoning. First, here's a less pressing worry that concerns premise (II): If S1 and S2 perform morally *praiseworthy* actions of the same type in a common choice situation, then it may turn out that S1 is *more* morally responsible for his action than S2 is for her action. Suppose, for example, that S1 has considerably less impulse control than S2, so that while S1 and S2 both made the right choice in their shared choice situation, making the right choice was significantly more difficult for S1 than it was for S2. If so, then it may be that S1 is more praiseworthy for his right choice than S2 is for hers, where this is due in part to the fact that S1 wasn't equipped as well as S2 was to face their common choice situation (= ~II).

Second, there's a more pressing worry that concerns premise (I) – and will, I believe, eventually yield a partial rebutter of MA-1. We can start working our way toward a promising attempted counterexample to premise (I) by considering the following cases that falsify analogs of (I) for other kinds of achievement than morally responsible action:

> S1 is an ordinary adult. S2 is an expert mathematician. S1 and S2 confront, and successfully solve, the same relatively easy arithmetical problem. Though S1's mathematical capacities are less developed than are S2's, S1 and S2 were equally well equipped to face their common mathematical task. (Writes Ryberg [2014: 396]: 'Confronted with the simple arithmetical problem, the fact that the mathematician possesses more developed arithmetical capacities [than the ordinary adult] is simply irrelevant'.)

> S1 is an ordinary adult. S2 is an NBA-caliber shooting guard. Under normal practice conditions, S1 and S2 attempt and make relatively easy lay-ups. Though S1's basketball abilities are less developed than are S2's, S1 and S2 were equally well equipped to face their common basketball task.

> S1 is an ordinary child. S2 is an expert bird watcher. Under normal perceptual conditions, S1 and S2 see blue jays in their respective backyards, and they are asked to classify the seen animal as either a blue jay or a bald eagle. Both form knowledge-constituting beliefs that the seen animal is a blue jay. Though S1's bird-identification capacities are less developed than are S2's, S1 and S2 were equally well equipped to face their common bird-identification task.

Reflection on such cases suggests that there may be analogous cases involving morally responsible actions that falsity (I) itself. Consider the following example:

> Subjects S1 and S2 differ significantly in the degrees to which their responsibility-relevant psychological capacities are developed: S1 is a normal child, say, and S2 is a normal adult. Despite the significant difference in the degrees to which their responsibility-relevant psychological capacities are developed, S1 and S2 now find themselves in identical choice situations. That is, S1 and S2 face a common set of available options, among which each must decide. Moreover, this shared choice situation is relatively easy, in the following ways: there are only two options – say, either tell the truth about some recent piece of behavior, or lie about it – and it's obvious to both agents which option is the right one – viz. tell the truth.

It may be that, although S1's responsibility-relevant capacities are less developed than are S2's, S1 and S2 are equally well equipped to (choose to) tell the truth in their shared choice situation. Of course, if they really *are* equally well equipped to (choose to) tell the truth in their shared choice situation, then this case constitutes a counterexample to (I). Without whole-heartedly endorsing this as a counterexample to (I), I do think that reflection on this case and relevantly similar ones casts enough doubt on (I) to keep the reasoning set out above from adequately supporting (MA-1).

Further, once (MA-1) has been undercut by such considerations, we can begin to glimpse at least a partial rebutter of (MA-1). Consider the following view concerning the relevance of degrees of development of responsibility-relevant capacities to moral responsibility:

> The degree to which an agent's responsibility-relevant psychological capacities are developed sets limits on the kinds of actions for which the agent can be morally responsible. However, the degree to which an agent's responsibility-relevant psychological capacities are developed does not set limits on the degree to which the agent can be morally responsible for actions of 'responsibility-eligible' types – that is, action-types whose tokens the agent can be morally responsible for, given the degree to which her responsibility-relevant capacities are developed.

Proponents of this view will agree with advocates of (MA-1) on this much: the degree to which your responsibility-relevant capacities are developed sets limits on how morally responsible you can be for what you do. Nevertheless, the view just sketched is clearly incompatible with (MA-1). Suppose that the view sketched above is correct. Then, while (say) a young child who has no grasp at all on the concept of death could not plausibly be thought morally responsible for killing something (cf. Blumenfeld 2011: 317–18), that very same child might be as morally responsible as an ordinary adult could be for choosing to tell the truth (or to lie) about some recent piece of behavior, in an easy choice situation such as the one described in the last paragraph. But, if a young child might be as morally responsible for some action of hers as an ordinary adult could be for such an action, then (MA-1) is false: the degree to which an agent can be morally responsible for an action is *not* limited by the degree to which the agent's responsibility-relevant capacities are developed. Since the view in question may be true, it serves to at least partially rebut (MA-1), thus preventing the Melean Argument from well supporting the denial of the Proximal Determination Requirement.[26]

6.3.2 Objections to Fischer's Argument

Matters are even worse for Fischer's argument against the Proximal Determination Requirement, for each of its premises is incompatible with the Freedom Requirement (that is, the thesis that S's being directly morally responsible for A strictly implies that S was free with respect to A). I will – at long last – offer some support for and defense of the Freedom Requirement later in this subsection. But first, I need to introduce and argue for one additional thesis, what I'll call the

Proximal *Non*determination Requirement: Necessarily, if S was free with respect to A, then A was *not* proximally determined.

Here's an argument for the Proximal Nondetermination Requirement that should strike many readers as familiar:[27]

Assume, for conditional proof, that (finite, temporal) S's action A was proximally determined (that is, logically entailed by the immediate past and laws of nature). This assumption entails that A's absence was, in the circumstances, *physically impossible* – that is, A's absence, conjoined with the whole truth about the immediate past, entails that some or other prevailing law of nature is false. Now suppose, for reductio, that it is logically possible that S was free in the circumstances to *omit* A. Since A's absence was in the circumstances physically impossible, the reductio assumption entails that it's (logically or metaphysically) possible that S was free to do something that was, in the circumstances, physically impossible. Simply put, it's possible that S was on this occasion free to perform a miracle. But necessarily, S wasn't then free to perform a miracle – that is, necessarily, S wasn't then free to do something that was, in the circumstances, physically impossible (cf. van Inwagen 2004: 349). So the reductio assumption must be false: necessarily, S was *not* in the circumstances free to omit A. Therefore, necessarily, if S's action A was proximally determined, then S was not free with respect to A – and this claim is, by contraposition, equivalent to the Proximal Nondetermination Requirement.

The only *potentially* questionable step in this argument is the premise that our arbitrarily selected (finite, temporal) agent, S, not only does not but could not have had it within her power to do something that was, in the circumstances, physically impossible. Putting it very mildly, this premise enjoys a great deal of prima facie intuitive plausibility.[28] Note well: the premise in question leaves wide open the possibility that some (finite, temporal) agent *make a causal contribution toward* the occurrence of something that was, in the circumstances, physically impossible. In other words, the key premise leaves wide open the possibility that some (finite, temporal) agent *play a causal role in* the occurrence of a miracle. This is because S's having it within her power to causally contribute toward E doesn't suffice for S's having it within her power (being free) to do (bring about) E. Consider: A young child may have it within her power to causally contribute toward (or, play a causal role in) her arriving at school on time – by, for example, cooperatively climbing into her car seat upon entering the car, rather than hunkering down in the back seat for several minutes – while not having it within her power (or, being free) to arrive at school on time (which requires a working car, an adult driver, and so on).

Having provided some support for the Proximal Nondetermination Requirement, we're now in a position to consider an argument against (FA-1) and (FA-2), in whose light these premises should at best seem highly questionable. Recall those premises:

> **(FA-1)** For some possible deterministic causal sequence CS-1 that involves a directly morally responsible action A done by subject S for reasons R, there's a possible causal sequence CS-2 exactly like CS-1 in which A is proximally *un*determined, being *nondeterministically* caused by R.

(FA-2) If S is directly morally responsible for A in CS-1 *and* CS-2 is exactly like CS-1, then (provided that S's epistemic circumstances in CS-2 are identical to those in CS-1) S is directly morally responsible for A in CS-2 as well.

Here's the argument against (FA-1) and (FA-2):

If the Freedom Requirement is true, then both (FA-1) and (FA-2) are false. The Freedom Requirement is true. So, both (FA-1) and (FA-2) are false.

What can be said on behalf of this argument's premises? First, an argument for the claim that (FA-1) is false *provided that* the Freedom Requirement is true. If (FA-1) is true, then it's possible that some agent, S, be directly morally responsible for a proximally determined act, A. But this is *not* possible if the Freedom Requirement is true. Again, the Freedom Requirement says that, necessarily, if S is directly morally responsible for A, then S was free with respect to A. But, necessarily, if S was free with respect to A, then A was not proximally determined (= the Proximal Nondetermination Requirement). So, if the Freedom Requirement is true, then necessarily, if S is directly morally responsible for A, then A was not proximally determined – which entails that (FA-1) is false.

Next, an argument for the claim that (FA-2) is false *provided that* the Freedom Requirement is true. Suppose that S is directly morally responsible for action A in causal sequence CS. Either S was free to omit A *or* S was not free to omit A. If S was not free to omit A, then there's a possible causal sequence, CS*, exactly like CS – viz. CS *itself* – in which S lacks the freedom to omit A. By (FA-2), S is directly morally responsible for A in CS* yet lacks the freedom to omit A – which entails that the Freedom Requirement is false. Now suppose instead that S *was* free to omit A in CS. Intuitively, S's being free to omit A is not among the causes of A. So, by (FA-2), there's a possible causal sequence CS* exactly like CS (epistemically relevant features included) such that S is directly morally responsible for A yet lacks the freedom to omit A – which, again, entails that the Freedom Requirement is false. We can conclude, then, that if (FA-2) is true, then the Freedom Requirement is false. Contrapositively, if the Freedom Requirement is true, then (FA-2) is false.

We turn, finally, to the Freedom Requirement itself. The Freedom Requirement enjoys a good deal of prima facie plausibility. In addition to its considerable intuitive appeal (cf. O'Connor 2000: 20–2), there's the following best explanation argument for it: One good way to defend yourself from an ascription of direct moral responsibility for some action is to provide the attributer with strong evidence that you were not in fact free with respect to said action. The truth of the Freedom Requirement is the obvious explanation of why such a defensive maneuver can successfully block an ascription of direct moral responsibility for some action.[29]

Considerations of this sort can't seal the deal for the Freedom Requirement all by themselves, however, for there are challenging attempted counterexamples to the Freedom Requirement, cases that trace their lineage back to an important and influential example that Harry Frankfurt described in his classic 1969 *Journal of Philosophy* article 'Alternate Possibilities and Moral Responsibility'. Here's a recent, and relatively promising, attempted counterexample to the Freedom Requirement, in the mold of the influential case that Frankfurt described in his article (such examples have – naturally enough, and as many readers will already know – come to be called **Frankfurt Cases**):

> *Bob's Choice:* Black initiates a certain internally deterministic process P in Bob's brain at t1 with the intention of thereby causing Bob to decide at t2 (an hour later, say) to steal Ann's car. The process, which is screened off from Bob's consciousness, will culminate in Bob's deciding at t2 to steal Ann's car unless he decides on his own at t2 to steal it or is incapable at t2 of making a decision (because, for example, he is dead by t2). The process is in no way sensitive to any 'sign' of what Bob will decide. As it happens, at t2 Bob decides on his own to steal the car, on the basis of his own indeterministic deliberation about whether to steal it, and his decision is not deterministically caused. But if he had not just then decided on his own to steal it, P would have issued, at t2, in his deciding to steal it. Rest assured that P in no way influences the indeterministic decision-making process that actually issues in Bob's decision. (Mele 2006: 88; cf. Mele and Robb 1998, 2003)

The Freedom Requirement's critic will invite us to intuit that, in the case at hand, Bob is directly blameworthy (and thus, directly morally responsible) for his decision to steal Ann's car, notwithstanding the fact that Bob was not free to omit that decision (and thus, not free with respect to that decision).

In reply, a defender of the Freedom Requirement can raise the following crucial question:

> Would the very same decision to steal Ann's car that Bob actually made still have happened had the process P caused Bob to decide to steal Ann's car?

If the Freedom Requirement's critic answers negatively, then the Freedom Requirement's defender can plausibly claim (contrary to the critic's follow-up commentary on the case) that Bob was indeed free to omit his actual decision to steal Ann's car (cf. Mele 2006: 91–2), and so that *Bob's Choice* is not a counterexample to the Freedom Requirement after all (regardless of whether Bob is directly blameworthy for his decision). By hypothesis, Bob was free to not decide to steal Ann's car *on his own*. Under the current assumption, had Bob exercised this freedom, the decision he actually made would not have occurred. So, on our current assumptions about the case, Bob was indeed free to omit the decision he actually made.

On the other hand, if the Freedom Requirement's critic answers affirmatively – that is, the critic maintains that Bob's actual decision would still have happened had the process P caused Bob to decide to steal Ann's car – then the Freedom Requirement's defender can set out the following promising argument for the conclusion that Bob isn't directly blameworthy for his decision to steal Ann's car (for development and defense of this line of reasoning, see Widerker 2000, 2005 and Palmer 2013; cf. Otsuka 1998, section II):

> If the very same decision to steal Ann's car that Bob actually made would still have happened had the process P caused Bob to decide to steal Ann's car, then Bob was going to make that very decision to steal Ann's car *no matter what*. Now, if Bob was going to make that very decision to steal Ann's car *no matter what*, then no morally competent observer who knows all the relevant non-moral facts about Bob's situation could reasonably expect or demand that Bob *omit* that decision. But, an agent S is directly blameworthy for some action A that s/he performed only if it at least *might* be reasonable for a morally competent observer who knows all relevant non-moral facts about S's situation to expect or demand that S omit A. Therefore, since (as we're now interpreting the case) Bob was going to make the very decision to steal Ann's car that he actually made *no matter what*, Bob is not directly blameworthy for that decision after all.

Here, then, is the upshot of our discussion so far: Whatever intuitive evidence one might initially have had for the judgment that Bob is directly blameworthy for – but not free with respect to – his decision to steal Ann's car, that evidence must be weighed against at least two pieces of counterevidence (in addition to whatever intuitive appeal the Freedom Requirement enjoys when considered in isolation): (i) the best explanation argument for the Freedom Requirement sketched above (again, the

Freedom Requirement is the obvious explanation why you can successfully defend yourself from an ascription of direct moral responsibility for some action by providing strong evidence that you were not in fact free with respect to said action); *and* (ii) the argument just sketched for the conclusion that, depending on how we answer the crucial question whether the very same decision to steal Ann's car that Bob actually made would have happened had the process P caused Bob to decide to steal Ann's car, *either* Bob was free to omit his decision *or* he isn't directly blameworthy for his decision. I submit that this body of counterevidence at least slightly outweighs whatever intuitive evidence one might initially have had for thinking that Bob is directly blameworthy for – but not free with respect to – his decision to steal Ann's car. Even in light of Frankfurt Cases such as *Bob's Choice*, then, we have on balance at least some reason to believe the Freedom Requirement (which, it should be noted, is not to say that the Freedom Requirement is on balance reasonable to believe [cf. Audi 2011: 197]). And finally, since (as I argued above) the Freedom Requirement entails that both premises (FA-1) and (FA-2) of Fischer's argument against the Proximal Determination Requirement are false, we are now in a position to conclude that Fischer's Argument fails to defeat the Proximal Determination Requirement.[30]

6.3.3 Defending the Possibility Argument

We've now seen that the arguments against the Proximal Determination Requirement that Fischer and Mele have suggested each involve at least one highly questionable premise. So, provided that each of the Possibility Argument's premises – (PO-1) and (PO-2) – is reasonable on balance, the Possibility Argument is considerably stronger than either of the other two arguments against the Proximal Determination Requirement considered above. Recall those premises:

(PO-1) Possibly, some (finite, temporal) agent is directly morally responsible for some action that s/he performed.

(PO-2) If it's possible that some agent is directly morally responsible for some action that s/he performed, then it's possible that some agent is directly morally responsible for a *proximally undetermined* action that s/he performed.

As I noted earlier, given the extremely plausible assumption that some (finite, temporal) agent is morally responsible for some action A only if s/he is *directly* morally responsible for some action A* (where A* may be identical with A), (PO-1) is logically equivalent to the highly intuitively plausible Possibility Thesis (= morally responsible action is possible), which thesis I've already defended from the most likely arguments against it (see Section 5.1 above). What remains, then, is to provide some support for and defense of (PO-2). That's what I'll do in the remainder of this subsection. I believe that, by the end of this subsection, we'll be well justified in concluding from (PO-1) and (PO-2) that the Proximal Determination Requirement is indeed false. Now, one obvious strategy for supporting (PO-2) involves deploying an argument for the impossibility of proximally determined directly morally responsible action. As I've already noted, however, I'll here be taking a different tack. The upcoming argument for (PO-2) will be neutral on the question whether proximally determined morally responsible action is possible.

I suspect that (PO-2) will have initially struck most readers as considerably less obvious than (PO-1). Be that as it may, there's a surprisingly strong argument for (PO-2) available, which runs as follows:[31]

> Assume, for conditional proof, that (PO-1) is true: Possibly, some agent S is directly morally responsible for some action A that s/he performed.
>
> Trivially, either the Freedom Requirement is true or it's false.
>
> Suppose, first, that the Freedom Requirement is *true*. Then, by the Proximal *Non*determination Requirement, S is directly morally responsible for A *only if* A was not proximally determined. So, given (PO-1), it's possible that S be directly morally responsible for a proximally undetermined action. Therefore, if the Freedom Requirement is true, then the Proximal Determination Requirement is false.
>
> Now suppose, instead, that the Freedom Requirement is *false*. If the Freedom Requirement is false, then it's possible that S be directly morally responsible for an action A that s/he was *not* free to omit. And if it's possible that S be directly morally responsible for an action that s/he was *not* free to omit, then surely it's also possible that S be directly morally responsible for an action that s/he *was* free to omit. Now, by the Proximal Nondetermination Requirement, if S performs an action that s/he was free to omit, then that action was not proximally determined. So, if it's possible that S be directly morally responsible for an action that s/he was free to omit, then it's possible that S be directly morally responsible for an action that was not proximally determined (that is, the Proximal Determination Requirement

is false). Therefore, if the Freedom Requirement is false, then (once again) the Proximal Determination Requirement is false.

And so we can conclude, by conditional proof, that (PO-2) is true: the possibility of directly morally responsible action (= PO-1) entails the possibility of *proximally undetermined* directly morally responsible action (= the denial of the Proximal Determination Requirement).

This argument for (PO-2) is clearly valid. It has only two substantive basic premises: the Proximal Nondetermination Requirement, and the claim that an agent could be directly morally responsible for an action that s/he was free to omit *provided that* s/he could be directly morally responsible for an action that s/he wasn't free to omit. Since we've already seen a compelling argument for the Proximal Nondetermination Requirement (Section 6.3.2), I will move immediately to defending the claim that an agent could be directly morally responsible for an action that s/he *was* free to omit provided that s/he could be directly morally responsible for an action that s/he *wasn't* free to omit. More fully: If the Freedom Requirement is false, then there is at least one possible case that falsifies the Freedom Requirement such that adding to it the detail that its protagonist was free to omit the relevant action *needn't* make that action any worse a candidate for directly morally responsible action than it is absent such freedom. Here's the reasoning behind this conditional claim:

> If there are possible cases in which an agent is directly morally responsible for an action that s/he wasn't free to omit, then 'indeterministic' Frankfurt Cases such as *Bob's Choice* are among such cases.[32] Now if, in *Bob's Choice*, Bob is directly morally responsible for his decision to steal Ann's car having lacked the freedom to omit that decision, then there's a possible case that is similar to (albeit more realistic than) *Bob's Choice* – call it **Bob's Choice*** – in which there are no fail-safe mechanisms like process P around, and as a result Bob is not only directly morally responsible for his decision to steal Ann's car but was also free to omit that decision.[33] So, if there are possible cases in which an agent is directly morally responsible for an action that s/he *wasn't* free to omit, then there are possible cases in which an agent is directly morally responsible for an action that s/he *was* free to omit.

So far as I can tell, a very broad range of theorists on either side of the current debate over the truth value of the Freedom Requirement (and related principles) will be amenable to this reasoning. Indeed,

Haji (2012: 202–3) is the only theorist I know of who would definitely reject the above argument. According to Haji, while certain Frankfurt Cases are counterexamples to the Freedom Requirement, indeterministic Frankfurt Cases such as *Bob's Choice* do not involve directly morally responsible action, and so cannot impugn the Freedom Requirement. If Haji is right about this, then the first step of the above argument is false. In what follows, I will simply grant Haji's (2012: 203ff.) contention that his favored Frankfurt Cases are in fact counterexamples to the Freedom Requirement, focusing instead on his reason for denying that *Bob's Choice* involves directly morally responsible action.

Why does Haji deny that Bob is (in *Bob's Choice*) directly morally responsible for his decision to steal Ann's car? In response to a recent suggestion of mine (Coffman 2010b: 163f.) that cases such as *Bob's Choice* should strike many theorists as persuasive counterexamples to the Proximal Determination Requirement *regardless* of whether the Freedom Requirement is true, Haji (2012: 203) says the following:[34]

> [I]t is not evident why a proponent of the luck objection should accept the view that an agent, such as Bob, in an 'indeterministic' Frankfurt case, is morally responsible for his decision.... After all, it is open to the proponent to argue that absent the fail-safe mechanism in [*Bob's Choice*], Bob is not morally responsible for his decision to steal Ann's car because the decision is a matter of luck. 'Addition' to the case of the fail-safe mechanism should not undermine this verdict unless one has an explanation to the contrary.

Haji reasons that, since Bob could not be directly morally responsible for his decision to steal Ann's car in a (relatively realistic) case such as *Bob's Choice** (which, recall, differs from *Bob's Choice* in that it's devoid of fail-safe mechanisms like process P), Bob couldn't be directly morally responsible for his decision to steal Ann's car in *Bob's Choice* either. Haji's reasoning here assumes that Bob could be directly morally responsible for his decision to steal Ann's car in *Bob's Choice* only if he could also be directly morally responsible for his decision to steal Ann's car in *Bob's Choice**. Haji and I obviously agree on this assumption. But whereas (under the assumption that the Freedom Requirement is false) I reason that Bob could be directly morally responsible for the relevant decision in *Bob's Choice** since he could be directly morally responsible for that decision in *Bob's Choice*, Haji reverses this reasoning: he infers that Bob couldn't be directly morally responsible for the relevant decision in *Bob's Choice* from the premise that Bob couldn't be directly morally responsible for that decision in *Bob's Choice**. Why does Haji endorse that premise?

Haji endorses that premise on the basis of an argument that he refers to as the 'luck objection' in the passage quoted above. Here's a version of what Haji calls the 'luck objection' applied specifically to Bob in *Bob's Choice** (for Haji's development and defense of this kind of argument, see his 2012: 195ff. and 2006: 186–7):

> **(1)** In *Bob's Choice**, Bob's deciding (at t2) *not* to steal Ann's car is logically consistent with the immediate past and laws of nature. **(2)** If Bob had decided (at t2) *not* to steal Ann's car, then that 'negative' decision would have resulted from exactly the same deliberative process that actually issued in Bob's 'positive' decision to steal Ann's car. **(3)** So, the deliberative process that actually issued in Bob's decision to steal Ann's car might (in the circumstances) have instead issued in the opposite decision *not* to steal Ann's car. **(4)** If a deliberative process might (in the circumstances) have issued in *either* of two opposing decisions, then whichever decision the process actually gives rise to is 'a matter of luck', in the sense that nothing about the deliberative process explains why the decision occurs. **(5)** So, nothing about the deliberative process that actually issues in Bob's decision to steal Ann's car explains that decision. **(6)** If Bob's decision to steal Ann's car isn't explained by anything about the deliberative process that gives rise to it, then Bob is not directly morally responsible for that decision. **(7)** So, in *Bob's Choice**, Bob is not directly morally responsible for his decision (at t2) to steal Ann's car.

Attentive readers will no doubt recognize this (1)–(7) argument as a slightly more elaborate version of the No Explanation Argument discussed in Section 6.1 above, applied specifically to Bob in *Bob's Choice**. The same objection that I pressed against the No Explanation Argument above applies also to the (1)–(7) argument. Specifically, a proponent of step (4) must *either* implausibly deny that a reason-state R's nondeviantly causing an action A suffices for A's being done for (or, based on) R *or* implausibly deny that we can explain why an action A happened by citing a reason R for which A was performed (or, on which A was based). So far as I can see, then, it remains reasonable on balance to accept the following portion of my overall argument for (PO-2):

> If the Freedom Requirement is false, then cases like *Bob's Choice* are among those that falsify it. And if cases like *Bob's Choice* falsify

the Freedom Requirement, then cases like *Bob's Choice** falsify the Proximal Determination Requirement. Therefore, if the Freedom Requirement is false, then the Proximal Determination Requirement is false as well.

I've now provided support for and defense of premises (PO-1) and (PO-2) of the Possibility Argument for the denial of the Proximal Determination Requirement. At this point, I think we can safely infer from (PO-1) and (PO-2) that the Proximal Determination Requirement is indeed false: it's at least *possible* that some agent be directly morally responsible for an action whose occurrence was not entailed by the immediate past and laws of nature, an action whose *absence* was logically consistent with the immediate past and laws.

* * *

My overarching goal in Chapters 5 and 6 has been to demonstrate that the (relatively weak and plausible) thesis that morally responsible action is at least *possible* can help us to see not only that none of the main visible luck-involving threats to the scope of metaphysically free and morally responsible action ultimately materializes but also that luck itself as well as various other luck-related phenomena – including, perhaps most prominently on the contemporary action-theoretical scene, an action's being proximally *un*determined – are a good deal more congenial to metaphysically free and morally responsible action than is typically thought.[35] I submit that the defensive and offensive arguments in support of this conclusion that I have presented and defended across the last chapter and this one jointly constitute a significant step in the direction of mitigating salient action-theoretical worries about the compatibility of metaphysical freedom and moral responsibility, on the one hand, with luck itself and various other luck-related phenomena, on the other.

Coda

Let me draw this book to a close by setting out a more detailed summary of its main results than I was in a position to provide back in the preface.

Contrary to what recent theorists of luck have assumed, their main target of analysis – viz. the concept of an event's being *lucky for* a subject – is actually a disjunctive concept that is parasitic on the more fundamental notion of an event's being a *stroke of luck for* a subject. This thesis serves as at least a partial diagnosis of the failure of the literature's leading accounts of lucky events. Roughly, a significant event is lucky for you just in case that event is *either* itself a stroke of luck for you *or* due primarily to something that was a stroke of luck for you, where a significant event is a stroke of luck for you just in case the event could well have failed to happen and is not something that you did intentionally. The Enriched Strokes Account of lucky events, which conjoins the following two biconditionals, constitutes a relatively precise statement of the theory of lucky events that I've settled on:

The Strokes Account: Event E is at t (un)lucky for subject S iff (i) E is in some respect good (bad) for S and (ii) there's a stroke of good (bad) luck for S, E*, such that *either* (a) E = E* *or* (b) E* is a primary (chief, main) contributor to E.

The Analysis: E is at t a stroke of good (bad) luck for S iff (1) E is in some respect good (bad) for S; (2**) in a wide class of possible worlds that are close to the actual world before t, E doesn't happen around t nor does the process that actually generated E yield around t an event as good (bad) for S as E is; and (3) E isn't something that S did intentionally.

Turning to some central epistemological issues, if the Enriched Strokes Account of lucky events is true, then several different basic roles that luck can play in cognition are compatible with knowledge. Specifically, it is possible that a subject S's belief, B, constitutes knowledge even though each of the following is a stroke of luck for S: S is an existing thinker; S holds B; S has some evidence for B's propositional content; B is based on some portion of S's evidence for B's content; B's content is true. So, luck is in many ways highly congenial to propositional knowledge. Reflection on luck thus seems unlikely to reveal surprising limits on the scope of such knowledge among thinkers like us.

The Risk of Misleading Justification Approach to gettiered belief – which differs importantly from each of the literature's two leading approaches to gettiered belief (viz. the Ease of Mistake and Lack of Credit Approaches) – provides the most promising substantive account of gettiered belief. I settled on the following strain of this approach:

> **RMJA$_2$**: Subject S's belief B that P held in way W is gettiered at t iff (B is justified and true but) S *either* actually is at t justified, in a way like W, in believing many P-like falsehoods *or* could well have been so justified then.

In addition to properly handling all the cases that bedevil competing accounts, this analysis yields its own plausible explanation of the (prima facie) superiority of knowledge over mere gettiered belief. If the Enriched Strokes Account of lucky events is correct, then my favored analysis of gettiered belief does not involve the concept of luck itself (though it does employ one of that notion's core conceptual components, what I earlier labeled '*decent* possibility'). Therefore, since what strikes me as the most promising substantive account of gettiered belief does not involve the concept of luck, reflection on luck seems to me unlikely (in and of itself) to shed much light on the nature of propositional knowledge.

Turning from epistemological to action-theoretical issues, if luck itself or some other luck-related phenomenon threatens to limit the scope of free and responsible action among agents like us, it does so by way of one or another luck-involving argument for the Proximal Determination Requirement: the thesis that no one could be directly morally responsible for an action whose absence was logically consistent with the immediate past and laws of nature. Against the backdrop of the Enriched Strokes Account, the thesis that morally responsible action is possible (= the Possibility Thesis) helps us to see that (i) an agent could be both free with respect to and morally responsible for an action whose occurrence was at least partly a matter of luck for that agent; (ii) every visible luck-involving argument for the Proximal Determination Requirement fails; and (iii) the Proximal Determination Requirement is false. The Possibility Thesis helps us to see that the Proximal Determination Requirement is false by way of this reasoning:

> Morally responsible action is possible. So, if the Freedom Requirement (= one is directly responsible for an action only if one was free to omit it) is true, then the Proximal Determination Requirement is false, since an agent was free to omit an action only if it was proximally undetermined. On the other hand, if the Freedom Requirement is false, then an agent could be directly responsible for an action s/he wasn't free to omit. But then an agent could also be directly responsible for an action s/he *was* free to omit, which entails the denial of the Proximal Determination Requirement, since (again) an agent was free to omit an action only if it was proximally undetermined. Either way, the Proximal Determination Requirement is false.

Not only do all the main visible luck-related threats to the scope of free and responsible action among agents like us fail to materialize, but luck itself as well as various other luck-related phenomena turn out to be a good deal more congenial to free and responsible action than is typically thought.

And so, as was forecast back in the preface, the overall view of luck's significance for human knowledge and agency that has emerged over the course of this book is at once both optimistic and pessimistic. The view is optimistic in that it sees knowledge and metaphysically free, morally responsible agency as compatible with a surprisingly wide range of luck-related phenomena. The view is pessimistic in that it sees reflection on the concept of luck as unlikely (in and of itself) to shed much light on the nature of knowledge and free, responsible agency or to reveal surprising limits on the scope of these important phenomena among people like us.

Notes

1 Lucky Events: The Current Debate and a New Proposal

1. Noteworthy contributions include Rescher (1995), Latus (2003), Pritchard (2005), Riggs (2007, 2009a), Lackey (2008), and Levy (2009, 2011a); other contributions include Coffman (2007, 2009).
2. Chapters 1 and 2 expand on Coffman (2014).
3. In these first two chapters, I'll draw on both Coffman (2007) and (2009). Anyone familiar with those works will notice that I now diverge from them at some key points. As I see it, a large part of what explains the fact that there are wide areas of agreement – but also some sharp disagreements – between my past and present selves over the nature of luck is that I haven't up till now been sufficiently clear on the (as I now see it) crucial point that some lucky events (the indirectly lucky ones) derive their status as such from *other* lucky events (the directly lucky ones) whose status as such is not so derived.
4. The last two sentences owe much to Bennett (1988) as well as Paul and Hall (2013).
5. Throughout, I'll be assuming that we have a sufficiently good intuitive sense of how much certain states of affairs differ from certain others.
6. For careful development of an influential version of the Modal Account, see Pritchard (2005). (Henceforth, I'll typically suppress the parenthetical 'occurrence' condition, which should be assumed in all the accounts of luck discussed below.)
7. This nuanced version of the Control Account is from Riggs (2009a). For simpler versions of the Control Account see Nagel (1979), Zimmerman (1987), Statman (1991), and Greco (1995). We'll consider Riggs' rationale for adding condition (ii) below.
8. For recent versions of the Mixed Account, see Coffman (2007), Riggs (2007), and Levy (2009, 2011a).
9. Thanks to Georgi Gardiner for helping me get clearer on the issues addressed in this paragraph.
10. This case is inspired by one from Williamson (2000: 123).
11. Recall from Section 1.1 that modally fragile doesn't entail undetermined. My claims here are therefore entirely neutral on the issue whether undetermined events can be acts done intentionally, freely, and knowingly. See Chapters 5 and 6 below for a thorough discussion of such action-theoretical issues.
12. To be fair, Riggs (2007: 338–9) thinks that even if such cases aren't clear counterexamples to the Modal Account's claim of sufficiency for luck, they nevertheless enable a somewhat subtler criticism of the account. I'm here defending such cases' status as clear counterexamples to the Modal Account's right-to-left conditional.
13. Incidentally, I believe that the kind of error theory sketched here will serve, *mutatis mutandis*, to defend Lackey's (2008: 259–60) 'Derek' counterexample

to the Control Account from the claim that the event she deems lucky for her subject (viz., the making of a close-range lay-up) really isn't. Matters are more complicated when it comes to Lackey's 'Demolition Worker' case, due to some problematic ambiguity in its details; see Section 2.2 below for discussion of this case.
14. See the introductory section of Chapter 5 for a more thorough characterization of the direct/indirect moral responsibility distinction.
15. Thanks to Devon Bryson, David Palmer, and Carolina Sartorio for helping me develop this analogy.
16. The first two examples are adapted from Bennett (1988: 21ff.).
17. The following argument can be adapted to show that replacing 'is a primary contributor to' with 'is counterfactually sufficient for' would also make the Strokes Account too weak. I leave such adaptation as homework for interested readers.
18. Thanks to Georgi Gardiner for suggesting an example that inspired this one.
19. Notably, a similar treatment applies as well to the following case from Coffman (2007: 395), which someone might initially regard as a counterexample to the Strokes Account's left-to-right conditional: 'A nefarious brain scientist, Ned, is *extremely* reliable – though not *infallible* – when it comes to predicting at t1 whether Jones will at t2 choose to perform a right action, A, at t3. Were he to predict at t1 that Jones will at t2 choose to A at t3, Ned would interfere so that Jones is unable to make the relevant choice at t2. Suppose Ned predicts that Jones *won't* make the relevant choice, and so leaves Jones alone. As it happens, Ned's prediction is wrong: Jones in fact chooses at t2 to A at t3.' (This case, which an anonymous referee suggested to me several years ago, is clearly inspired by Harry Frankfurt's [1969] famous attempted counterexample to what he calls the 'Principle of Alternate Possibilities'.) A critic of the Strokes Account's left-to-right conditional might claim that Jones wasn't at t2 *lucky* that he chose to A, despite the fact that his choice was good for him and due primarily to a prior stroke of good luck for him – viz., Ned's incorrect prediction. I accept the claim that Jones wasn't lucky that he chose to A, but I reject the claim that Jones's choice to A was due *primarily* to Ned's mistaken prediction (though I'm open to the claim that the latter made at least a fairly large contribution to the former). Rather, the case is best understood so that Jones's choice to A was due *primarily* to his having whatever reasons he had in favor of A-ing (perhaps along with an intention to make up his mind about A-ing).
20. Of course, 'is a primary contributor to' is vague. But that's not obviously a strike against analyzing luck in terms of primary contribution. Indeed, the observation may well count in favor of such an analysis, given the vagueness of 'is (un)lucky for'.
21. Thanks to Georgi Gardiner, Maria Lasonen-Aarnio, and Douglas MacLean for suggesting cases that inspired this one.
22. I note, in passing, an interesting structural difference between *Drawing Marbles* and *Buried Treasure*. *Drawing Marbles* features a fragile outcome of multiple individually robust phenomena. By contrast, *Buried Treasure* should be interpreted as featuring a robust outcome of phenomena at least some of which were individually fragile (cf. Lackey 2008: 263–4). See Section 2.4 below for additional pertinent discussion of *Buried Treasure*. (Thanks to Lee Whittington for comments that led me to add this note.)

23. Thanks to Georgi Gardiner and Lee Whittington for helping me think through this objection to the Strokes Account.
24. For a brief but helpful survey, see Zagzebski 2011 (especially Section 2.3).
25. Here and elsewhere, '[P]' abbreviates 'the proposition that P'.

2 What Is a Stroke of Luck? Enriching the Strokes Account

1. Following other recent theorists of luck (for example, Pritchard 2005, Levy 2011a), I here employ a familiar notion of objective chance (or risk) on which the chance (or risk), just before t, that an event E will happen at t is equal to the size of the set of worlds that are close to actuality before t in which E happens at t, divided by the size of the whole set of worlds that are close to actuality before t. (This note is indebted to van Inwagen [1997: 231ff.] and also to Williamson [2000: 123–4].)
2. In line with my relatively broad use of 'do' (see the last paragraph of the introductory section of Chapter 1), I here use 'produce' ('prevent') in a broad sense that covers both *causal production* (*causation of omission*) for events proper and *actualization* (*keeping from obtaining*) for states of affairs.
3. Something like the claim to which this note is appended animates the 'Luck Argument(s)' (as they're called) against libertarianism about metaphysical freedom (the thesis that metaphysical freedom exists and is incompatible with the truth of causal determinism). For a helpful critical survey of historical and contemporary luck-driven objections to libertarianism, see Franklin (2011). In Chapters 5 and 6, I'll bring the overall theory of luck currently under construction to bear on some of the most prominent objections to libertarianism.
4. According to Mele and Moser (1994: 45), it doesn't follow from the fact that an act, A, was not done intentionally that it was done *un*intentionally: 'There is a middle ground between A-ing intentionally and A-ing unintentionally. We locate "side-effect actions" of the kind in question on that ground. Insofar as such actions are not done unknowingly, inadvertently, or accidentally, they are not unintentional. Insofar as the agent is not aiming at the performance of these actions, either as ends or as means to (or constituents of) ends, they are not intentional either.'
5. Mele (2006: 25) presents the following intriguing case: 'Intending to vote for Gore, [Al] pulled the Gore lever in a Florida voting booth. Unbeknownst to Al, that lever was attached to an indeterministic randomizing device: pulling it gave him only a 0.001 chance of actually voting for Gore. Luckily, he succeeded in producing a Gore vote. It is very plausible that Al's voting for Gore was too lucky to count as an intentional action... However, if there are free actions, it is difficult to see why Al's voting for Gore is not among them, other things being equal.' Suppose Al freely votes for Gore in this case. Then, since it's very plausible that his successfully voting for Gore was a stroke of luck for Al, it's very plausible that there could be a free action that's a stroke of luck for its agent. But even if this is correct, since Al's voting for Gore is clearly only an *indirectly* free action – that is, a free action that owes its status as such to some *prior* free action – the case doesn't establish the logically stronger, and initially quite counterintuitive, claim that there could be a *directly* free action that's also a stroke of luck for its agent.

6. There are at least a couple of fairly obvious and straightforward arguments that one might employ in an effort to bolster the indicated assumption's plausibility. Here's the first: (P1) All directly free acts are decisions (cf. Widerker 1995, Pereboom 2001, Mele 2006). (P2) All decisions are intentional actions (cf. Mele 2003a). (C1) All directly free acts are done intentionally. The problem with this argument is (P1), for it's arguable that there can be directly free overt acts (cf. Clarke 2003: 122–3, Coffman 2011a: 272–3). Briefly (cf. Coffman 2011a: 273): Suppose you think that even the simplest overt free acts – for example, freely blinking or nodding – must derive their freedom from some prior free mental act (for example, a free decision to blink/nod). Because the required mental act seems no simpler or easier than the relevant overt act, it seems you're committed – on pain of treating like cases differently – to saying that the required mental act is itself free *only if* it's preceded by a further free mental act (for example, a free choice to decide to blink/nod). Parallel considerations will then force you to say that the second required mental act is itself free *only if* it's preceded by yet another free mental act. Upshot: You're committed to thinking that any free act whatsoever is preceded by infinitely many free acts – not a pretty picture! We should conclude, then, that there can indeed be directly free overt acts: free overt acts that don't derive their freedom from any prior free acts (mental *or* overt).

    Here's a second, much more promising argument for the thesis in question: (P1) Any directly free act is an act its agent does for a reason (cf. Levy 2011a: 64). (P2) Any act an agent does for a reason is something its agent does intentionally (cf. Mele and Moser 1994: 64). (C1) All directly free acts are done intentionally. If a skeptical interlocutor pressed for further reasons to accept the claim that any directly free act is something its agent does intentionally, I'd lead with the argument just set out.
7. Cf. Nagel (1979), Zimmerman (1987), Statman (1991), Greco (1995), Coffman (2007, 2009), and Levy (2009, 2011a).
8. See the introductory section of Chapter 5 for additional discussion of the concept here expressed by 'free to', which is often called 'metaphysical freedom'.
9. See Coffman (2009: 503–4).
10. Wayne Riggs has been especially influential on this front.
11. Of course, you intentionally placed the cat in potentially lethal circumstances; but that's not the same thing as intentionally killing the cat.
12. For further discussion of so called 'resultant moral luck' as well as a related phenomenon that is sometimes called 'act-focused situational moral luck', see Section 5.1 below.
13. See the introductory section of Chapter 5 for further discussion of the direct/indirect moral responsibility distinction.
14. In fact, I suspect that the claim to which this note is appended will turn out to be false; see Section 5.3.1 for pertinent discussion. For present purposes, though, I'm simply setting this worry aside.
15. Mele (2003b: 447) distinguishes among three kinds of 'specific abilities' (that is, 'an ability an agent has at a time to A then or to A on some specified later occasion'): *simple* ability to A, a kind of ability you have provided that you actually perform A; ability to A *intentionally*; and *promise-level* ability to A, a

kind of ability you must take yourself to have in order to *sincerely promise* to A. We can understand *Rigged Lottery* and *Two Buttons* as involving any of the three kinds of specific abilities that Mele distinguishes (I leave such modification as homework for interested readers). Those two cases thus serve to support all the most likely readings of Theses 1 and 2.

16. Special thanks to Doug MacLean and Susan Wolf for extremely helpful conversations about the issues explored over the last several paragraphs.
17. I don't mean to attribute this objection to Lackey. Her commentary on the case clearly commits her to the following: the warehouse's explosion is, for Ramona, a lucky event that she (indirectly) freely caused (by freely pressing the button). This claim is consistent with both the Strokes Account and the Analysis, and I'm now happy to accept it (contrast Coffman 2009, which I now view as mistaken). An event's being lucky for a subject doesn't entail that the event is a stroke of luck for the subject, and an act's being *indirectly* free doesn't suffice for its being done intentionally (cf. Mele 2006: 25). So, since Lackey is not obviously committed to the objection to which this note is appended, I refrain from attributing it to her. I want to consider an initially troubling objection to the left-to-right conditional of the Analysis that a critic might base on Lackey's example, even if Lackey would not press such an objection.
18. Interpreted in this way, the example is structurally identical to Lackey's 'Derek' case (2008: 259–60). Everything I say about this second interpretation of *Demolition Worker* extends easily to the 'Derek' case.
19. Happily (and as readers can easily verify), neither the Strokes Account nor the Analysis entails the principle currently under discussion.
20. If acts can be done more or less intentionally – an issue I take no stand on here – then (3) also helps capture such comparative facts about luck.
21. Contrast Coffman (2007: 390f.), which I now regard as mistaken.
22. According to Levy (2011a: 17), 'the degree of chanciness necessary for an event to count as lucky is *sensitive* to the significance of that event for the agent' (my emphasis). However, Levy (2011a: 17) also explicitly agrees with me that 'there is a threshold, even for an event as significant for the agent as the death [S] risks, below which surviving is merely fortunate and not lucky (suppose that the probability of the gun's firing was 0.00001%).'
23. Compare this with Levy's (2011a: 21–2) own claims about the case he calls 'Buried Treasure*', discussed in Section 1.2 above.
24. Thanks to Lee Whittington for suggesting that such a move should be considered.
25. Morris (1986) is a contemporary classic in defense of this possibility.
26. Notably, Levy (2011a: 30) concedes the plausibility of the claim that one isn't lucky relative to properties one exemplifies *necessarily* or *essentially*.
27. It seems clear that an event can be *fortunate* for you even if it's not directly caused by a stroke of good luck for you. For example, it's fortunate for me that the sun is now shining, even if the sun's now shining isn't directly caused by anything that counts as a stroke of good luck for me.
28. Similar points can be applied, I believe, to paradigm ascriptions of circumstantial luck (cf. Nagel 1979) – for example, 'lucky to have been outside Germany when the Nazis came to power', 'lucky to have such a wonderful family', and so on. For a complementary perspective on such ascriptions of

luck that also takes into account fascinating recent psychological work on luck ascriptions, see Pritchard and Smith (2004), especially p. 12 and p. 24.
29. Note well: I'm *not* claiming that Vincent didn't intentionally choose to plant roses in his mother's memory on the northwest part of the island. Rather, my claim here is just that Vincent didn't intentionally form an intention possessed of the relevant counterfactual property – viz. *being such that he'd find buried treasure were he to execute it*.
30. My earlier defense of the claim that, in a wide class of possible worlds that are close to the actual world just beforehand, Vincent (in *Buried Treasure*) doesn't form an intention with the pertinent counterfactual property around the relevant time will apply here as well, *mutatis mutandis*. If we interpret *African Expedition* in such a way that antecedent factors aligned so as to *guarantee* that Smith would become so constrained around the relevant time, then whatever sense we may initially have had that Smith was *lucky* to visit the area during a period when there would be a life-saving eclipse will start to evaporate – his visiting the area then will instead start seeming *fated*.
31. But what about *Smith's* stroke of good luck – viz. his becoming constrained to visit the area during the relevant period? Wasn't that a stroke of good luck for *Jones* too? No, because Smith's *becoming* constrained to visit the area during that period wasn't, when it happened, in any way good for Jones; remember, at that point, Smith hadn't yet invited Jones along for the ride. Now I'm willing to grant that Smith's *being* constrained to visit the area during the indicated period was, *when Smith issued his invitation*, good for Jones. But since there was just beforehand no chance that Smith *wouldn't* be so constrained then (that is, when issuing his invitation), it's not at all plausible that Smith's being so constrained then was a *stroke of luck* for Jones – which is of course just as the Analysis would have it, in virtue of condition (2**).

3 Knowledge and Luck I: Gettiered Belief and the Ease of Mistake Approach

1. As Schafer (2014) helpfully emphasizes, there are two importantly different readings of the epistemological anti-luck platitude (alternatively, there are two importantly different such anti-luck platitudes). On one reading, the platitude is supported by reflection on lucky guess cases, and it essentially amounts to the claim that knowledge requires epistemically justified (or rational) belief. On the other reading, the platitude is supported by reflection on Gettier Cases, and it essentially amounts to the claim that knowledge requires *un*gettiered belief. As this introductory section will make clear, I'm here focusing on the *second* of the two readings of the anti-luck platitude just distinguished. For a discussion of the *first* reading of the platitude, Bergmann (2006) is an excellent starting point; see especially Chapters 1, 2, and 5.
2. Chapters 3 and 4 expand on Coffman (forthcoming).
3. My treatment of the issues taken up in this section obviously owes much to Unger (1968), Engel (1992), and Pritchard (2005).
4. Thanks to Rodrigo Borges and Georgi Gardiner for urging me to ferret out and defend this thesis.

5. Here's a prime example (Goldman 1976: 772–3): 'Henry is driving in the countryside with his son. For the boy's edification Henry identifies various objects on the landscape as they come into view. 'That's a cow,' says Henry, 'That's a tractor,' 'That's a silo,' 'That's a barn,' etc. Each of the identified objects has features characteristic of its type.... [U]nknown to Henry, the district he has just entered is full of papier-mâché facsimiles of barns. These facsimiles look from the road exactly like barns, but are really just façades, without back walls or interiors, quite incapable of being used as barns. They are so cleverly constructed that travelers invariably mistake them for barns. Having just entered the district, Henry has not encountered any facsimiles; the object he sees is a genuine barn.'
6. Here's a prime example (Greco 2012: 11): 'Smith has an epistemic guardian angel who is keen to reward Smith's competent performances. On this occasion Smith competently reasons to a false belief, the angel sees as much, and so changes the world around so as to make the belief true.'
7. Those who group fake barn and hidden helper cases with the Classics include Plantinga (1993), Hiller and Neta (2007), Stone (2013), Freitag (2014), and Schafer (2014). Theorists who group fake barn cases with the Classics include Howard-Snyder, Howard-Snyder, and Feit (2003), Lackey (2009), Reed (2009), Turri (2012), and Pritchard (2012a). Theorists who group hidden helper cases with the Classics include Turri (2011) and Greco (2012).
8. Here, I have in mind (a) the 'double luck' recipe (Zagzebski 1994) and (b) the 'lack of proper connection between justificatory and truth-making factors' recipe (Howard-Snyder, Howard-Snyder, and Feit 2003). I distinguish such general recipes for constructing Gettier Cases from substantive accounts of gettiered belief – and concentrate on the latter – for (at least) this reason: Each of the general recipes is left sufficiently vague so that quite different substantive accounts of gettiered belief can all claim, with equal plausibility, to have honored it. For example, proponents of the Ease of Mistake Approach (Pritchard 2005) as well as advocates of the Lack of Credit Approach (Turri 2011) can claim, with equal plausibility, to have honored the double luck recipe for constructing Gettier Cases (Zagzebski 1994). The general recipes are thus best understood, I submit, not as substantive accounts of gettiered belief, but rather as expressions of relatively loose adequacy constraints on such accounts – constraints that could, in principle, be met by more than one kind of substantive account of gettiered belief.
9. One may of course have such an intuitive reaction to the indicated cases *even if* one is also committed to denying Omnipresence. Cf. Sosa (2011: 84ff.), who ultimately ascribes (first-order) knowledge in fake barn cases – and so, must deny Omnipresence – on the basis of his apt belief account of knowledge, but also shares with readers the following description of how such cases can strike him: 'We are thus led to a quandary. Apt discerning of surface color is true belief that manifests the believer's good color sight. And this seems unaffected by the nearby presence of fakes. Yet if the believer might too easily have been viewing a fake instead of a genuinely red surface, then he seems not to *know* the seen surface to be red. It is then plausible to conclude that *apt belief is one thing and knowledge quite another*' (84, emphasis in original).
10. Similar cases include Neta and Rohrbaugh's examples *A* and *B* (2004: 399–400), as well as Comesaña's *Halloween Party* (2005: 397) and Baumann's example *k* (2014: 540–1).

11. For others who suggest that cases such as *Lucky Subitizer* refute the Ease of Mistake Approach's right-to-left conditional, see the papers cited in the last note.
12. Incidentally, *Coffee Cup* strikes me as a much more promising attempted counterexample to the safety requirement on knowledge than the literature's leading candidates (cf. Hawthorne and Lasonen-Aarnio 2009). Roughly, proponents of the safety requirement maintain that a belief, B, held in way W by subject S constitutes knowledge *only if* B would be true were S to hold B via W (cf. Pritchard 2004, 2005, 2007). See Bogardus (2014) for a defense of the safety requirement from attempted counterexamples described by Neta and Rohrbaugh (2004), Comesaña (2005), and Kelp (2009), along with a novel but (in my view) problematic attempted counterexample to the requirement. For critical discussion of Bogardus's case ('Atomic Clock'), see Section 4.6.2 below. My treatment of Sosa's *Lucky Subitizer* in the main text resembles Bogardus's (2014: 297–9) treatment of the cases he discusses from Neta and Rohrbaugh and from Comesaña. But our positions on Kelp's attempted counterexample differ significantly: whereas Bogardus claims that the key belief in Kelp's case constitutes knowledge but is safe, I allow that the belief is unsafe but argue that it falls short of knowledge. See Section 4.6.1 below for a critical discussion of Kelp's case ('Demonic Clock').
13. Similar cases include Levy's *Young Jack** (2011a: 28) and Pritchard's *Temp* (2012a: 260).
14. What I'm calling the 'Minimal Creditability Requirement' is an expression of what Pritchard (2012a) calls the 'ability intuition', whose truth I'm happy to accept here.

4   Knowledge and Luck II: Three More Approaches to Gettiered Belief

1. For an excellent introduction to the relevant portions of the virtue-theoretic movement, see Greco and Turri (2012, 2013).
2. For worries about this kind of attempt to explain the putative superiority of knowledge to gettiered belief, see Section 4 of Pritchard, Millar, and Haddock (2010).
3. This detail – that *all* the adults in Morris's vicinity are knowledgeable, well-intentioned, and so on – is crucial. I don't want this example to have even the faintest whiff of a fake barn-type case about it.
4. Cf. Greco and Turri (2011, Section 9).
5. For further discussion of related issues, see Coffman (2011b) and Coffman (2011c).
6. See Sections 3.3 and 3.5 above for supporting arguments for and defense of my assumption here that the ignorance-inducing phenomenon illustrated by the Classics is present also in hidden helper cases such as *Hobbled*. Note also the following interesting difference between *Hobbled* and *Religious Sheep Rock* (Section 3.5): while both cases are of the hidden helper variety, they differ in that Watson's abilities saliently explain why he believes accurately, whereas Roddy's don't.

7. Cf. Sosa (2007: 23): 'Beliefs can be true...independently of the believer's competence in so believing, as in Gettier cases.'
8. Compare Bratman (1984: 387): 'Further, on a natural reading of 'knowingly', you did not hit target 1 knowingly; for you did not know that it was target 1, rather than target 2, that you were hitting.' But contrast Gross (1979: 84–5): 'A routine fumigation might have been carried on for the purpose of ridding the ship of rats, with knowledge that a sailor was sleeping below, or at least with *good reason to believe* [my emphasis] that he was. Death, we would then say, is caused *knowingly*'. Since you can have good reason to believe P without knowing P, the sufficient condition that Gross suggests for acting knowingly conflicts with KRAK.
9. Sosa (2010) defends ascribing first-order knowledge in fake barn-type cases by arguing that the contrary intuition is in fact a mistaken response to a lack of *second-order* knowledge. Applied to *Fake Fruits*: While Sara knows that there's an apple in the bowl, she doesn't know that she knows this; and Sara's lack of second-order knowledge can prompt us to mistakenly deny her first-order knowledge. Kelp (2013: 9–10) persuasively criticizes this kind of defense. Briefly, Kelp's reply runs as follows: If our first-order ignorance intuition regarding fake barn-type cases really is a response to the subject's *second-order* ignorance, then we should be able to elicit a first-order ignorance intuition regarding a normal case by stipulating that the subject lacks second-order knowledge. But this exercise does not elicit a first-order ignorance intuition. Consider, for example, a conceptually impoverished subject in normal countryside who believes she's facing a barn. By hypothesis, she can't so much as entertain the thought that she *knows* she's facing a barn, and so, she lacks second-order knowledge. On Sosa's proposal, this thinker's lack of second-order knowledge should elicit from us a *first-order* ignorance intuition (that is, a sense that she doesn't know she's facing a barn). But the case needn't elicit such a sense from us. This strongly suggests that our first-order ignorance intuition regarding fake barn-type cases is a reaction to something other than the subject's second-order ignorance (for example, the subject's first-order ignorance).
10. Crisp (2000: 48) seems to detect these two senses as well but doesn't pause to carefully disentangle them.
11. To further clarify, the epistemic notion in play here is what epistemologists typically label 'propositional justification', the relation expressed by 'P is justified for S' (as opposed to, say, 'S justifiedly believes P'). For more discussion, see Section 1.3.2 in Ichikawa and Steup (2012).
12. Thanks to Kirk Ludwig and Jennifer Nagel for helpful discussion.
13. To get the variant from the original, replace the original's last three sentences with the following material: 'In β – which is close to α before t – Ernie is at t justified in believing (via degraded subitizing ability) many falsehoods like [There are three objects present]. So, in *some* world that's close to α before t, Ernie is at t justified in believing (via subitizing ability) many relevant falsehoods. Further, since *many* tainted cups were equally available to Ernie, there are *many* other worlds like β that are close to α before t and such that Ernie chooses a tainted cup at t*, ingesting its contents shortly thereafter. So, in a *wide class* of worlds that are close to α before t, Ernie is at t justified in believing (via subitizing ability) many relevant falsehoods.'

14. See Whiting (2013) for a thorough and compelling case for the thesis that believing falsely is always bad (other things being equal) – which thesis, incidentally, is perfectly compatible with the view that believing truly is not always (prima facie) good.
15. Many readers will immediately see the reason for the label (which, so far as I know, was coined by Comesaña [2013]): the examples in question bear an obvious structural similarity to a famous one that Frankfurt (1969) describes, in which (allegedly) an agent is morally responsible for an act despite the existence of a counterfactual intervener whose presence makes performing the act inevitable for the agent. I discuss such cases in Section 6.3.2 below.
16. Cf. Bogardus (2014: 304): '*Atomic Clock*... points out a way in which knowledge and safety can indeed part ways. Smith can know that P at t even if either *some event E has a high chance of happening at t* or *E will almost certainly happen soon after*, where E would put Smith in an inferior position with respect to P. As long as E hasn't occurred *yet*, knowledge is still possible even using the threatened faculties or the imperiled methods. That is, one may know even under epistemic threat, so long as the threat is *as of yet* unrealized.'
17. Cf. Plantinga (1996: 315–16): 'An exercise of my cognitive powers, therefore, even when those powers are functioning properly...in the maxi-environment for which they are designed, can be counted on to produce a true belief with respect to *some* cognitive mini-environments but not with respect to others. Some mini-environments are *favorable* for a given exercise of cognitive powers; others are *misleading*, even when my faculties are functioning properly. These mini-environments, we might say, are such that my faculties are not designed to produce a true belief in or with respect to them – even though they include the maxi-environment for which my faculties have indeed been designed (by God or evolution).'
18. The following speech is, obviously enough, modelled on the quotation from Bogardus (2014: 301–2) above in which he ascribes various epistemic good-making features to Smith's belief about the time.
19. Notably, a proponent of $RMJA_2$ can coherently ascribe inferential knowledge from a false premise to thinkers in cases such as those described by Warfield (2005), Klein (2008), and Fitelson (2010). Here's a representative example from Warfield (2005: 407–8): 'Counting with some care the number of people present at my talk, I reason: "There are 53 people at my talk; therefore my 100 handout copies are sufficient." My premise is false. There are 52 people in attendance – I double counted one person who changed seats during the count. And yet I know my conclusion.' Let 'Fritz' denote this example's protagonist. Granted, Fritz is justified in believing many falsehoods similar to the content of his false 'premise' belief about the number of people in attendance. But despite this fact, we can understand the case so that Fritz is not justified in believing many falsehoods similar to the content of his *true* 'conclusion' belief that he's got enough handouts for everyone in attendance; nor need it be true that he *could well* have been so justified at the time in question. $RMJA_2$ is therefore consistent with the claim that Fritz's true 'conclusion' belief amounts to knowledge (and so isn't gettiered). (Thanks to Rodrigo Borges for urging me to consider $RMJA_2$'s bearing on such alleged 'knowledge from falsehood' cases.)

5 Freedom, Responsibility, and Luck I: The Possibility of Moral Responsibility and Literal Arguments for the Proximal Determination Requirement

1. Cf. Franklin (2011: 202): 'The luck argument is especially troubling for libertarians who maintain not only that free will and moral responsibility are compatible with indeterminism, but that they *require* it.' For what is arguably the most detailed and influential contemporary development of the standard libertarian position, see Kane (1996, 1999). For development of a 'non-standard' libertarian position on which there can be proximally determined directly morally responsible action, see Ekstrom (2000: 106ff.) and Mele (2006: 9–14). I briefly discuss such a position in note 31 to Chapter 6.
2. As is indicated by the first parenthetical bit in the sentence to which this note is appended, in this chapter and the next one I'm focusing exclusively on finite agents such as us who exist at times.
3. For a sampling of similar characterizations of morally responsible action (along with references to additional important discussions of the topic), see Zimmerman (2002: 555–6), Clarke (2005: 21–2), and Fischer and Tognazzini (2011: 390–1). S's deserving moral praise (blame) for A does not entail that any actual person is at all justified in praising (blaming) S for A (cf. Zimmerman 2002: 555–6, Fischer and Tognazzini 2011: 390ff.). The deserved moral praise (blame) in question may be as mild as the private hosting of one or another of what Strawson (1962) called the 'reactive attitudes' upon learning of S's performance of A (standard examples of such attitudes include resentment, indignation, guilt, gratitude, and so on). Finally, these definitions of morally responsible action leave it open that the pertinent desert facts always obtain in virtue of some *other* facts about the agent in question (cf. Zimmerman 2002: 555–6).
4. The concepts at play in this definition can be illustrated by way of the following kind of case (cf. Carlson 2000: 280–1): You confront a locked safe whose correct combination is 8675309. Since your brain and fingers are working properly, you have it within your power to dial any seven-digit combination (including, of course, 8675309). But you are also totally clueless as to the safe's correct combination. So, while you have it within your power to open the safe, you don't know how to open the safe. At present, then, you aren't free to open the safe.
5. By 'visible argument for P', I mean an argument for P that someone has actually presented *or* an argument for P to which our attention can naturally be drawn through consideration of some argument for P that someone has actually presented.
6. By 'nonpartisan argument', I mean an argument that doesn't presuppose the truth of some substantive account of metaphysically free and/or morally responsible action.
7. While Levy (2011a) occasionally describes his overall target conclusion as the thesis that morally responsible action is impossible, he much more frequently describes his target as the thesis that no agent is in fact morally responsible for anything s/he does. The latter description is better since (a) some of Levy's key arguments depend on empirical claims that are at best contingently true (see, for example, his objection to 'quality of will' theories

of moral responsibility at p.184ff.), and (b) Levy sometimes endorses claims that seem to commit him to thinking that morally responsible action is at least possible (see, for example, his proposed counterexample to what he calls the 'no difference principle' at p.48). See Section 5.3.3 below for critical discussion of a crucial step of Levy's luck-driven argument against the existence of morally responsible action.

8. For helpful exposition and critical discussion of this kind of argument for the impossibility of morally responsible action, see Zimmerman (1987: 376–9).
9. This standard, rough-and-ready characterization of resultant moral luck is all we'll need for present purposes. For the best available discussion of resultant moral luck, including a more thorough and precise characterization of the phenomenon than what I offer here in the main text, see Sartorio (2012b).
10. For helpful exposition and critical discussion of this kind of argument for the impossibility of morally responsible action, see Clarke (2005).
11. For another endorsement of claims along the lines of (ZA-1) and (ZA-2), see Greco (1995: 86ff.).
12. Writes Copp (1997: 449–50): '[A] person is blameworthy for [X] just in case she deserves blame on the basis of [X].' The sentence to which this note is appended expresses the right-to-left conditional of the biconditional that Copp asserts in the above quotation. One upshot of the argument now under consideration in the main text is that, if the right-to-left conditional of Copp's biconditional is indeed true, then the possibility of responsibility tout court is incompatible with (SA-3) of the Strawsonian Argument, and thus, the Strawsonian Argument fails due to a false premise *if* Zimmerman's Argument succeeds. (As we'll soon see, however, there are plausible counterexamples to the indicated portion of Copp's biconditional.)
13. *Question:* Are the initial premises of this argument consistent with the above definition of responsibility tout court? *Answer:* Yes. Responsibility tout court, recall, is moral responsibility in the absence of moral responsibility for any *action(s)*. Now note two points. First point: it is certainly coherent – indeed, it is extremely plausible (cf. Zimmerman 2002: 564–5) – to say that *if* responsibility tout court is possible, then its exemplification can't be brute but must instead be grounded in or based on certain features of an individual. So, the first premise (after the initial supposition), with its implication that responsibility tout court is grounded in or based on certain further features, is consistent with the definition of responsibility tout court. Second point: the possession of a potentially act-influencing reason state isn't itself, and needn't have resulted from, a morally responsible action (or omission, for that matter). So, the second premise, with its implication (at least when combined with the first premise) that moral responsibility requires moral responsibility for some (not necessarily actional) responsibility-grounding feature, is consistent with the above definition of responsibility tout court.
14. Here, I'm simply going to grant that it's possible that there be true 'counterfactuals of freedom' (as they're called) – that is, true counterfactuals of the form < S would have freely performed A had S been in (prior) circumstances C >. In fact, following van Inwagen (1997), I'm inclined to deny that any such counterfactual could be true (see Zimmerman 2002: 572–4 for pertinent discussion). Briefly: If some such counterfactual could be true, then there's a possible free action, A, such that its agent, S, would have performed A had

s/he been in the relevant prior circumstances, C. Necessarily, S performs A *freely* given prior circumstances C only if C's obtaining is nomologically consistent with A's absence (see Section 6.3.2 below for a familiar line of argument in support of this claim). If C's obtaining is nomologically consistent with A's absence, then A (metaphysically) might not have happened had C obtained. And if A might not have happened had C obtained, then it's false that A would have happened had C obtained. So, necessarily, S performs A freely given prior circumstances C only if it's false that A would have happened had C obtained. So, no possible free action A is such that its agent S would have performed A had s/he been in the relevant prior circumstances C. So, no counterfactual of the form < S would have freely performed A had S been in (prior) circumstances C > could be true. But again, I'll here simply set aside such objections to the coherence of the notion of responsibility tout court.

15. Again, for the best available discussion of resultant moral luck, including a more thorough and detailed description of the general structure of such scenarios than I offer in the main text here, see Sartorio (2012b).
16. According to Hieronymi (2006: 56; cf. Levy 2011a: 77), '[i]t is now quite standard, in philosophy of action, to think of intending as settling the question of what one will do. Having settled that question...leaves one open to certain questions and criticisms....I can be asked why I think [A-ing] is the thing for me to do, and my intention to [A] can be inconsistent, in familiar ways, with both my other attitudes and my actions. Further, it seems that I am rightly subject to these particular requests for justification and charges of inconsistency only insofar as I intend to [A]. Thus an intention...seems at least in part commitment-constituted. An intention is a commitment to doing something'. Pretty clearly, anyone who accepts this view of intentions should think that Choosy Assassin's actively forming an intention to kill the target could make him at least a *bit* more deserving of moral criticism than is Choiceless Assassin. Such a theorist will maintain that, whereas *Choosy* Assassin has (actively) settled the question whether to kill the target in a way that clearly conflicts with the target's best interests, *Choiceless* Assassin hasn't yet so settled that question. Such a settling (or commitment) difference between the two assassins could arguably ground at least a small responsibility difference between them. (See Section 6.1 below for a bit of related additional evidence against ZA-2.)
17. Though there's an important wrinkle that needs ironing out. The expression 'A is S's fault' admits of two readings: *A is due to a character fault (flaw) of S's* and *S is to blame for A*. Arguably, the former doesn't entail the latter (cf. Watson 1996, Fischer and Tognazzini 2012). A psychopath, for example, may be such that some of his actions are due to his character faults (flaws), notwithstanding the fact that he doesn't deserve blame for any of the relevant actions (Fischer and Tognazzini 2012: 386–7). I'm interpreting van Inwagen's 'That is *your* fault' as meaning *You are to blame for that* (= *You deserve blame for that*).
18. The general defensive strategy here obviously resembles one that G.E. Moore (1953) employs in defending ordinary empirical knowledge ascriptions from Humean skeptical argumentation in his 'Hume's Theory Examined'. Compare also van Inwagen's (1983: 149–50) final objection to the key premise of what he calls the 'third strand of the *Mind* argument'. (Thanks to David Palmer for

probing comments on an earlier version of the argument of the last few paragraphs. This acknowledgment, I hasten to add, should not be understood as implying that I think David will or should be fully satisfied by the changes I've made in light of his probing comments.)

19. Cf. Stump and Fischer's (2000: 47) distinction between what they (and many others) call 'indirect' and 'direct' arguments for the incompatibility of causal determinism and moral responsibility: 'It is useful to divide contemporary arguments for the incompatibility of causal determinism and moral responsibility into two types: indirect and direct. The indirect arguments present reasons why causal determinism is incompatible with the possession of the relevant kind of alternative possibilities [= metaphysical freedom] and conclude from this that causal determinism is incompatible with moral responsibility. It is, of course, a presupposition of the indirect arguments that moral responsibility requires alternative possibilities. The direct arguments contain no such presupposition, although some of their proponents may believe that moral responsibility does indeed require alternative possibilities.'

20. (IA-3) is obviously quite similar to what Frankfurt (1969) calls the 'Principle of Alternate Possibilities'. Notably, (IA-3) seems not to rule out, but also not to entail, the possibility of resultant moral luck scenarios (cf. Otsuka 1998: 699–700).

21. See Levy (2011a: 42–3) for a recent statement of what I classify as a version of the Direct Argument (p.42) that grows into a version of the Indirect Argument when he adds premises along the lines of (IA-2) and (IA-3) that posit connections among luck, control, and responsibility (p.43).

22. Note that this claim is neutral on the question whether your wearing the soles down at t was proximally determined (see Section 1.1 above). Even proximally determined events can be modally fragile, in the relevant sense.

23. Recall from Section 2.1 that, according to Mele and Moser (1994: 45), it doesn't follow from the fact that A was not done intentionally that A was done *un*intentionally: 'There is a middle ground between A-ing intentionally and A-ing unintentionally. We locate "side-effect actions" of the kind in question on that ground. Insofar as such actions are not done unknowingly, inadvertently, or accidentally, they are not unintentional. Insofar as the agent is not aiming at the performance of these actions, either as ends or as means to (or constituents of) ends, they are not intentional either.'

24. Two notes in one. First, if the envisaged case really is one in which you're free with respect to an action that was just a stroke of good luck for you, then we can obtain a case in which you're free with respect to an action that was just a stroke of *bad* luck for you by highlighting (or, if necessary, adding) a respect in which your wearing the soles down is bad for you at t. Second, since the action in question (wearing down your shoes' soles) could only be indirectly or derivatively free (cf. Graham 2010: 290ff.), this case's status as a counterexample to (IA-2j) is consistent with the following claims that I endorsed back in Section 2.1: no *directly* free action can be a stroke of luck for its agent; any *directly* free action is done intentionally.

25. Given the First Proposed Equivalence, the 'just a matter of luck' reading of (DA-2) is obviously true: the First Proposed Equivalence clearly entails that

one is not in any way morally responsible for something that is *just* a matter of luck for one.
26. Here is Franklin's (2011: 203–5) helpful characterization of (what I'm calling) 'action-centered event-causal libertarian' accounts of metaphysically free and morally responsible action: 'Event-causal theories of action seek to analyze the notion of an agent making something happen solely in terms of certain events and states making something happen.... An action is an event that is caused, in the appropriate way, by agent-involving mental events.... Event-causal *libertarians* maintain that, crucial to transforming a mere action into a free action is that the mental events that caused the action do so nondeterministically.... According to [action-centered] event-causal libertarianism, if [an] action was free, then it was nondeterministically [and proximally] caused, in the appropriate way, by agent-involving mental events... [Action-centered event-causal libertarianism] locates indeterminism between our reasons, desires, beliefs, preferences, etc. – states which lead to action – and choice and overt action.'
27. Assume the Proposed Equivalences and that A was (un)lucky for S. Trivially, either A was a stroke of good (bad) luck for S or A wasn't. Suppose first that A *was* a stroke of good (bad) luck for S. Trivially, either S was praiseworthy (blameworthy) for A or s/he wasn't. If S was praiseworthy (blameworthy) for A, then A was only partly a matter of luck for S (Second Proposed Equivalence), and so, A was at least partly a matter of luck for S (Third Proposed Equivalence). On the other hand, if S was *not* praiseworthy (blameworthy) for A, then A was just a matter of luck for S (First Proposed Equivalence), and so, A was at least partly a matter of luck for S (Third Proposed Equivalence). So, if A was a stroke of good (bad) luck for S, then A was at least partly a matter of luck for S. Now suppose that A was *not* a stroke of good (bad) luck for S. Then A was (un)lucky for S but was not itself a stroke of good (bad) luck for S, and so, A was only partly a matter of luck for S (Second Proposed Equivalence), and so, A was at least partly a matter of luck for S (Third Proposed Equivalence). Hence, given the Proposed Equivalences and that A was (un)lucky for S, it follows that A was at least partly a matter of luck for S.
28. Attentive readers will notice that this case bears certain structural similarities to some of the epistemic luck cases described and discussed in Sections 3.1 and 3.2 above.
29. Cf. Strawson (1994: 6): '[T]o be truly responsible for how one is, mentally speaking, in certain respects, one must have [responsibly] brought it about that one is the way one is, mentally speaking, in certain respects.'
30. Readers can easily verify that the Proposed Equivalences jointly entail that A was at least partly a matter of luck for S *only if* A was (un)lucky for S.
31. Cf. Clarke (2003: 80), who writes: '[T]here is nothing in...the concept of action...that supports a view that nondeterministic causation of an event threatens or can undermine its status as an action.'
32. Notably, several of Levy's (2011a) other luck-driven arguments depend on the success of his luck objection to action-centered event-causal libertarianism (cf. Levy forthcoming).
33. Say that an action, A, performed by subject S is **basic** iff S performed A but *not* by way of performing some other action, A*.

34. Incidentally, note the conflict between this commitment and the parenthetical qualification in Levy's definition of 'direct control'.
35. And if the attempted counterexample discussed in Section 5.3.1 succeeds, then (c) an agent could be free with respect to an action whose occurrence was *just* a matter of luck for that agent.

6 Freedom, Responsibility, and Luck II: Stipulative Arguments for the Proximal Determination Requirement and Three Arguments against It

1. Because there's a large literature surrounding each of the arguments considered in Sections 6.1 and 6.2, I'll generally move a little more quickly here than I do elsewhere in this book, often referring readers to key portions of the relevant literature for further discussion.
2. Again, by 'nonpartisan argument', I mean an argument that doesn't presuppose the truth of some substantive account of metaphysically free and/or morally responsible action.
3. Strictly speaking, the argument that Haji develops in the cited works is not an argument for the Proximal Determination Requirement (at least, it's not a valid argument for that requirement). Here's what the indicated argument's premises entail, at most: If a proximally undetermined action conflicts with its agent's best judgment *and* with its agent's stronger motives, then its agent is not directly morally responsible for it. However, as we'll see in Section 6.3.3 below, Haji clearly thinks that the argument developed in the cited works can be adapted so as to apply to proximally undetermined action in general. Since only such an adaptation is relevant here – where we're considering (valid) arguments for the Proximal Determination Requirement – such an adaptation is what I formulate and assess in the main text.
4. Proponents of 'noncausal' accounts of action like Ginet (2008) would reject the upcoming argument.
5. Proponents of noncausal accounts of action, mentioned in the last note, *can* endorse the upcoming argument against (NE-1) since this argument does not depend on the claim that any possible action done for a reason must have been caused.
6. For further critical discussion of the No *Complete* Explanation Argument, see (among other things) Clarke (2003, 2004), Coffman (2010b, 2011a), Franklin (2011), and de Calleja (2014).
7. Cf. Clarke (2003: 77, footnote 8): 'One can take a moral stand *by making a decision.*' Recall also from Section 5.1 above Hieronymi's (2006: 56; cf. Levy 2011a: 77) helpful description of a view of intentions common on the contemporary actional-theoretical scene: 'It is now quite standard, in philosophy of action, to think of intending as settling the question of what one will do. Having settled that question...leaves one open to certain questions and criticisms.... I can be asked why I think [A-ing] is the thing for me to do, and my intention to [A] can be inconsistent, in familiar ways, with both my other attitudes and my actions. Further, it seems that I am rightly subject to these particular requests for justification and charges of inconsistency only insofar as I intend to [A]. Thus an intention...seems at least

in part commitment-constituted. An intention is a commitment to doing something'. Pretty clearly, anyone who accepts this view of intentions will find appealing the claim that one can take and disclose a moral stand on some issue or question *by* actively forming a relevant intention. Note also that any theorist who, for whatever reason, inclines toward the view that one can take a moral stand by forming an intention should also be inclined to reject (ZA-2) of Zimmerman's Argument for the possibility of responsibility tout court (see Section 5.1 above). More specifically, such a theorist should be inclined to accept the following claim about the pertinent assassin cases: 'Choosy Assassin's actively forming an intention to kill another person could make him at least a *bit* more deserving of moral criticism than is Choiceless Assassin.' If one can take a moral stand by actively forming an intention, then Choosy Assassin has taken a moral stand regarding the target's life that Choiceless Assassin has not (yet) taken. This moral stand difference between the two assassins could arguably ground at least a small responsibility difference between them.
8. As noted above (Section 5.2), the Freedom Requirement (= IA-3) is obviously quite similar to what Frankfurt (1969) calls the 'Principle of Alternate Possibilities'.
9. I've elected to omit discussion in the main text of two kinds of arguments that readers familiar with the relevant literature might have expected to encounter here. The two kinds of arguments that I have in mind are (a) arguments for the Unfreedom Lemma that employ a 'transfer of unfreedom' principle (for example, an agent is not free with respect to logical consequences of facts that s/he is not free with respect to) *and* (b) the 'Rollback Argument' (as employed by, for example, Levy 2011a: 50–1). I omit discussion of arguments for the Unfreedom Lemma that employ a transfer of unfreedom principle (cf. van Inwagen 1983: 146–50; Nelkin 2001) because, as Graham (2010: 279–86; cf. Shabo 2013: 295–7) has demonstrated, every visible attempt to formulate an argument for the Unfreedom Lemma that depends on such a principle suffers from some or other fatal flaw (for complementary critical discussion of recent attempts to formulate such an argument for the Unfreedom Lemma, see Finch and Warfield 1998 along with Smith and Coffman 2010). Now for the 'Rollback Argument', proponents of which (for example, Levy 2011a: 50–1) invite us to conclude that (something like) the Unfreedom Lemma is true *simply* on the basis of imagining a series of replays of an initial proximally undetermined choice such that the choice happens in only about half the replays. (Importantly, although van Inwagen [2000: 14ff.] carefully develops and discusses such a thought experiment, he does *not* invite readers to infer the Unfreedom Lemma *simply* on the basis of considering such a thought experiment. Rather, van Inwagen uses the indicated thought experiment to bolster MI-1, and he attempts to support MI-2 with what I'm calling the 'Promising Argument' [cf. Franklin 2012: 412, footnote 24].) I omit discussion of the Rollback Argument because, as Franklin (2012: 406ff.) persuasively argues, (i) such a thought experiment is in all probability metaphysically impossible (as it seems to imply that there are true contradictions about what an agent does at a given time) and, in any case, (ii) the 'argument' amounts to little more than the *assertion* that (something like) the Unfreedom Lemma is true. For further critical discussion of the Rollback

Argument, see Clarke (2003: 164–70) and Franklin (2011: 215–19, 2012: 406–9).
10. For discussion of such reasoning, see van Inwagen (1983: 128–9) and Warfield (2003: 623).
11. For discussion of such reasoning, see van Inwagen (1983: 129–42) and Clarke (2003: 37–9).
12. Shabo (2014: 153) appears to deny this extremely plausible assumption when, in setting out his 'Assimilation Argument' (discussed below) for (something like) the Proximal Determination Requirement, he claims that 'a causally undetermined human action *could* in principle be a truly random outcome...just as other types of events, such as a particle's swerving one way when another way was possible, or some radioactive material's decaying at one rate when another rate was possible, could be random outcomes.' Shabo goes on to suggest that any theorists who 'take [arguments like the *Mind* Argument] seriously' will accept his assumption that 'an undetermined action could be a random outcome' (153). I would point to van Inwagen (1983), Clarke (2003), and Mele (2006) as three of the most prominent among a large group of theorists who take arguments like the *Mind* Argument seriously yet reject the claim that 'an undetermined action could be a truly random outcome'.
13. Van Inwagen (1983: 142–6) provides an early and highly influential discussion of what I'm calling the 'Device Argument'. The specific reconstruction of this argument that I offer and assess in the main text is guided by Graham's (2010) outstanding critical discussion of other extant reconstructions of the argument (including van Inwagen's [1983: 146–8] own reconstruction), and formulated so that it's clearly a valid argument for the Proximal Determination Requirement (on potential formal pitfalls here, see section II of Warfield 2000). Readers should keep in mind that, despite having done as much as any other contemporary theorist to articulate and defend a successful version of the *Mind* Argument, van Inwagen does not ultimately endorse the argument. In an enlightening and entertaining paper in which he sets out his main views on the free will debate entirely in the third person, van Inwagen (2004: 225) writes: 'Free will is a mystery because, although it obviously exists,...it seems to be incompatible with both determinism and indeterminism....Van Inwagen, of course, believes that the arguments he has given for the incompatibility of free will and determinism contain *no* flaws...and that there is some flaw, or are some flaws, in the familiar arguments for the incompatibility of free will and indeterminism. But as to the latter class of arguments – well, he's damned if he knows what the flaws in them might be. He simply hasn't a clue.'
14. Say that an action, A, performed by S is **basic** iff S performs A but *not* by way of performing some other action, A*. Say that an action, A, performed by S is **non-basic** iff S performs A by way of performing some other action, A*.
15. Shabo's actual presentation of the Assimilation Argument employs five different examples, the first two of which can be safely omitted here. Omitting those first two examples requires lightly editing Shabo's description of Case 3 (I retain Shabo's labels for this and the remaining two examples, Cases 4 and 5). Nothing about my upcoming critical discussion of Shabo's Assimilation Argument depends on omitting his Cases 1 and 2 or on the aforementioned

light editing of his description of Case 3. Cases 4 and 5 are quoted directly from Shabo's article.
16. For development and critical assessment of a somewhat similar line of argument, see van Inwagen (1983: 129–42).
17. The argument that follows is a somewhat streamlined version of a more elaborate argument that Finch develops in sections 6–7 of her 2013 article 'Against Libertarianism'. I'm confident that the following argument is sufficiently similar to the one that Finch actually presents so that the objection I will eventually press against the former, or at least an objection very similar to it, will also impugn the argument that Finch actually presents.
18. In what follows, let 't1' denote a time just prior to the time denoted by 't2'.
19. Equivalently: Necessarily, if S was at t1 free with respect to whether s/he performs A at t2 *and* S performs A at t2, then S performs A freely at t2.
20. Cf. Clarke (2003: 145–6).
21. Again, let 't1' denote a time just prior to the time denoted by 't2'.
22. Once more, by 'nonpartisan argument', I mean an argument that doesn't presuppose the truth of some substantive account of metaphysically free and/or morally responsible action.
23. Writes Fischer (2011: 97; cf. Sartorio 2011: 1077): 'Whatever underlies the responsibility-grounding relationship – whatever constitutes the relevant glue that binds together the prior states of the agent with his choice – is...a matter of *the way the prior states of the agent lead to the choice in question*'.
24. Cf. Mele (2006: 131–2): 'Moral responsibility is very commonly and very plausibly regarded as a matter of degree. *If* young children and adults are morally responsible for some of what they do, it is plausible...that young children are not nearly as morally responsible for any of their deeds as some adults are for some of their adult deeds. When we combine our recognition of that point with the observation that the good and bad deeds of young children are relatively trivial in themselves, we should be struck by the implausibility of stringent standards for deserved moral praise and blame of young children – including standards the satisfaction of which requires [proximal determination].' I say that Mele has 'inspired' and 'suggested' (rather than 'presented' or 'defended') the argument that I'll call 'The Melean Argument' (as opposed to 'Mele's Argument') in an effort to be duly sensitive to the impressive subtlety of Mele's critical discussion of the Proximal Determination Requirement (cf. Mele 2013: 253–4).
25. Recall from Chapter 5's introductory section that, by 'choice situation', I mean a situation in which 'an agent...has several options available to her, among which she must decide' (Maier forthcoming: 8). This concept is commonly invoked in both everyday as well as more formal – for example, decision-theoretical – contexts.
26. For additional complementary critical discussion of the Melean Argument, see Clarke (2004), Blumenfeld (2011), Coffman (2010b), and Levy (2011a: 34–5, footnote 15).
27. For a sampling of recent statements of arguments along these lines, see van Inwagen (1983, 2004), Warfield (2003), and Finch (2013).
28. For helpful recent discussion of some of the issues here, see Section 3 of van Inwagen (2004).

29. For helpful recent discussion of some of the issues here, see Warfield (1996, 2003, 2008). Notably, I think that the best explanation argument sketched in the paragraph to which this note is appended supports not only the claim that direct *blameworthiness* for an action requires metaphysical freedom with respect to that action but also the claim that direct *praiseworthiness* for an action requires metaphysical freedom with respect to that action. Though they may (for a variety of reasons) occur less frequently than situations wherein one tries to block a charge of direct blameworthiness for an action, one can find oneself in a situation wherein one wishes to block an ascription of direct praiseworthiness for an action. Providing the attributer with strong evidence that one was not in fact free with respect to the pertinent action could, I believe, be as effective here as it would be in a case of blameworthiness ascription. Cf. Chisholm (1964: 3–5): 'I think we can say ... that if a man is responsible for a certain event or a certain state of affairs..., then that event or state of affairs was brought about by some act of his, and the act was something that was in his power either to perform or not to perform. ... One may object: But surely if there were such a thing as a man who is really *good*, then he would be responsible for things that he would do; yet, he would be unable to do anything other than just what it is that he does do. ... The answer, I think, is suggested by a comment that Thomas Reid makes upon an ancient author. The author had said of Cato, "He was good because he could not be otherwise," and Reid observes: "This saying, if understood literally and strictly, is not the praise of Cato, but of his constitution, which was no more the work of Cato than his existence." If Cato was himself responsible for the good things that he did, then Cato, as Reid suggests, was such that, although he had the power to do what was not good, he exercised his power only for that which was good.'
30. Thanks to David Palmer for helpful comments on an earlier version of this section's defense of the Freedom Requirement.
31. An interesting side point: If (PO-2) is true, then the so called (by Clarke 2003) 'deliberative libertarian' position is (not just false but) incoherent. According to deliberative libertarianism (as defended by, for example, Ekstrom 2000), directly morally responsible action is possible and must be proximally determined but is also incompatible with global determinism, and so must have some undetermined causes in the deliberative process that gives rise to it. (PO-2) says that directly morally responsible action is possible only if *proximally undetermined* directly morally responsible action is possible. Obviously, if that's right, then two core claims of deliberative libertarianism – directly morally responsible action is possible; such action must be proximally determined – are jointly inconsistent. For different – and, I believe, somewhat less decisive – objections to deliberative libertarianism, see Clarke (2003, 2011) and Franklin (2011).
32. Note that this claim is neutral on both the truth value of the Freedom Requirement itself, as well as the question whether fully deterministic Frankfurt Cases may also constitute counterexamples to the Freedom Requirement (if the Freedom Requirement is false). For helpful recent discussion and defense of the claim that any potentially successful Frankfurt Case must be indeterministic, see Palmer (2005) as well as Ginet and Palmer (2010).

For dissent, see Fischer (2010); for a persuasive reply to Fischer's dissent, see Palmer (2014).
33. Note, in this connection, that theorists who wield Frankfurt Cases against theses like the Freedom Requirement commonly stipulate that the protagonist in such a case would (or at least, *might*) have performed, and been morally responsible for, the pertinent action had the relevant fail-safe mechanism been absent (cf. Fischer 2011: 244).
34. Briefly, my thought in Coffman (2010b: 163–4; cf. Coffman and Warfield 2007: 185–8) was that Bob seems directly morally responsible for choosing *on his own* at the relevant time to steal Ann's car, which was (by hypothesis) proximally undetermined (that is, Bob's not choosing *on his own* at that time to steal Ann's car was consistent with the immediate past and laws of nature). (Notice that, since the details of *Bob's Choice* leave it open that Bob was free with respect to so choosing at that time, the relevant thought seems consistent with the Freedom Requirement.) If that thought is right, then *Bob's Choice* looks to be a counterexample to the Proximal Determination Requirement (one that, to repeat, seems compatible with the Freedom Requirement). However, for purposes of constructing the Possibility Argument, I assert and defend only the logically weaker claim that *Bob's Choice* can be 'converted into' a counterexample to the Proximal Determination Requirement (= *Bob's Choice**) *provided that* the Freedom Requirement is false.
35. I'm therefore in agreement with theorists such as Kane (1999) and Mele (2006) who claim that we needn't – and therefore shouldn't – invoke the possibility of 'agent causation' (the view that *agents themselves*, in addition to 'agent-involving' events, can contribute causally to events) in order to mitigate luck-involving worries about the scope of metaphysically free and morally responsible action.

References

Audi, R. 1994. 'Dispositional Beliefs and Dispositions to Believe.' *Noûs* 28: 419–34.

Audi, R. 2011. *Epistemology*. New York: Routledge.

Ballantyne, N. 2011. 'Anti-Luck Epistemology, Pragmatic Encroachment, and True Belief.' *Canadian Journal of Philosophy* 41: 485–503.

Ballantyne, N. 2012. 'Luck and Interests.' *Synthese* 185: 319–34.

Ballantyne, N. 2014. 'Does Luck Have a Place in Epistemology?' *Synthese* 191: 1391–1407.

Baumann, P. 2014. 'No Luck with Knowledge? On a Dogma of Epistemology.' *Philosophy and Phenomenological Research* 89: 523–51.

Bennett, J. 1988. *Events and Their Names*. Indianapolis, IN: Hackett.

Bergmann, M. 2006. *Justification without Awareness*. Oxford: Oxford University Press.

Blumenfeld, D. 2011. 'Lucky Agents, Big and Little: Should Size Really Matter?' *Philosophical Studies* 156: 311–19.

Bogardus, T. 2014. 'Knowledge Under Threat.' *Philosophy and Phenomenological Research* 88: 289–313.

Bratman, M. 1984. 'Two Faces of Intention.' *Philosophical Review* 93: 375–405.

Carlson, E. 2000. 'Incompatibilism and the Transfer of Power Necessity.' *Noûs* 34: 277–90.

Carter, J.A. 2013. 'A Problem for Pritchard's Anti-Luck Virtue Epistemology.' *Erkenntnis* 78: 253–75.

Chisholm, R. 1964. 'Human Freedom and the Self.' The University of Kansas Lindley Lecture.

Chisholm, R. 1977. *Theory of Knowledge*. Englewood Cliffs, NJ: Prentice-Hall.

Clarke, R. 2003. *Libertarian Accounts of Free Will*. Oxford: Oxford University Press.

Clarke, R. 2004. 'Reflections on an Argument from Luck.' *Philosophical Topics* 32: 47–64.

Clarke, R. 2005. 'On an Argument for the Impossibility of Moral Responsibility.' *Midwest Studies in Philosophy* 29: 13–24.

Clarke, R. 2010. 'Because She Wanted To.' *The Journal of Ethics* 14: 27–35.

Clarke, R. 2011. 'Alternatives for Libertarians.' In R. Kane (ed.), *The Oxford Handbook of Free Will* (2nd edition). Oxford: Oxford University Press.

Coffman, E.J. 2007. 'Thinking about Luck.' *Synthese* 158: 385–98.

Coffman, E.J. 2009. 'Does Luck Exclude Control?' *Australasian Journal of Philosophy* 87: 499–504.

Coffman, E.J. 2010a. 'Misleading Dispositions and the Value of Knowledge.' *Journal of Philosophical Research* 35: 241–58.

Coffman, E.J. 2010b. 'How (Not) to Attack the Luck Argument.' *Philosophical Explorations* 13: 157–66.

Coffman, E.J. 2011a. 'Clarke's Defense of the Contrast Argument.' *dialectica* 65: 267–75.

Coffman, E.J. 2011b. 'Does Knowledge Suffice for Warrant to Assert?' *Philosophical Studies* 154: 285–300.
Coffman, E.J. 2011c. 'Two Claims about Epistemic Propriety.' *Synthese* 181: 471–88.
Coffman, E.J. 2013. 'Can Virtue Epistemology Capitalize on JTB's Appeal?' *Philosophical Issues* 23: 199–222.
Coffman, E.J. 2014. 'Strokes of Luck.' *Metaphilosophy* 45: 477–508.
Coffman, E.J. Forthcoming. 'Gettiered Belief.' In R. Borges, C. de Almeida, and P. Klein (eds), *Explaining Knowledge: New Essays on the Gettier Problem*. Oxford: Oxford University Press.
Coffman, E.J. and T. Warfield. 2007. 'Alfred Mele's Metaphysical Freedom?' *Philosophical Explorations* 10: 185–94.
Cohen, D. 2006. 'Openness, Accidentality and Responsibility.' *Philosophical Studies* 127: 581–97.
Comesaña, J. 2005. 'Unsafe Knowledge.' *Synthese* 146: 395–404.
Comesaña, J. 2013. 'Sosa on Safety and Epistemic Frankfurt Cases.' In J. Turri (ed.), *Virtuous Thoughts*. Dordrecht: Springer.
Copp, D. 1997. 'Defending the Principle of Alternate Possibilities: Blameworthiness and Moral Responsibility.' *Noûs* 31: 441–56.
Crisp, T. 2000. 'Gettier and Plantinga's Revised Account of Warrant.' *Analysis* 265: 42–50.
Dancy, J. 1985. *Introduction to Contemporary Epistemology*. Oxford: Blackwell.
Davison, S. 1999. 'Moral Luck and the Flicker of Freedom.' *American Philosophical Quarterly* 36: 241–51.
de Calleja, M. 2014. 'Cross-World Luck at the Time of Decision is a Problem for Compatibilists as Well.' *Philosophical Explorations* 17: 112–25.
DeRose, Keith. 2009. *The Case for Contextualism*. Oxford: Oxford University Press.
Dretske, Fred. 1970. 'Epistemic Operators.' *The Journal of Philosophy* 67: 1007–23.
Ekstrom, L. 2000. *Free Will: A Philosophical Study*. Boulder, CO: Westview.
Engel, M. 1992. 'Is Epistemic Luck Compatible with Knowledge?' *Southern Journal of Philosophy* 30: 59–75.
Feldman, R. and E. Conee. 1985. 'Evidentialism.' *Philosophical Studies* 48: 15–34.
Finch, A. 2013. 'Against Libertarianism.' *Philosophical Studies* 166: 475–93.
Finch, A. and T. Warfield. 1998. 'The *Mind* Argument and Libertarianism.' *Mind* 107: 515–28.
Fischer, J. 2010. 'The Frankfurt Cases: The Moral of the Stories.' *Philosophical Review* 119: 315–36.
Fischer, J. 2011. 'Indeterminism and Control: An Approach to the Problem of Luck.' In J. Fischer (ed.), *Deep Control: Essays on Free Will and Value*. Oxford: Oxford University Press.
Fischer, J. 2014. 'Toward a Solution to the Luck Problem.' In D. Palmer (ed.), *Libertarian Free Will: Contemporary Debates*. Oxford: Oxford University Press.
Fischer, J. and N. Tognazzini. 2011. 'The Physiognomy of Responsibility.' *Philosophy and Phenomenological Research* 82: 381–417.
Fitelson, B. 2010. 'Strengthening the Case for Knowledge from Falsehood.' *Analysis* 70: 666–9.
Frankfurt, H. 1969. 'Alternate Possibilities and Moral Responsibility.' *The Journal of Philosophy* 66: 829–39.

Frankfurt, H. 1978. 'The Problem of Action.' *American Philosophical Quarterly* 15: 157–62.
Franklin, C. 2011. 'Farewell to the Luck (and Mind) Argument.' *Philosophical Studies* 156: 199–230.
Franklin, C. 2012. 'The Assimilation Argument and the Rollback Argument.' *Pacific Philosophical Quarterly* 93: 395–416.
Freitag, W. 2014. 'Safety, Sensitivity and "Distant" Epistemic Luck.' *Theoria* 80: 44–61.
Gendler, T. and J. Hawthorne. 2005. 'The Real Guide to Fake Barns: A Catalogue of Gifts for Your Epistemic Enemies.' *Philosophical Studies* 124: 331–52.
Gettier, E. 1963. 'Is Justified True Belief Knowledge?' *Analysis* 23: 121–3.
Ginet, C. 2008. 'In Defense of a Non-Causal Account of Reasons Explanation.' *The Journal of Ethics* 12: 229–37.
Ginet, C. and D. Palmer. 2010. 'On Mele and Robb's Indeterministic Frankfurt-Style Case.' *Philosophy and Phenomenological Research* 80: 440–6.
Goldman, A. 1976. 'Discrimination and Perceptual Knowledge.' *The Journal of Philosophy* 73: 771–91.
Graham, P. 2010. 'Against the *Mind* Argument.' *Philosophical Studies* 148: 273–94.
Greco, J. 1995. 'A Second Paradox Concerning Responsibility and Luck.' *Metaphilosophy* 26: 81–96.
Greco, J. 2003. 'Knowledge as Credit for True Belief.' In M. DePaul and L. Zagzebski (eds), *Intellectual Virtue*. Oxford: Oxford University Press.
Greco, J. 2010. *Achieving Knowledge*. Cambridge: Cambridge University Press.
Greco, J. 2012. 'A (Different) Virtue Epistemology.' *Philosophy and Phenomenological Research* 85: 1–26.
Greco, J. and J. Turri. 2012. *Virtue Epistemology: Contemporary Readings*. Cambridge, MA: MIT Press.
Greco, J. and J. Turri. 2013. 'Virtue Epistemology.' In E. Zalta (ed.), *The Stanford Encyclopedia of Philosophy* (Winter 2013 Edition). URL = <http://plato.stanford.edu/archives/win2013/entries/epistemology-virtue/>.
Gross, H. 1979. *A Theory of Criminal Justice*. Oxford: Oxford University Press.
Haji, I. 1999. 'Indeterminism and Frankfurt-type Examples.' *Philosophical Explorations* 1: 42–58.
Haji, I. 2001. 'Control Conundrums: Modest Libertarianism, Responsibility, and Explanation.' *Pacific Philosophical Quarterly* 82: 178–200.
Haji, I. 2006. 'The Principle of Alternate Possibilities and a Defeated Dilemma.' *Philosophical Explorations* 9: 179–202.
Haji, I. 2012. 'Reason, Responsibility, and Free Will: Reply to My Critics.' *The Journal of Ethics* 16: 175–209.
Harman, G. 1976. 'Practical Reasoning.' *Review of Metaphysics* 79: 431–63.
Hawthorne, J. 2004. *Knowledge and Lotteries*. Oxford: Oxford University Press.
Hawthorne, J. and M. Lasonen-Aarnio. 2009. 'Knowledge and Objective Chance.' In P. Greenough and D. Pritchard (eds), *Williamson on Knowledge*. Oxford: Oxford University Press.
Hieronymi, P. 2006. 'Controlling Attitudes.' *Pacific Philosophical Quarterly* 87: 45–74.
Hiller, A. and R. Neta. 2007. 'Safety and Epistemic Luck.' *Synthese* 158: 303–13.
Howard-Snyder, D., F. Howard-Snyder, and N. Feit. 2003. 'Infallibilism and Gettier's Legacy.' *Philosophy and Phenomenological Research* 66: 304–27.

Ichikawa, J.J. and M. Steup. 'The Analysis of Knowledge.' In E. Zalta (ed.), *The Stanford Encyclopedia of Philosophy* (Fall 2013 Edition). URL = <http://plato.stanford.edu/archives/fall2013/entries/knowledge-analysis/>.
Kane, R. 1996. *The Significance of Free Will*. Oxford: Oxford University Press.
Kane, R. 1999. 'Responsibility, Luck, and Chance: Reflections on Free Will and Indeterminism.' *The Journal of Philosophy* 96: 217–40.
Kelp, C. 2009. 'Knowledge and Safety.' *Journal of Philosophical Research* 34: 21–31.
Kelp, C. 2013. 'Knowledge: The Safe-Apt View.' *Australasian Journal of Philosophy* 91: 265–78.
Klein, P. 2008. 'Useful False Beliefs.' In Q. Smith (ed.), *New Essays in Epistemology*. Oxford: Oxford University Press.
Kim, J. 1974. 'Noncausal Connections.' *Noûs* 8: 41–52.
Lackey, J. 2007. 'Why We Don't Deserve Credit for Everything We Know.' *Synthese* 158: 345–61.
Lackey, J. 2008. 'What Luck Is Not.' *Australasian Journal of Philosophy* 86: 255–67.
Lackey, J. 2009. 'Knowledge and Credit.' *Philosophical Studies* 142: 27–42.
Lackey, J. 2011. 'Assertion and Isolated Secondhand Knowledge.' In J. Brown and H. Cappelen (eds), *Assertion: New Philosophical Essays*. Oxford: Oxford University Press.
Latus, A. 2003. 'Constitutive Luck.' *Metaphilosophy* 34: 460–75.
Levy, N. 2009. 'What, and Where, Luck Is: A Response to Jennifer Lackey.' *Australasian Journal of Philosophy* 87: 489–97.
Levy, N. 2011a. *Hard Luck: How Luck Undermines Free Will and Moral Responsibility*. Oxford: Oxford University Press.
Levy, N. 2011b. 'Luck and Free Will.' In J. Aguilar, A. Buckareff, and K. Frankish (eds), *New Waves in Philosophy of Action*. New York: Palgrave Macmillan.
Levy, N. Forthcoming. 'Luck and Agent Causation: A Response to Franklin.' *Criminal Law and Philosophy*.
Lewis, D. 1986. 'Causation.' In D. Lewis (ed.), *Philosophical Papers II*. Oxford: Oxford University Press.
Maier, J. Forthcoming. 'The Agentive Modalities.' *Philosophy and Phenomenological Research*.
Mele, A. 1992. 'Acting for Reasons and Acting Intentionally.' *Pacific Philosophical Quarterly* 73: 355–74.
Mele, A. 1997. 'Introduction.' In A. Mele (ed.), *The Philosophy of Action*. Oxford: Oxford University Press.
Mele, A. 1999. 'Ultimate Responsibility and Dumb Luck.' *Social Philosophy and Policy* 16: 274–93.
Mele, A. 2003a. *Motivation and Agency*. Oxford: Oxford University Press.
Mele, A. 2003b. 'Agents' Abilities.' *Noûs* 37: 447–70.
Mele, A. 2006. *Free Will and Luck*. Oxford: Oxford University Press.
Mele, A. 2013. 'Moral Responsibility and the Continuation Problem.' *Philosophical Studies* 162: 237–55.
Mele, A. and P. Moser. 1994. 'Intentional Action.' *Noûs* 28: 39–68.
Mele, A. and D. Robb. 1998. 'Rescuing Frankfurt-style Cases.' *Philosophical Review* 107: 97–112.
Mele, A. and D. Robb. 2003. 'Bbs, Magnets, and Seesaws: The Metaphysics of Frankfurt-style Cases.' In M. McKenna and D. Widerker (eds), *Moral Responsibility and Alternative Possibilities*. Aldershot, UK: Ashgate.

Moore, G.E. 1953. *Some Main Problems of Philosophy*. London: George Allen & Unwin Ltd.
Morris, T. 1986. *The Logic of God Incarnate*. Ithaca, NY: Cornell University Press.
Nagel, T. 1979. 'Moral Luck.' In T. Nagel (ed.), *Mortal Questions*. Cambridge: Cambridge University Press.
Nelkin, D. 2001. 'The Consequence Argument and the *Mind* Argument.' *Analysis* 61: 107–15.
Neta, R. and G. Rohrbaugh. 2004. 'Luminosity and the Safety of Knowledge.' *Pacific Philosophical Quarterly* 85: 396–406.
O'Connor, T. 2000. *Persons and Causes*. Oxford: Oxford University Press.
Orozco, J. 2010. 'I Can Trust You Now ... But Not Later.' *Acta Analytica* 25: 195–214.
Otsuka, M. 1998. 'Incompatibilism and the Avoidability of Blame.' *Ethics* 108: 685–701.
Palmer, D. 2005. 'New Distinctions, Same Troubles: A Reply to Haji and McKenna.' *The Journal of Philosophy* 102: 474–82.
Palmer, D. 2013. 'Capes on the W-Defense.' *Philosophia* 41: 555–66.
Palmer, D. 2014. 'Deterministic Frankfurt Cases.' *Synthese* 191: 3847–64.
Paul, L.A. and N. Hall. 2013. *Causation: A User's Guide*. Oxford: Oxford University Press.
Pereboom, D. 2001. *Living without Free Will*. Cambridge: Cambridge University Press.
Plantinga, A. 1993. *Warrant and Proper Function*. Oxford: Oxford University Press.
Plantinga, A. 1996. 'Respondeo.' In J. Kvanvig (ed.), *Warrant in Contemporary Epistemology*. Lanham, MD: Rowman and Littlefield.
Pritchard, D. 2004. 'Epistemic Luck.' *Journal of Philosophical Research* 29: 193–222.
Pritchard, D. 2005. *Epistemic Luck*. Oxford: Oxford University Press.
Pritchard, D. 2007. 'Anti-Luck Epistemology.' *Synthese* 158: 277–97.
Pritchard, D. 2012a. 'Anti-Luck Virtue Epistemology.' *Journal of Philosophy* 109: 247–79.
Pritchard, D. 2012b. 'In Defense of Modest Anti-Luck Epistemology.' In K. Becker and T. Black (eds), *The Sensitivity Principle in Epistemology*. Cambridge: Cambridge University Press.
Pritchard, D., A. Millar, and A. Haddock. 2010. *The Nature and Value of Knowledge*. Oxford: Oxford University Press.
Pritchard, D. and M. Smith. 2004. 'The Psychology and Philosophy of Luck.' *New Ideas in Psychology* 22: 1–28.
Reed, B. 2009. 'A New Argument for Skepticism.' *Philosophical Studies* 142: 91–104.
Rescher, N. 1995. *Luck: The Brilliant Randomness of Everyday Life*. New York: Farrar, Straus and Giroux.
Riggs, W. 2007. 'Why Epistemologists are So Down on Their Luck.' *Synthese* 158: 329–44.
Riggs, W. 2009a. 'Luck, Knowledge, and Control.' In A. Haddock, A. Millar, and D. Pritchard (eds), *Epistemic Value*. Oxford: Oxford University Press.
Riggs, W. 2009b. 'Two Problems of Easy Credit.' *Synthese* 169: 201–16.
Ryberg, J. 2014. 'Responsibility and Capacities: A Note on the Proportionality Assumption.' *Analysis* 74: 393–7.

Sartorio, C. 2011. 'Actuality and Responsibility.' *Mind* 120: 1071–97.
Sartorio, C. 2012a. 'Causation and Freedom.' *The Journal of Philosophy* 109: 629–51.
Sartorio, C. 2012b. 'Resultant Luck.' *Philosophy and Phenomenological Research* 84: 63– 86.
Schafer, K. 2014. 'Knowledge and Two Forms of Non-Accidental Truth.' *Philosophy and Phenomenological Research* 89: 373–93.
Schlosser, M. 2014. 'The Luck Argument against Event-Causal Libertarianism: It is Here to Stay.' *Philosophical Studies* 167: 375–85.
Shabo, S. 2013. 'Free Will and Mystery: Looking Past the *Mind* Argument.' *Philosophical Studies* 162: 291–307.
Shabo, S. 2014. 'Assimilations and Rollbacks: Two Arguments against Libertarianism Defended.' *Philosophia* 42: 151–72.
Skyrms, F.B. 1967. 'The Explication of "X Knows that *p*".' *The Journal of Philosophy* 64: 373–89.
Smith, D. and E.J. Coffman. 2010. 'The Fall of the *Mind* Argument and Some Lessons about Freedom.' In J. Campbell, M. O'Rourke, and D. Shier (eds), *Action, Ethics and Responsibility*. Cambridge, MA: MIT Press.
Sosa, E. 2007. *A Virtue Epistemology*. Oxford: Oxford University Press.
Sosa, E. 2010. 'How Competence Matters in Epistemology.' *Philosophical Perspectives* 24: 465–75.
Sosa, E. 2011. *Knowing Full Well*. Princeton, NJ: Princeton University Press.
Statman, D. 1991. 'Moral and Epistemic Luck.' *Ratio* 4: 146–56.
Steglich-Petersen, A. 2010. 'Luck as an Epistemic Notion.' *Synthese* 176: 361–77.
Stone, J. 2013. '"Unlucky" Gettier Cases.' *Pacific Philosophical Quarterly* 94: 421–30.
Strawson, G. 1994. 'The Impossibility of Moral Responsibility.' *Philosophical Studies* 75: 5– 24.
Strawson, P. 1962. 'Freedom and Resentment.' *Proceedings of the British Academy* 48: 187– 211.
Stump, E. and J. Fischer. 2000. 'Transfer Principles and Moral Responsibility.' *Philosophical Perspectives* 14: 47–56.
Turri, J. 2011. 'Manifest Failure: The Gettier Problem Solved.' *Philosophers' Imprint* 11: 1– 11.
Turri, J. 2012. 'Is Knowledge Justified True Belief?' *Synthese* 184: 247–59.
Turri, J. Forthcoming. 'Unreliable Knowledge.' *Philosophy and Phenomenological Research*.
Waller, B. 1988. 'Free Will Gone Out of Control.' *Behaviorism* 16: 149–57.
Warfield, T. 1996. 'Determinism and Moral Responsibility are Incompatible.' *Philosophical Topics* 24: 215–26.
Warfield, T. 2000. 'Causal Determinism and Human Freedom are Incompatible: A New Argument for Incompatibilism.' *Philosophical Perspectives* 14: 167–80.
Warfield, T. 2003. 'Compatibilism and Incompatibilism: Some Arguments.' In M. Loux and D. Zimmerman (eds), *The Oxford Handbook of Metaphysics*. Oxford: Oxford University Press.
Warfield, T. 2005. 'Knowledge from Falsehood.' *Philosophical Perspectives* 19: 405–16.
Warfield, T. 2008. 'Metaphysical Compatibilism's Appropriation of Frankfurt.' *Oxford Studies in Metaphysics* 3: 283–95.

Watson, G. 1996. 'Two Faces of Responsibility.' *Philosophical Topics* 24: 227–48.

Whiting, D. 2013. 'The Good and the True (or the Bad and the False).' *Philosophy* 88: 219– 42.

Widerker, D. 1995. 'Libertarianism and Frankfurt's Attack on the Principle of Alternative Possibilities.' *The Philosophical Review* 104: 247–61.

Widerker, D. 2000. 'Frankfurt's Attack on the Principle of Alternative Possibilities.' *Philosophical Perspectives* 14: 181–201.

Widerker, D. 2005. 'Blameworthiness, Non-Robust Alternatives, and the Principle of Alternative Expectations.' *Midwest Studies in Philosophy* 29: 292–306.

Williamson, T. 2000. *Knowledge and Its Limits*. Oxford: Oxford University Press.

Unger, P. 1968. 'An Analysis of Factual Knowledge.' *The Journal of Philosophy* 65: 157–70.

van Inwagen, P. 1983. *An Essay on Free Will*. Oxford: Oxford University Press.

van Inwagen, P. 1997. 'Against Middle Knowledge.' *Midwest Studies in Philosophy* 21: 225–36.

van Inwagen, P. 1998. 'The Mystery of Metaphysical Freedom.' In P. van Inwagen and D. Zimmerman (eds), *Metaphysics: The Big Questions*. Malden, MA: Blackwell.

van Inwagen, P. 2000. 'Free Will Remains a Mystery.' *Philosophical Perspectives* 14: 1–19.

van Inwagen, P. 2004. 'Freedom to Break the Laws.' *Midwest Studies in Philosophy* 28: 334–50.

van Inwagen, P. 2008. 'How to Think about the Problem of Free Will.' *The Journal of Ethics* 12: 327–41.

van Inwagen, P. 2011. 'A Promising Argument.' In R. Kane (ed.), *The Oxford Handbook of Free Will* (2nd edition). Oxford: Oxford University Press.

Vargas, M. 2012. 'Why the Luck Problem Isn't.' *Philosophical Issues* 22: 419–36.

Zagzebski, L. 1994. 'The Inescapability of Gettier Problems.' *Philosophical Quarterly* 44: 65–73.

Zagzebski, L. 2009. *On Epistemology*. Belmont, CA: Wadsworth.

Zagzebski, L. 2011. 'Foreknowledge and Free Will.' In E. Zalta (ed.), *The Stanford Encyclopedia of Philosophy*. URL = <http://plato.stanford.edu/archives/fall2011/entries/free-will-foreknowledge/>

Zimmerman, M. 1987. 'Luck and Moral Responsibility.' *Ethics* 97: 374–86.

Zimmerman, M. 2002. 'Taking Luck Seriously.' *The Journal of Philosophy* 99: 554–76.

Zimmerman, M. 2006. 'Moral Luck: A Partial Map.' *Canadian Journal of Philosophy* 36: 585–608.

Index

Abilities Question, 26, 27–32, 170n15
actions
  basic, 126–7, 181n33, 184n14
  done for a reason, 131, 135–6, 162, 170n6, 182n5
  done knowingly and propositional knowledge, 76–7
  and strokes of luck, 26–7, 119, 127
  non-basic, 184n14
  non-causal accounts of, 126, 182n4, 182n5
  reason-explanation of, 131, 162, 168n19
  uncontrolled vs. contingent on uncontrolled factors, 102–3
  see also free actions, intentional actions, morally responsible actions
agent causation, 187n35
anti-luck platitude in epistemology, 49–50, 52, 66, 95–6, 172n1
  see also epistemic luck, Gettier Cases, gettiered belief, Omnipresence
assertion, 44, 71–2
Audi, Robert, 78, 158

Ballantyne, Nathan, 3, 4, 96
Bennett, Jonathan, 15, 167n4, 168n16
Bergmann, Michael, 75, 172n1
Blumenfeld, David, 153, 185n26
Bogardus, Tomás, 90, 91, 92, 93, 94, 174n12, 176n16, 176n18
Bratman, Michael, 26, 175n8
Bryson, Devon, 168n15

Carlson, Erik, 177n4
Carter, J. Adam, 74
causal determinism, 4
  see also proximal determination, Proximal Determination

Requirement, Proximal Nondetermination Requirement
causation, *see* contribution relations
chance, 4, 7–8, 20, 40, 169n1, 171n22
  see also probability, Unfreedom Lemma: arguments for
Chisholm, Roderick, 49, 186n29
choice, 133–4
choice situation, 99, 150–3, 185n25
circumstantial luck, 171n28
Clarke, Randolph, 126, 131, 132, 133, 136, 137, 143, 170n6, 177n3, 178n10, 181n31, 182n6, 182n7, 184n9, 184n11, 184n12, 185n20, 185n26, 186n31
Classics, 49–50, 57–9, 61–2, 66, 68, 77–9, 173n7
cognitive abilities
creditability of believing truly to:
  and divine revelation, 74–5
  and environmental reliability, 73–4
  explanatory salience account of, 68–73
  and fake barn cases, 75–6
  and hidden helper cases, 65–6
  power manifestation account of, 68–9, 73–7
  true belief as creditable to vs. merely resulting from, 68, 71
  true belief as manifestation of vs. saliently explained by, 73–4
  see also gettiered belief: Lack of Credit Approach to, Minimal Creditability Requirement
Cohen, Daniel, 131
Comesaña, Juan, 173n10, 174n12, 176n15
Conee, Earl, 82
Connections Question, 26–7
constitutive luck, 41–2
control, 26–8, 41–2, 102–3, 105, 107, 126–7, 132–3, 136

195

Index

contribution relations
  causal, 14–15, 43, 88–9, 126, 131, 136, 148, 154–5, 162, 169n2, 181n31, 187n35
  large, 17–18, 168n19
  and lucky events, 13–19
  non-causal, 15
  primary
    and counterfactual dependence, 16–17
    explanation of, 13–15
    non-transitivity of, 18
Copp, David, 178n12
counterfactuals of freedom, 109, 178n14
Crisp, Thomas, 175n10

Dancy, Jonathan, 49, 50, 95
Davison, Scott, 111
de Calleja, Mirja Pérez, 182n6
decision, 133–4
DeRose, Keith, 12
dispositions to believe, 78, 80–1
  see also gettiered belief: Risk of Misleading Dispositions Approach to
disvalue of false belief, 85–6
doing, broad conception of, 3
  see also actions
Dretske, Fred, 28

Ekstrom, Laura, 177n1, 186n31
Engel, Mylan, 60, 61, 172n3
Epistemic Frankfurt Cases, 86–90, 176n15
epistemic justification, 71–2, 78–9, 172n1, 175n11
  see also gettiered belief: Risk of Misleading Justification Approach to
epistemic luck, 51–6, 60–1
  see also Gettier Cases, gettiered belief
events, 2–3, 125
  see also states of affairs
examples
  African Expedition, 9, 11, 46, 172n30, 172n31
  Atomic Clock, 90–5, 174n12, 176n16

Bad Lottery, 5, 13, 19
Bob's Choice, 156–8, 160–3, 187n34
Bob's Choice*, 160–3, 187n34
Buried Treasure, 5–8, 12, 20, 42, 44–6, 47, 168n22, 172n29, 172n30
Buried Treasure*, 6–8, 171n23
Case 3, 140–3, 184n15
Case 4, 140–3
Case 5, 141–3
choiceless and choosy assassins, 110–11, 179n16, 183n7
Coffee Cup, 64–7, 68, 80–1, 83, 85, 174n12
Derek's lay-up, 11, 167n13, 171n18
Demolition Worker, 11, 34–7, 168n13, 171n18
Demonic Clock, 86–90, 174n12
Device Scenario, 136–8
Discreditable Fact, 138–40
Distracted Driver, 11–12, 20, 37–8, 47, 53
Divine Revelation, 75, 85
Doctor, 72
Drawing Marbles, 20–2, 38–9, 168n22
Fake Fruits, 75–7, 84, 87, 92, 94, 175n9
Field Trip, 70–2, 73, 74, 85
Game Show, 32–4
Good Lottery, 5, 7–8, 13, 19–20, 22
Hobbled, 72–3, 84, 174n6
Kidnapping, 10–11, 47
Katelyn's sunrise, 10, 47
Lucky Subitizer, 62–4, 69, 85, 174n11, 174n12
new assassins, 113–14, 179n16, 183n7
Oxfam donation choice, 8–9, 46
Pocket Change, 49, 57–9, 61, 78, 79, 84
Pyromaniac, 83–4
Religious Sheep Rock, 65–7, 68, 80–1, 82–3, 174n6
Rigged Lottery, 28, 29, 171n15
Schrödinger's Cat, 29, 30
Sheep Rock, 49, 57–9, 62, 65, 73, 76, 78, 79, 84
Successful Assassin, 106–7, 110–11
toddler survival, 15–16

examples – *continued*
  Two Buttons, 28, 31–2, 171n15
  Two Lotteries, 33–4
  Unsuccessful Assassin, 106–7, 110–11
  exploiting an event for a purpose, 3, 5, 9–11, 47
  see also lucky events: Control Account of

fake barn cases, 57, 59, 76, 87, 173n5, 173n7, 173n9, 175n9
  see also Gettier Cases, gettiered belief
Feit, Neil, 173n7, 173n8
Feldman, Richard, 82
Finch, Alicia, 135, 143, 183n9, 185n17, 185n27
Fischer, John Martin, 101, 130, 134, 147, 148, 149, 150, 153, 158, 177n3, 179n17, 180n19, 185n23, 187n32, 187n33
Fitelson, Branden, 176
fortune, 42–3
Frankfurt, Harry, 88, 156, 168n19, 176n15, 180n20, 183n8
  see also Epistemic Frankfurt Cases, Frankfurt Cases
Frankfurt Cases, 156–8, 160–3, 168n19, 176n15, 186n32, 187n33, 187n34
  see also Freedom Requirement
Franklin, Christopher, 97, 120, 123, 132, 133, 137, 139, 142, 145, 146, 169n3, 177n1, 181n26, 182n6, 183n9, 186n31
free actions
  direct vs. indirect, 26
  and intentional actions, 27, 170n6, 171n17, 180n24
  mental vs. overt, 170n6
  and power to select one course of action over another, 145–6
  and proximal determination, 153–4
  and strokes of luck, 27, 169n5
  see also Freedom Requirement, metaphysical freedom, practical abilities, relative freedom

freedom with respect to an event, *see* relative freedom
Freedom Requirement, 134, 153–8, 159–63, 166, 183n8, 186n32, 187n33, 187n34
  see also Frankfurt Cases
free will, 143
  see also free actions, metaphysical freedom, practical abilities, relative freedom
Freitag, Wolfgang, 173n7

Gardiner, Georgi, 167n9, 168n18, 168n21, 169n23, 172n4
Gendler, Tamar, 76
Gettier, Edmund, 49, 57, 61
  see also Gettier Cases, gettiered belief
Gettier Cases, 49
  different kinds of, 57–9, 173n7
  general recipes for constructing, 173n8
  intuitive diagnosis of ignorance in, 58
  see also epistemic luck, gettiered belief
gettiered belief, 50
  Ease of Mistake Approach to, 60–7
  as inferior to propositional knowledge, 69, 85–6
  Lack of Credit Approach to, 68–77
  and liability to mislead, 58–9, 77–9, 176n17
  Risk of Misleading Dispositions Approach to, 77–81
  Risk of Misleading Justification Approach to, 78–9, 81–95
  scope of, 57–9, 173n7
  see also epistemic luck, Gettier Cases
Ginet, Carl, 182n4, 186n32
Goldman, Alvin, 173n5
Graham, Peter A., 135, 136, 137, 140, 180n24, 183n9, 184n13
Greco, John, 30, 68, 69, 70, 167n7, 170n7, 173n6, 173n7, 174n1, 174n4, 178n11
Gross, Hyman, 175n8
guidance, 88–9

Haddock, Adrian, 174n2

Haji, Ishtiyaque, 130, 131, 133, 135, 145, 161, 162, 182n3
Hall, Ned, 18, 167n4
happening, broad conception of, 3
Harman, Gilbert, 26
Hawthorne, John, 61, 64, 76, 83, 174n12
hidden helper cases, 57, 59, 65–6, 73, 173n6, 173n7, 174n6
   see also Gettier Cases, gettiered belief, Minimal Creditability Requirement
Hieronymi, Pamela, 179n16, 182n7
Hiller, Avram, 173n7
Howard-Snyder, Daniel, 173n7, 173n8
Howard-Snyder, Frances, 173n7, 173n8

Ichikawa, Jonathan Jenkins, 175n11
incompatibility of freedom and lack of proximal determination, *see* Unfreedom Lemma
incompatibility of freedom and proximal determination, *see* Proximal Nondetermination Requirement
incompatibility of moral responsibility and lack of proximal determination, *see* Proximal Determination Requirement
intentional actions
   vs. actions done knowingly, 26–7, 119, 169n4, 169n5, 170n6, 180n23
   and free actions, 27, 170n6, 171n17, 180n24
   and lucky events, 12
   proximally undetermined, 117, 124–7
   and reliability, 35–6
   and strokes of luck, 25–7, 35–7
   see also lucky events: Control Account of, lucky events: Mixed Account of, strokes of luck: the Analysis of
intentions, 111, 133–4, 140–3, 179n16, 182n7
Inverse Proportionality Thesis, 40–1

   see also luck ascriptions, lucky events: relative rarity of

Kane, Robert, 177n1, 187n35
Kelp, Christoph, 66, 74, 86, 87, 174n12, 175n9
Kim, Jaegwon, 15
Klein, Peter, 176n19
Knowledge Requirement on Acting Knowingly, 76–7

Lackey, Jennifer, 1, 5, 7, 8, 11, 12, 16, 34, 36, 40, 42, 45, 47, 48, 70, 71, 72, 75, 167n1, 167n13, 168n22, 171n17, 171n18, 173n7
Lasonen-Aarnio, Maria, 83, 168n21, 174n12
Latus, Andrew, 8, 39, 40, 167n1
Levy, Neil, 4, 5, 6, 7, 12, 16, 21, 23, 39, 41, 42, 43, 44, 98, 100, 116, 120, 126, 127, 167n1, 167n8, 169n1, 170n6, 170n7, 171n22, 171n23, 171n26, 174n13, 177n7, 179n16, 180n21, 181n32, 182n34, 182n7, 183n9, 185n26
Lewis, David, 15
libertarianism
   action-centered event-causal, 123, 126, 181n26
   deliberative, 186n31
   and luck, 98, 120, 169n3
   standard, 98
   see also Proximal Determination Requirement, Proximal Nondetermination Requirement, Unfreedom Lemma
luck
   as a disjunctive notion, 13–14
   vs. fortune, 42–3
   just a matter of vs. partly a matter of, 31, 118
   as relation between subjects and events broadly construed, 2–3
   see also luck ascriptions, lucky events, strokes of luck

luck ascriptions, 11–12, 23, 44, 171n28
  see also luck, lucky events, strokes of luck
lucky events
  and accidental necessity, 22–3
  Control Account of, 3, 9–12, 47, 167n7, 167n13
  directly vs. indirectly, 13–14, 19–20
  Enriched Strokes Account of, 37–48, 164–5
  ignorance requirement on, 7–8, 20
  Mixed Account of, 3–4, 8, 12, 20, 25, 42, 45–8, 167n8
  Modal Account of, 3, 5–9, 12, 20, 46, 167n6, 167n12
  relative rarity of, 15–16, 40–1
  Strokes Account of, 13–24, 25, 36, 37–48, 51, 120–1, 123, 125, 164–5, 168n17, 168n19, 171n17
  vs. strokes of luck, 13–14
  see also luck, luck ascriptions, strokes of luck
Ludwig, Kirk, 175n12

MacLean, Douglas, 168n21, 171n16
Mele, Alfred, 14, 26, 31, 35, 88, 98, 100, 101, 116, 119, 126, 130, 131, 132, 136, 147, 148, 149, 150, 156, 157, 158, 169n4, 169n5, 170n6, 170n15, 171n17, 177n1, 180n23, 184n12, 185n24, 187n35
metaphysical freedom, 27, 99, 100, 101, 115, 170n8, 186n29
  see also free actions, relative freedom
Millar, Alan, 174n2
Mind Argument, 101, 135–46, 179n18, 183n9, 184n12, 184n13
  see also Rollback Argument, Unfreedom Lemma
Minimal Creditability Requirement, 66, 75, 174n14
Moore, G.E., 179n18
moral luck
  act-focused situational, 103–7, 110–11

  resultant, 30–1, 103–7, 110–11, 178n9, 179n15, 180n20
  see also circumstantial luck, constitutive luck, moral responsibility, morally responsible actions, responsibility tout court
moral responsibility
  basic, 149
  degrees of vs. extent of psychological development, 148–9, 150–3
  in virtue of vs. for, 109, 178n12, 178n13
  see also Freedom Requirement, morally responsible actions, Possibility Thesis, responsibility tout court
morally responsible actions, 98, 177n3
  and attributability, 179n17
  and blameworthiness, 29–31, 98, 118, 156–8, 177n3, 178n12, 179n17, 181n27, 186n29
  and contingency on uncontrolled factors, 102–3
  directly vs. indirectly, 14, 98
  and explanation, 130–3
  first, 104, 112–15
  and praiseworthiness, 31, 98, 118, 177n3, 181n27, 186n29
  and reasonable demands of knowledgeable morally competent observers, 157
  and responsibility for influencing reasons, 112–15
  and taking a moral stand, 133–4
  see also Freedom Requirement, moral responsibility, Possibility Thesis, Proximal Determination Requirement
Morris, Thomas V., 171n25
Moser, Paul, 26, 35, 119, 126, 169n4, 170n6, 180n23

Nagel, Jennifer, 175n12
Nagel, Thomas, 100, 101, 102, 103, 167n7, 170n7, 171n28
Nelkin, Dana, 183n9

Neta, Ram, 69, 173n7, 173n10, 174n12
nomological grounding
  of free will, 143
  see also Unfreedom Lemma: Nomological Grounding Argument for
non-causal consequence, 15

O'Connor, Timothy, 155
Omnipresence, 57–9, 65–6, 73, 76–7, 173n9
Orozco, Joshue, 74
Otsuka, Michael, 157, 180n20

Palmer, David, 157, 168n15, 179n18, 186n30, 186n32
Paul, L.A., 167n4
perceptual experience, justificatory properties of, 82–3
Pereboom, Derk, 170n6
Plantinga, Alvin, 58, 77, 93, 94, 173n7, 176n17
possibility
  close, 3, 61, 63, 81, 169n1
  decent, 81
  easy, 61, 63, 81
  see also causal determinism, proximal determination
Possibility Thesis, 99
  arguments against
    Nagelian Argument, 101–3
    Strawsonian Argument, 103–15
  argument for, 114–15
  see also moral responsibility, morally responsible actions, responsibility tout court
practical abilities, 27–32, 143, 170n15
prevention, broad conception of, 26, 169n2
Principle of Alternate Possibilities, 168n19, 180n20, 183n8
  see also Frankfurt Cases, the Freedom Requirement
Pritchard, Duncan, 1, 4, 49, 50, 51, 53, 54, 55, 56, 60, 61, 65, 74, 87, 91, 95, 167n1, 167n6, 169n1, 171n28, 172n3, 173n7, 173n8, 174n12, 174n13, 174n14, 174n2

probability, 7, 20, 129, 135
  see also chance, Unfreedom Lemma: arguments for
production, broad conception of, 26, 169n2
propositional knowledge
  ability intuition about, 174n14
  and actions done knowingly, 76–7
  as better than gettiered belief, 69, 85–6
  from false premises, 176n19
  Minimal Creditability Requirement on, 66, 75, 174n14
  and non-accidentally true belief, 94
  safety requirement on, 60–7, 91, 92, 174n12, 176n16
  virtue-theoretic accounts of, 68–77
proximal determination, 97
  see also Proximal Determination Requirement, Proximal Nondetermination Requirement, Unfreedom Lemma
Proximal Determination Requirement, 97
  arguments against
    Fischer's Argument, 148, 149, 153–8
    the Melean Argument, 149–53, 185n24, 185n26
    the Possibility Argument, 101, 130, 147–8, 149–50, 158–63, 187n34
  arguments for
    literal, 115–28
    stipulative, 115–16, 129–47
Proximal Nondetermination Requirement, 153–4
Pryor, James, 82

randomness, 100, 129, 135–6, 184n12
reactive attitudes, 177n3
Reed, Baron, 173n7
Reid, Thomas, 186n29
relative freedom, 99
  and actional outcomes of prior actions, 140
  and non-actional outcomes of prior actions, 137–8

relative freedom – *continued*
  and strokes of luck, 27–32, 170n15
  see also free actions, metaphysical freedom, Freedom Requirement
Rescher, Nicholas, 7, 41, 42, 167n1
responsibility tout court, 105
  as entailing possibility of morally responsible action, 109–10
  Zimmerman's Argument for possibility of, 105–12
  see also moral responsibility, morally responsible actions, moral luck, Possibility Thesis
Riggs, Wayne, 7, 8, 9, 10, 11, 46, 47, 68, 71, 167n1, 167n7, 167n8, 167n12, 170n10
Rohrbaugh, Guy, 69, 173n10, 174n12
Rollback Argument, 183n9
  see also the *Mind* Argument, Unfreedom Lemma
Russian roulette, 39–41
Ryberg, Jesper, 150, 151

Sartorio, Carolina, 18, 168n15, 178n9, 179n15, 185n23
Schafer, Karl, 172n1, 173n7
Schlosser, Markus, 131, 135, 145
Shabo, Seth, 135, 140, 145, 183n9, 184n12, 184n15
Skyrms, F.B., 83
Smith, Donald, 183n9
Smith, Matthew, 172n28
Sosa, Ernest, 16, 62, 64, 68, 69, 73, 173n9, 174n12, 175n7, 175n9
states of affairs, 3
  see also events
Statman, Daniel, 167n7, 170n7
Steglich-Petersen, Asbjørn, 7, 8, 20
Steup, Matthias, 175n11
Stone, Jim, 65, 173n7
Strawson, Galen, 100, 102, 104, 181n29
Strawson, Peter, 177n3
strokes of luck
  and actions done knowingly, 26–7, 119, 127
  as admitting of degrees, 37–8
  the Analysis of, 25–48, 52–3, 94, 119, 125, 164, 172n31

  and closure under entailment, 28–9
  as composite, 21–2, 39
  control over, 27–32, 170n15
  and free actions, 27, 169n5, 170n15
  and intentional actions, 25–7, 35–7
  vs. lucky events, 13–14
  and moral responsibility, 31, 118
  and time, 22–3
  see also luck, luck ascriptions, lucky events

Tognazzini, Neal, 177n3, 179n17
Turri, John, 68, 69, 72, 73, 76, 173n7, 173n8, 174n1, 174n4

Unfreedom Lemma, 134–6, 183n9
  arguments for
    Assimilation Argument, 140–3
    Device Argument, 136–8
    Nomological Grounding Argument, 143–5
    Promising Argument, 138–40
    Selection Argument, 145–6
  see also the *Mind* Argument, Rollback Argument
Unger, Peter, 94, 172n3

van Inwagen, Peter, 4, 99, 114, 135, 136, 138, 139, 154, 169n1, 178n14, 179n17, 179n18, 183n9, 184n10, 184n11, 184n12, 184n13, 185n16, 185n27, 185n28
Vargas, Manuel, 148

Waller, Bruce, 131
Warfield, Ted, 176n19, 183n9, 184n10, 184n13, 185n27, 186n29, 187n34
Watson, Gary, 179n17
Whiting, Daniel, 176n14
Whittington, Lee, 168n22, 169n23, 171n24
Widerker, David, 157, 170n6

Williamson, Timothy, 167n10, 169n1
Wolf, Susan, 171n16

Zagzebski, Linda, 68, 169n24, 173n8

Zimmerman, Michael, 30, 102, 103, 104, 105, 106, 107, 109, 110, 167n7, 170n7, 177n3, 178n8, 178n13, 178n14

CPSIA information can be obtained at www.ICGtesting.com
Printed in the USA
LVOW01*1656080215

425997LV00002BB/142/P